The Voodoo Queen

The Voodoo Queen

a novel by

ROBERT TALLANT

PELICAN PUBLISHING COMPANY
GRETNA 2005

First published by Putnam
Pelican paperback edition
First printing, October 1983
Second printing, September 1992
Third printing, March 2000
Fourth printing, June 2005

Library of Congress Cataloging in Publication Data

Tallant, Robert, 1909-1957.
    The voodoo queen.

    Reprint. Originally published: New York: Putnam,
c1956.
    1. Laveau, Marie, 1794-1881 Fiction. I. Title
PS3539.A36V6 1983   813'.54   83-8160
ISBN-13: 978-0-88289-332-7

Printed in Canada
Published by Pelican Publishing Company, Inc.
1000 Burmaster Street, Gretna, Louisiana 70053

The Voodoo Queen

Introduction

MARIE LAVEAU was the last great American witch. Yet her art bore no more resemblance to that of the New England witches, for instance, than Boston resembles New Orleans, the city in which she lived and practiced. Hers was jungle-born, African in origin, for she was the queen of the voodoos, and by far the most important voodooienne ever to reign on this continent.

As such she was accused, by town gossip, of almost every crime of which humans are capable. She was never convicted of any, but it was whispered, especially during her later years, that she consorted with Satan, who appeared to her in the forms of snakes, goats, and other beasts; that she was a thief, a blackmailer and a procuress; that she had been the mistress of a legion of men; that she had committed murder.

Of none of this is there much evidence nor any proof. To be sure, she did use a little blackmail of a sort, usually by creating fear in slaves or servants so that they would be co-erced into advising their masters and mistresses into seeking her services. This was a common practice among voodoo-iennes. The rest of the gossip was probably circulated by her enemies and rivals, and much of it after she was too old to defend herself from such attack. In a few instances wild stories about her also appeared in the newspapers of the day. For while she was still alive she became a legend.

Yet there was another kind of legend, too. To many people

3

she was known as a kind, charitable, almost saintly woman. She lived a very long time, and it is known that she tended the wounded brought back from the Battle of New Orleans in 1815, that she nursed numerous victims of the terrifying yellow fever epidemics, that she was considered a "saint" by prisoners in the parish jail, among whom she visited for decades, bringing them food and clothing, as well as voodoo charms. It is said that in times of financial depression she gave away all her money to the poor in her neighborhood.

Also, according to the standards of her time and class, she seems to have been a moral woman, at least sexually. She bore fifteen children to the same man. At her rites, of course, there were the usual practices of all voodoo rites, but the queen did not take part in these.

Marie Laveau has fascinated me for most of my life. Since childhood, like all New Orleans children, I have been hearing the stories about her, and about twelve years ago I began trying to sort the stories out, to find old, old people who might remember her or at least recall what their parents had said. In 1946, when a book of mine, *Voodoo in New Orleans*, was published, I included in its contents all the stories, fact and legend, that I knew about Marie up to that time. Ever since then I have wanted to write a novel about her.

So this is a novel. I have tried to make it as factual as possible, but the whole truth about Marie cannot be known, so I have taken some dramatic liberties. Despite years of research it is difficult to separate fact and fiction. Even in the case of other writers hearsay and gossip has been accepted as fact, and no writer has dwelt upon her at length except myself. There is such confusion in regard to the truths of her life that her own living descendants tell different stories about her.

However, I believe I have come close to the truth. All the principal characters in this book were real people, including her parents, her husbands, her children and her closest friends. In nearly all of these cases I have used their real names. When

I have not it is either because they could not be found or because the use of them might injure someone's feelings.

Of her beauty there can be no doubt. I have described her as she is always described. There were many beautiful women among her race.

I have quoted her age correctly, and that was easy, although it is a curious fact that many other authors have misquoted it. But since her funeral in 1881 was described at length in the newspapers of New Orleans, and since her marriage to Jacques Paris in 1819 is a matter of record in the archives of the St. Louis Cathedral in this city, and shows her then to have been twenty-five years old, it is obvious she was born in 1794.

Voodoo is still a living religion, and right here in the United States. It may easily be that this is due almost entirely to the influence of Marie Laveau. Traces of it can be found all over the country. In her late years Marie trained a few people in its practice, and many others stole her secrets and carried them to New York, to Charleston, to Chicago, to the West Coast. Everywhere voodoo practitioners know her name, recite it with awe, and tell tales of her, true, false and foolish.

Voodoo has changed a great deal, but it had changed from its origins even in the days of Marie Laveau. Originally snake worship, imported from Africa, and coming to Louisiana with slaves from the West Indies, its character had been altered to suit the purposes of its practitioners. It had become almost entirely a matriarchy, with women ruling the cults. The Mamaloi and Papaloi, the Mamma and Papa, who had usually ruled together in Santo Domingo, no longer existed as such. Mamma was all. When men attempted to found cults they usually failed to have much success. Also, other things had been left behind in what is now Haiti. It is doubtful if the snake was really ever worshiped in Louisiana. It was still used as a symbol and often as an oracle. The custom of making an image of a human in the form of a doll was also left behind, or at least was unknown in the time of Marie Laveau. Much of voodoo had become the selling of the charms known as *gris-gris*, of which there were two kinds, good and evil.

It was Marie Laveau who popularized voodoo. The meetings held at Bayou St. John, just outside the city, were regularly attended by hordes of people. She also managed to get the "business" of many people, some of them of high social strata, who would never have dreamed before of seeking help from a voodoo queen.

Much of this was due to her own personality, to her magnetism as a woman. Apparently no one who saw her once ever forgot her. It is this about her that has interested me most, for from that came her real power, without a doubt. Here was a woman who was born when Spain still owned a third of this nation, who lived through wars, epidemics, disasters of many kinds, through wealth and ruin in her personal life, who always won her battles in her strange way, and who still survived in a period so close to us that she was known by persons still living, a wise and mysterious and beautiful woman, who was our last great witch.

There is one thing more I should like to add here. The charms, or *gris-gris*, I have described in this novel are all purportedly ones used by Marie Laveau. Any reader is welcome to try them. Personally, I prefer not to do so.

ROBERT TALLANT

New Orleans

Chapter 1

SHE hurried through the market, afraid she would miss him. She had not been able to come yesterday, and her day had been long and lonely without the morning to remember. It must not happen again.

It was still more night than day, yet the market and the streets were alive with movement and almost terrifying with noise. Heavy wagons rumbled by, the hoofs of the horses thunderous on the great cobblestones that had come over the sea long ago as ballast for the sailing ships. On every side the fishmongers and the dark vegetable women shrieked and screamed at each other, and at the world, fighting for preferred places for the day and for the attention of the few servants beginning to enter the market, their baskets empty as yet, ready for the bargaining and heckling demanded by their pride and by their mistresses. Along the walls and pillars the Choctaws had already arranged their wares, and they now sat in silence, waiting to be approached. Over it all hung the smell of the market, half stench, half perfume, spice and fish, July flowers and rotting cabbages.

She regretted having come this way. It slowed her. Every few feet she had to encircle coops of clucking fowl, caged rabbits, or wooden tubs filled with damp moss, above which living crabs flailed the air with angry claws. Parrots squawked at her, a tiny monkey gibbered in a friendly fashion, and canaries sang. At some places there was barely a space of a foot's width through which to pass, and she had to almost stop, to almost crawl. Once a naked Indian baby with an old face and an immensely swollen belly tumbled, gurgling wildly, across her path and she nearly fell, but she caught her balance and rushed on.

When she climbed the rickety wooden steps to a higher level of the levee there was less hindrance, but here, too, there was a long line of market people, stretching almost as far as the eye could see, their stalls and tables already set up, their blankets and squares of canvas spread out upon the still dark grass. Women and men, white, Indian, Negro, and all the mixtures of blood and shades of color possible, they were prepared for the day with their fish and poultry, fruit and vegetables, dry goods and tinware and trinkets. All were talking at once, or crying out their wares, or quarreling with their neighbors. A line of black slaves stood waiting for whatever was to be their fate, their necks linked together with a heavy rope, under the guard of a burly white man whose right fist held a thick black whip.

Now there was pale light in the sky above the river, and specks of gold splashed down upon the two round turrets on the Cathedral of St. Louis beyond the Place d'Armes. But she did not see the cathedral turrets nor look up at the sky. She ran on toward a grove of orange trees, running like a child, her long, loosened black hair flying behind her.

He saw her first. He came out from the gloom among the trees and strode toward her.

"Marie!"

Almost out of breath, she whispered his name. "Jacques!"

They did not kiss. He put his hands on her shoulders for a moment. Their bodies did not touch, but the yearning was in both, and it hurt.

She gave him the small bundle in the gleaming white napkin she had carried all the way. "It's a fig cake," she told

8

him. "I made it last night. The figs are from our own trees. They are fine this year."

"I missed you yesterday," he said, taking the wrapped cake and holding it in both hands, and thanking her by holding it with special tenderness.

"Mamma was sick again," she said. "I can't come when she has these attacks. The pain was dreadful this time. Each time it seems worse."

"Poor thing."

She moved her head gently. "The doctor came and gave her a new medicine. It is strong and evil. I tasted it. But it is worthless. They all are."

"I know," he said quietly.

"I call him only because people would think me wicked if I did not," she said. She glanced away from him for an instant, her eyes almost closing. "Gossip! Gossip!" she added. "One cannot stop the tongues."

Her expression had betrayed her. Now his own became severe, his brows met in a frown. "And what did you do?"

"Nothing." She forced a smile, then laughed lightly.

He lifted her left hand, which he noticed she kept clenched into a fist, and began prying open her fingers, gently but stubbornly. "Let me see, Marie!"

"No, Jacques!"

"Let me see," he insisted, looking at her and thinking as he always did that he had never seen a woman like her. She was as tall as he was, and nearly as broad of shoulder. Her unparted black hair streamed behind her delicate ears and down her back almost to her waist. In this dim light her skin was dark red with flecks of gold on her temples and cheekbones, and now her immense eyes glowed, a clear white line of iris shining beneath each huge pupil. "Don't fight me," he told her. "I am stronger than you are."

Laughing again, but nervously, she opened her hand. In her tawny-pink palm there were two cowpeas.

9

"Witch!" He was not really angry, but he was not pleased. He did not touch the peas. "You know what I think of that," he reminded her.

"It can do no harm, Jacques." Her red lips pouted childishly. "One is for Mamma. The other is for us. I will leave them in the church, and if they are still there tomorrow we will have luck. You will see."

"I don't like it."

"What harm is it?" she asked. "It is a very little *gris-gris*." She raised her chin. "It will work as well as the medicine the doctors give people."

"Pray to God," he said. "Ask the saints and the Holy Mother for help! Isn't God enough?"

"There are powers you have forgotten," she murmured. Her lashes shadowed her cheeks for a moment. "We must not quarrel."

"Marie, I am not quarreling."

She laid a hand on his sleeve. "I have something to tell you," she said. "He is coming this evening, Jacques."

His expression changed. "Monsieur Laveau?"

"Yes, Jacques." She squeezed his arm with excitement. "Mamma sent him a message. He will come. He always does when she asks him."

He smiled faintly, but doubtfully. "In any case," he said, "no matter what happens I'm going to stop this. I'm tired of only these meetings. We have to change this."

"I've explained all that to you," she said patiently. "Mamma permits no one in our house without his consent. But I know it will be all right. My father has always been good and gentle to me. He is a kind and gentle man."

"Marie," he told her, "it doesn't matter!"

"He will be glad," she promised. "I'm twenty-five. He should be relieved that I'm marrying. But there has never been anyone else, Jacques. Never anyone but you."

"It doesn't matter," he repeated, curling his lips a little, narrowing his eyes. "Even if he hates me I am going to marry you. Do you think white fathers love us? Mine showed no trace of it!"

"Darling," she said, and she put her forehead against his shoulder for a moment. His shoulder felt warm and strong. Now she began to cry a little.

"My God!" he whispered, and laid the back of a hand on her breast.

She raised her head and stared straight into his eyes, and then they talked a little more. When he left for his work at Monsieur Louis Mazereau's a few minutes later, without further caresses between them, she stood very still, watching after him. He walked south on the levee, slowly, with reluctance, his carpenter's kit in one hand, her fig cake in the other. He was tall in a city of short men, as she was tall in comparison with the petite women. He was magnificent, she thought. His eyes were always before her, soft gray, except when he was angry. His features were finely cut. His black hair was crisp and curly, but no curlier than that of many a Spaniard.

She held fast to her cowpeas as she left the levee and descended the creaking, rotting steps. Over and over again she thought: Never anyone but you, Jacques! Never, never, never . . . !

The sun was coming out as she crossed through the Place d'Armes, and already the heat beat down upon the neglected old square, with its broken fences, its heaps of stones, its paths of worn earth, where no grass grew. Marie walked swiftly, as she always did, her back straight, her head held high and proudly, her lips curved into a half smile, her thoughts still of Jacques. The mean shops and stores that lined the streets on both sides of the square were opening now. These were in buildings of two stories each, most of them roofed with red and black tiles, and all having balconies over the *banquettes* which were supported by pillars running down to the curbs of the open gutters. Lights were burning only in the windows of remoulet's Hotel, a somewhat more substantial building than the others, its ground floor also occupied by shops.

A roughly dressed white man, obviously drunk, tried to block her way as she left the square to cross the Rue Condé to the cathedral on the other side of the street. She did not go around him, but stood perfectly still, raising her head even higher on her strong, sculptured throat, her eyes cold and arrogant. She waited for him to move. He muttered indecencies in English, which she understood perfectly, but pretended not to, and then he walked around her, shaking his head and giggling in a silly manner. An American, she thought with scorn, an ignorant fool, as they all were. And what had happened to the curfew, established two years ago? All the cafés were supposed to be closed at nine o'clock and all people off the streets. It was evident this fellow had been drinking all night, violating the law as only Americans did. It had been the Americans, at least such of them as this one, who had made the curfew necessary in New Orleans. How she hated them!

Outside the cathedral she put the two cowpeas into her mouth under her tongue and stood there a moment, watching a chain gang of slaves who were cleaning the street. She sighed, wishing she had a slave of her own—just one to help with the housework and to run errands. It would be so nice for Mamma. She pulled her scarf up and arranged it over her hair and entered the church.

There were only a few old women kneeling in the rear, and none paid any attention to her as she went up the center aisle and knelt before the huge crucifix at one side before the altar. She said her prayers slowly and anxiously, trying to feel them deep inside. When she was through she took the cowpeas from her lips and quickly placed them in a seam in the stone that formed the base of the cross. Then she rose and left the cathedral as quickly as she had come, pausing only at the holy water font to dip her fingers and cross herself hastily.

Passing through the mud streets beyond Rue Royale that led to her home, her thinking was of Jacques again. How strange it was, she reflected, that he felt as he did about some things. It was strangest because he had himself come to New Orleans from Santo Domingo just as had her mother. It was true he had come as a child, but his mother should have taught him with more wisdom. He had no faith at all in the Old Ones! She knew that Jacques was wrong. Later she would teach him.

All afternoon Marie was busy with preparations for the visit of her father. She knew he would arrive soon after dark, as he always did, and she wanted everything to be nice. The little house was always neat and clean, but she went all over it again, dusting where there was no dust, straightening where there was no need for it, polishing furniture that always gleamed. Afterwards she baked the fish and got ready the vegetables for supper, hoping her father would stay to eat with them.

Through it all her mother lay on the sofa in the small parlor, or moved restlessly to her bed, and then back again to the sofa, as if she could not bear to remain in one place, yet could bear moving about even less. Watching her, Marie knew her mother was in pain and was trying to conceal it. She wondered, too, how Marguerite felt now about her father. Years ago she had always been so excited when she expected him, darting about the house on her tiny feet, doing all the tasks Marie now did, and spending half the day primping and preening before the mirror; filling vases with flowers from the garden. And dying after he left, and being a shadow until word came that he was on his way again.

Marie had been a child then, and she remembered how pretty her mother had once been. A little dark perhaps, darker than herself, but finely formed and exquisite, so tiny —for all Marie's height and proportions had come from

Charles Laveau. Marguerite had been a bronze doll with high Indian cheekbones and black eyes that slanted slightly and a small pursed mouth like a scarlet pomegranate.

Just before dusk Marie did her mother's hair, and as she worked with it she noticed as she did every day now how Marguerite had changed. She was only a few years past forty, but the pomegranate lips were already dry and pale and thicker in appearance. The hair Marie brushed and brushed, then oiled, and brushed some more, was dry, too, and more crinkled than it had seemed years ago, and no longer inky black, but faded into shades of brown and red, and streaked with gray. The once bright and beautiful eyes were faded, also, their lights dimmed, the irises stained with yellow. White people said the beauty of quadroon women did not last. Would she be like this herself in fifteen or twenty years? But then she was more white than her mother, and her mother was sick. Sometimes Marie wondered if she should blame her father for this, but she wondered it without bitterness; it was the way things were. Yet his visits had become less and less frequent during the last five years. He had not remained overnight for nearly ten. How did her mother feel about him now? She said nothing, but she was still more animated than usual when he was coming, and in all the years she had never looked at another man. She will always love him, Marie told herself. Always. I am like her in that way. There will never be anyone for me but Jacques. There never was before. There could never be again.

"You must hurry," Marguerite said, as Marie pinned the last of the braids about the small head. "You haven't even started to dress, child!"

"It won't take me long, darling," Marie promised.

"Your white muslin. It is so warm, and you must look fresh for Monsieur Charles." She had always called him "Monsieur Charles" to Marie.

"Yes, Mamma."

"And do up your hair."

Marguerite fanned herself slowly, peering anxiously into the mirror.

"Mamma, you will like Jacques," Marie said.

"We will see what Monsieur Charles says," Marguerite told her, as if upon that depended whether or not she would like Jacques, and it did. "Am I ugly, Marie?"

"You are beautiful."

"Get my little lace fan from the bureau," Marguerite directed, waving the old palmetto one she had been using. "You are sweet to lie, my child, but I know I am ugly. Marie, pull all the curtains, and not too many candles! Anyway, Monsieur Charles never liked too many lights. And hurry! You must be ready when he arrives!" Marguerite turned back to her mirror and bit her lips. "And fetch me a red rose from the garden, Marie. I will crush the petals. My mouth is so pale."

Marie washed herself all over out in the kitchen across the courtyard behind the cottage. She put on her new white dress and her white slippers, and lifted her heavy hair and bound it into a great pile high on her head. Then she twisted strands of it and made curls that lay before each ear on each cheek.

All the time she was dressing she was thinking of her father. He had been a good father, she felt, despite the way things were and the rules by which they all must live. He had done his best for them. He was generous. Money came at regular periods, and gifts, too, both for Marguerite and for herself. During her childhood, when he came often to the house, and when he had been a bachelor, he would often take her on his lap and be as affectionate as any other father. Sometimes he had played games with her, and he had taught her to read a little and to write a little, which was all the education she had ever received. It had been her father who had not wanted her to go to the balls.

15

These were the quadroon balls, as they were known, where young girls of her race went to dance with young white men, many of them wealthy and of the aristocracy. It was at such a ball that Charles and Marguerite had met.

The only time Marie could remember seeing her father angry was one evening when Marguerite had suggested that perhaps Marie should go. Marie had then been fifteen.

"Oh, no!" he had cried, almost with horror. "I will not have it. Marie is my daughter, too, Marguerite." •

"But we met there, Monsieur Charles," Marguerite said, but timidly, looking as if it had never occurred to her that Charles would object. "What is she to do? How else can a girl like Marie find a protector?"

"She will marry," Charles said. "If not, I will provide for her." His voice softened. "Believe me, Marguerite, I am glad I met you, but I don't want Marie at the balls. Let us hear no more about it."

And they had not. Marguerite never argued with her beloved Monsieur Charles.

Actually, Marie had almost wanted to go to the balls then, at that age. At least she had been curious to see one. She knew girls who had already gone and she had heard descriptions of them. The ballrooms were beautiful and glittering with light, the girls wore white dresses, the young men were handsome.

There was nothing evil or wicked about the balls. Indeed, they were conducted with great propriety. The girls were chaperoned by their mothers. When a young man wished to select one as a mistress he must consult with her mother, or get his father to do so, as was often the case. If he was accepted he must make certain promises, among them one of some financial arrangement should he marry or break off his affair for some other reason. He must also provide, too, for any children that might be born of the union. In most cases the girl would never take any other lover, although in

16

some instances, after the relationship was severed, she might marry a man of her own race.

But Monsieur Charles had not wanted this for Marie, he had said, and that had been the end of it. Yet Marie knew that in her heart Marguerite had often worried about her future. What would become of her one day? Sometimes Marguerite had come out with it when they were alone, and said firmly that Marie needed a protector. She would never mention it to Monsieur Charles, Marguerite would say, but in this one thing he was wrong.

After the time had passed when Marie had wanted to attend the balls she had tried to assure her mother that she would manage. Perhaps she would marry. And what would that mean, Marguerite would argue. It would mean a hard life as the wife of a poor quadroon—a tradesman of some sort, a blacksmith perhaps, a carpenter—a carpenter like Jacques. And already she was getting so old. Marguerite would use the Creole expression about her age. At twenty-five a woman must throw her corset on top of her *armoire*, her wardrobe. It was that hopeless that she would ever get a husband.

There were other things she could do, Marie would say. She sewed well. Or she could be a hairdresser; she had a way for and a flair with the arrangements of coiffures. These things women like her could do for a living. Their neighbor, Madame Laclotte, made a profession of going out to the houses of white ladies to do their hair for special social occasions, and already she had taught Marie much. Anyway, Marie reminded her mother, Monsieur Charles would provide for her, as he had promised. Anything could happen, Marguerite answered. She had known of cases when after a man's death his "other family" had come to great poverty and suffering.

Now Marie thought, as she dressed for her father, there will be no more of that argument. She would marry Jacques. Both her parents should be pleased. She had not tossed her corset on her *armoire*.

That evening was the first time in her life Marie had ever thought her mother pathetic. She had long felt a sadness for her, for her fading health, for the ending of her love. But this evening what she felt was worse than that. Marguerite skipped about the room, chirping, chirping, being vivacious, striving to seem young, and at what cost in pain only she knew, chattering incessantly, laughing high false laughter, touching her Monsieur Charles with her pink fingertips, with her closed fan.

Marie watched her father's face, and she was convinced he felt as she did. He smiled, he made a joke or two, but his blue eyes remained grave. Now and then their glances met. Marie would look up at him, for he was tall, a handsome man, with wings of white in his fair hair, and it was as if they were talking to each other in a language her mother could not understand, and saying to each other, "Poor Marguerite! Poor Marguerite! What can either of us do now?"

He had brought presents—a fine silk scarf for Marguerite, a bottle of wine, and for Marie a pair of earrings, gold hoops, big ones and real gold, he assured her. She loved them, and held them to her ears. "Put them on," Charles said, and then did it for her, attaching each through her pierced lobes. The gold hoops complemented the tones of her skin, they dangled and danced with every movement of her head. She was proud, as she examined herself in the mirror, and proud and warm that her father had put them on her with his own hands. For a moment one of his hands had lingered against her cheek and she had seen his eyes fill with affection, and her heart had warmed. We are like each other, she had thought; there is understanding between us; we are father and daughter in the truest way.

When he said he would be delighted to stay for supper Marguerite looked about to swoon with pleasure. Throughout the meal they did not mention the subject that was the real purpose of his visit. It was their way to let that come with time. While Marguerite chattered and made a fuss over him, refilling his glass and selecting special morsels for his plate, Marie continued to think about him and about his other life, his real life. She thought of that often, for she was curious about it, and actually she knew little about it. What was Madame Laveau like, and the children? There were two girls and one son, her mother had told her. It never occurred to Marie to think of them as her sisters and her brother. They were too remote for that. They were simply her father's other children. Madame was her father's wife. Their world was far away, on a huge plantation somewhere up the Mississippi River, almost to Baton Rouge, her mother had said. It was never discussed. Monsieur Charles never mentioned it, nor did they, but rumors came to them. Now and then he brought Madame to New Orleans, and friends and neighbors had seen them on the street and run to Marguerite with the news. Marguerite had always been interested. What was Madame wearing? Was it true she was fat? And how did Monsieur Charles look?

As Marie brought in coffee from the kitchen to the round table in the parlor where they were eating, she heard Marguerite broach the subject. Monsieur Charles listened attentively, his face serious and interested. At last he turned to Marie. "Tell me about him," he said. "What is his name?"

"Jacques Paris." She hesitated. "He's a carpenter." She tried to think of what else she should say.

Charles was smiling, and she knew what he was thinking. This was the first time there had ever been any discussion of her in regard to any man. This was the first time there had ever been any man.

"I am twenty-five," she said.

"Is it possible?" asked Charles. "You make me feel elderly!"

Marguerite fanned herself violently. "More wine, Monsieur Charles?" She filled his glass before he answered. "Twenty-five, it is old," she agreed with Marie. "A poor carpenter! But at her age perhaps one cannot choose?"

Marie felt fire beating against her eyes. "Mamma, it is not like that!" she cried.

"It is romance," said Marguerite. "I know, my dear. I know." She turned to Charles. "When I am gone I do not want her to be alone." She sighed. "Perhaps it is better than nothing."

He looked straight into Marie's eyes. "She must not be alone," he said, rising. "Marguerite, you must meet the young man. He must call." He rose, gripping the back of his chair, his gaze still fixed to Marie's face. "As for his being poor," he added, "perhaps I can help a little. I will have my attorney search for a house for them, provided of course that you like him, Marguerite."

"Papa!" It was the first time Marie had called him that since she had been a small child.

"It will be my wedding present," Charles told her. "Now come walk to the gate with me. It is late, and I will be in trouble because of the curfew."

By the time they reached the gate set in the high board fence fronting the cottage Marie's eyes were filled with tears. There was a full moon and she twisted her head so that he would not see them, but he put a hand gently on her chin and turned her face back toward him. "My first-born," he said, with a sigh. "You're a very beautiful woman, Marie." He hesitated, then he added, "A fortunate one, besides. You may marry for love."

She nodded, knowing what he meant. He would find suitable husbands for his other daughters. They would have no choice, for no matter what he felt in his heart, he would follow the old custom. He would find suitable husbands for those daughters, and only by the most fortunate coincidence

20

would either of them be the girl's choice. Suddenly she was filled with elation that she was not one of them.

She put a hand in his, timidly, her gratitude to him huge and warm, and her affection. "You are good," she said. "I've told Jacques how good and kind you are."

He chuckled. "Not so good, I'm afraid. I'll find a larger cottage for you than this, and you must take Marguerite with you. Then some day I will come to see you and meet your Jacques. Perhaps Marguerite can let this, and that will provide all of you with a little more money. She doesn't look well, Marie. Doctor Ducote still comes?"

"He does no good," she said.

"I'll see him before I leave the city," he promised. He paused a moment, then patted her arm. "You've never hated me, Marie?" he asked suddenly.

"Hate you!"

"I have strange thoughts," he said. "It isn't the kindest of fates fathers such as I bestow on children like you. It doesn't bother most men, I suppose, but I've wondered. Marie, I loved your mother."

"I know that," she said, unable to meet his gaze.

"You have been as dear to me in your way," he said, "as my other children." He removed his hand and his arm dropped to his side. "Be happy, Marie," he whispered, and went out quickly, closing the gate behind him.

She walked back slowly through the small flower garden toward the candlelighted window, her emotions oddly confused. She was happy about Jacques, and that her father had agreed so easily to their plans, but there was sadness in her, too. Marguerite now lay on the sofa in the parlor, the fan still and limp in one hand, her face tired and gray. "Bring me my pills and a little wine, Marie," she begged. "My pains have been terrible this evening. Do you find Monsieur Charles looking well?"

The cowpeas wrapped carefully in a handkerchief and hidden in the bosom of her dress so that Jacques would not see them, she hurried across the Place d'Armes. As usual he was already at their meeting place. She told him quickly, happily, her eyes glowing. He was to come to supper this evening. She would make him a gumbo. Mamma was better this morning.

He caught her to him and they both rocked with laughter, not caring now that the market people stared and whispered and giggled. Of course he would come, straight from work, he promised. They would be married at once, as soon as it could be arranged with the priest. Marie told him she would speak to her good friend, Père Antoine, herself. She knew him better than Jacques, and he would arrange everything for them.

But at dusk Doctor Ducote bent over Marguerite's bed. She had been in agony since before noon, and now, at last Doctor Ducote had come. Marie watched the doctor's probings with eyes devoid of faith or any trust. When he straightened his small back he said, "She must go to the hospital."

Marguerite tossed her head on the pillow. "No."

Marie echoed it. "No!" There was only one, for them. She could not remember knowing many who had come out of the Charity Hospital after having been a patient there.

Doctor Ducote moved away from the bed and walked to the door between the bedroom and the parlor. He signaled Marie with a nod and she followed him.

"She will be a great care," Doctor Ducote said.

Marie looked down on the short man. "I am strong," she told him. "I don't mind. Is she very ill?"

The doctor did his best to look wise. "In the hospital we could do more," he said.

"What could you do?" Marie asked.

He shrugged. "We could see."

"Goodnight, doctor," she said.

He lowered his lids. "I will come in the morning."

"Thank you," she said, walking with him to the door.

She returned to her mother and grasped her hand. "Get Dédé," Marguerite said.

Marie hesitated. "Are you sure, Mamma?" She held her breath. Despite her own experiments with voodoo, Sanité Dédé frightened her.

"Of course," said Marguerite, scowling childishly. "Get Dédé."

"Yes, Mamma." Marie took a towel from the rack on the washstand and wiped the perspiration from her mother's forehead. "I'll go in a few minutes."

"Tell me about Jacques," said Marguerite. "Where did you meet him, child?"

Marie wrapped her hands in the towel, squeezing parts of it with her fingers until they ached. "At the market, Mamma," she said. "We started talking. I don't know how it happened."

"He is a good man?" asked Marguerite. "He is nice?"

"I love him, Mamma. Yes, he is a good man, too."

Marguerite smiled thinly. "I am very happy," she said. "Get Dédé."

"Yes, dear."

Marie rose, her skirts swirling, and left the room quickly. If she hurried she might be back with Dédé before Jacques got there. It was only a few blocks to Dédé's house. She would run all the way. But when she opened the gate Jacques was already there, an arm raised to pull the bell rope, a great smile of surprise showing his white teeth. He came in with a rush, slamming the gate behind him. His arms encircled her. His mouth was on hers before she could speak.

For a moment she gave herself to his mouth, to his lean, strong, carpenter's arms, to the beat of his heart. When she could breathe again she told him about Marguerite. "Go talk to her, Jacques. I'll only be gone a little while."

He pressed a thigh between hers. "Where are you going?"

She had to tell him, and he frowned.

"It's to please her, Jacques," she begged.

The wrinkles left his forehead. "Of course," he said. "I'll be with her. But hurry."

"I'll hurry." She put her arms around him.

"Marie," he said, "I hate voodoo."

She wriggled free. "Go talk to her, Jacques. I'll be back in a few minutes. Please, Jacques!"

Marguerite opened her eyes, it seemed with effort. It was difficult for him to know what to say, but they talked. At last Marguerite went to sleep again, and then as quickly awakened, her eyes wide again, and staring into his. He thought how beautiful she must have been, how very beautiful; unlike Marie, for there was no resemblance at all. He thought of his race, and its strangeness, unconscious of his own beauty.

"Dédé?" Marguerite moaned.

"Marie will be back soon," he promised.

"Monsieur Charles?" Marguerite asked.

He put a large pale brown hand on her shoulder. "Sleep a little," he said.

She smiled faintly. "So long to sleep, Jacques. I have been thinking, dear. Marie will need you."

Suddenly Marie was there, the woman with her, an old black woman with a black veil over her face. Dédé waited in the door. She frowned at them, and pulled back the veil, showing her thick dark features. She moved toward the bed slowly, walking with a slight limp, but with a regal air, her manner professional and serene. She set the small cloth bag she carried on a chair by the bed and stood there a moment, closing her eyes. Then she opened them and gazed steadily into the watching eyes of Marguerite. "You have a crab in you," she told Marguerite. "It's biting your insides. I see it well."

Marie heard Jacques make a grunting noise. Dédé heard

24

it, too, and her eyes flashed. "Nobody else must be in this room," she said sternly. "The work will not be good."

"Come, Jacques." Marie led him outside, back into the front garden.

Jacques didn't look at her. "Does your mother believe this?" he asked.

Questioning it worried her. "You mustn't ask things like that," she told him. "Of course my mother believes it. In Santo Domingo my mother's people had great power. My mother's mother was a famous worker. She taught Mamma a great deal of knowledge, but she never used it."

"My mother believed it," he admitted in a weary tone.

"Then why not you, Jacques?"

"It is ignorance," he said.

She shuddered. "You frighten me! I don't know what I believe sometimes. Dédé frightens me, too, a little. I know only what I have seen, and I believe you're wrong. I'm sure of that at least. Monsieur Mazereau has told you it is ignorance, hasn't he?" She knew that Monsieur Mazereau had much influence over Jacques. Lately she had been thinking he had too much. He had taught Jacques to read and write, and he lent Jacques books to read. Jacques had told her all this and about some of his reading. It worried her. Too much education was not good for them.

"He and others," Jacques replied. "I feel they are right." But then he put his arms around her. "Let's not talk about it now," he begged.

When Dédé passed them silently, without speaking a word, Jacques said, "I must go now. You'll be busy with your mother." He silenced her when she protested that she had invited him to supper, that she had promised to make him a gumbo. "I'll stop by at the same time tomorrow," he told her.

He came every day for nearly two weeks after that, until the day Marguerite died. Dédé had been called too late, but the end was quiet and without pain. The crab was dead, Dédé explained, but it had done too much damage before she had been there to put the tub of cold water with the floating stale bread beneath the bed, to sprinkle the corners of the room with ginger root soaked in sweet oil, to give Marguerite a potion of blackberry tea and powdered cat's eyes.

Chapter 2

JACQUES watched as she went down the path cutting through the tall weeds, and as she paused a moment before the door of the shack. He was too far away to hear her knock, but he saw the door open to admit her. She walked through the black rectangle and into what seemed to be darkness. He pressed a fist against his mouth and cursed in his mind.

He left his hiding place, feeling despicable because he had spied on her. Yet he had felt he must know if what he had long suspected was true. Marie was visiting Sanité Dédé, and he was positive she had been doing so since she first discovered she was pregnant, if not before.

As he walked back toward the Rue du Rampart Jacques wondered if she had not been going there ever since Marguerite's death. He knew Marie still felt Dédé could have saved her mother had she summoned the woman earlier, and that it was Doctor Ducote she had always blamed. He had never argued with her about it, hoping the notion would pass, that it was the fanciful notion of a woman.

They had been married six months now. Less than one month after Marguerite's funeral they had been married in the Cathedral of St. Louis by old Père Antoine. Marie's neighbors shook their heads and said to each other that it was shameful she did not wait for a full year of mourning, and indecent that she had never worn black, but she had seen no use in doing either. Nothing could help Marguerite.

So she and Jacques had been married quietly, with only Monsieur Mazereau as a witness. Charles Laveau had not come, as he had not come to Marguerite's funeral. But he had sent notes and, with one, money for the expenses. Then, three weeks after her marriage, he had visited them, and told them their house was ready. Marie had been glad to leave Marguerite's cottage, where she had spent all her life. She had found tenants with ease, and soon they were settled in their own home, blocks away, and out of the old city, below the Esplanade, the wide street that divided the original city from a newer section. Three months after their wedding the baby made known its existence. Jacques had trembled with happiness, and Marie's eyes had grown brighter yet more gentle each week.

Crossing a muddy street, Jacques thought his face must be on fire. It was not so much anger that blazed in him as humiliation. He couldn't understand it. He had always prided himself that he had never had anything to do with voodoo. That was for black people, for slaves. He knew some of his own race practiced it in secret, and that even some white people did so. But to him it was evil and cursed. He must do something about Marie, he told himself. He must be patient and not blame her too much; his own mother had believed in it. Yet this could not go on.

It was a silver-green Sunday afternoon in February, warm and still sunny although it grew late, but it had rained almost all the night before. The streets were black slush, the ditches bubbled and gurgled, overflowing with filth. Jacques picked his way with care, remaining, where they existed, on the wooden *banquettes,* as sidewalks were called in New Orleans. He had decided not to go home yet. Walking might help clear his mind. Farther uptown on the Rue du Rampart the streets were better, the *banquettes* more dependable. Then he began to hear the drums.

He knew what they were and where they were. He had

28

come far. It was the Sunday afternoon bamboula in the square just off the Rue du Rampart and across the street from where the Rue d'Orleans ended, and where once had stood one of the old forts guarding the city. Cleared now, it was a meeting place each Sunday for the blacks, most of them slaves, where they danced and sang and amused themselves from noon until dusk.

When he reached it, Jacques stood outside the low picket fence surrounding the square, and watched for a few minutes. But for a few tall sycamore trees, the square was devoid of foliage. Even the grass had been stomped down and killed by years of dancing feet, and the earth was naked beneath the crowd that now filled it. He judged that there were three or four hundred people there, almost all black, with only a few brown and yellow faces among them. No wonder it was coming to be known as Congo Square!

Two drums beat. An old man sat astride one of a cylindrical shape, his back bent, his head down, both hands beating out his rhythm; he used both the heels of his hands and his fingers, faster, faster, faster. Another man accompanied him on a round drum, held between his knees as he crouched on his haunches. The only other musical instrument was a curious stringed one that Jacques knew was of a type imported from Africa. Fashioned from a calabash, it had but two strings, attached to two pegs, and at the end of its finger board was the crudely carved figure of a man or a god, an image slightly obscene. This instrument was played by the oldest man of all, a tiny withered creature with snowy hair and arms like pipe stems who might have been nearly a hundred years of age.

The noise the musicians made was harsh, cacophonous, brutal. Jacques leaned against the fence, more sickened than ever. These people would deny that this had anything to do with voodoo. Perhaps it didn't, but he knew many of them, perhaps most, were believers, that many practiced it in one

29

form or another. Were these the people with whom Marie felt a sisterhood? He was both grieved and revolted by the thought.

All about the musicians in the square the people danced. They went round and round in circles, sometimes holding hands, sometimes not, shaking themselves, writhing and twisting, men and women coming together and parting, squirming like snakes, often in a parody of love. Some of them sang, usually the women, yet it could hardly be called singing. A woman would release one note, a barbarous screeching, howling sound that went up and up toward the sky. Then another, and another, until it seemed the incredible noise must be heard in every part of the city. Then there would be silence but for the music. A moment later they would begin again.

A man began singing. This was a chant, obviously in some African tongue, for it was not French. Now most of the dancers ceased, crowding about the singer to listen; the three musicians altered their rhythm to accompany him. Then a dozen women formed a circle about him, and the others stepped back to create a clearing. The women each held a colored handkerchief up over their heads, grasping a corner of it in each hand. They began shuffling about the singer in a slow and solemn circle, moving the handkerchiefs from left to right, then dropping their arms to form other patterns with them, moving the handkerchiefs in front of them, behind them. The man continued to sing; there was little tune; the words seemed to repeat, over and over, monotonously. The effect was weird, hypnotic, savage.

Jacques grasped the pickets until his hands turned white. Sweat ran in streams down his face. His body felt chilled beneath his clothes. One of the dancing women screamed out a single note. Another took it up, then still another. Jacques turned away suddenly and left the place as fast as he could walk, wanting to run. A few blocks away the cathedral bells began to ring the hour, and he crossed himself. He thought of going to the Father, to Père Antoine, but he was too ashamed for that.

The candles were lighted by the time Marie came home. In the last moment of dusk she came through their garden, and he stood in the door watching her. He was calmer now, but he still had no idea what he would say, or even if he would say anything yet.

She kissed him impulsively, and he put his hands on her hair and kept them there for a moment. "Foolish," she asked, "why did you follow me?"

He gaped stupidly, amazed. "You saw me!"

She shook her head, still held lightly in his hands. "No. Dédé told me. Of course she knew you were outside, Jacques."

Then Dédé had seen him. Somehow she had spied him from the house, perhaps from a window he hadn't noticed. Naturally she would try to make her knowledge of his presence seem due to her magic. "Why did you go?" he asked, putting his hands on her shoulders, but gently.

"She was ill," Marie said. "She's been ill for some time. She has a powerful enemy, but she will win. She will rise from her bed."

He turned his back on her and walked away. When he flung himself into a chair, facing her again, he didn't look at her. "How can you believe that kind of nonsense, Marie?" he asked dully. "If the woman is ill, she is ill. It has nothing to do with enemies! My God! What has she been teaching you?"

She came over slowly and sat at his feet, resting one cheek against his thigh, her head turned away from him, her black hair falling to the floor. She closed her eyes.

"She has taught me nothing wrong, Jacques," she said. "Only what is good for us. Actually she hasn't taught me anything in the way you mean. But I have learned."

"It's all ignorance!" he stormed, angry that she had admitted this much. Would it have been better not to have had her confession, not to have heard the truth? "You must know it is. We aren't savages! Besides, it is dangerous. You used to fear that woman."

"I don't any more," she said sleepily, almost purring. "Isn't it strange?" She waited a moment, and then she asked, "If you believe it is dangerous then you must believe in Dédé's powers a little, don't you think? Either it is nothing or it is real. It can only be dangerous if it is real. Don't you see? Everyone believes a little."

He grasped her shoulders and raised her forcibly, and their eyes met. Hers were smiling, but his were hard and angry. "It isn't that at all," he told her. "You know what I mean. Some of those people make their evil work real! They use tricks—even poison! You know that as well as I do! You must give me your promise that you won't go to Dédé's house again."

The smile left her face. "Don't ask me that, Jacques."

"Yes, I must ask you that."

"She is ill," she argued. "I am the only one who goes to her. I am her only friend. I must do that for Mamma. She was her friend. It would be wrong of me to desert her."

He stared down steadily. "And when she is well?"

"That will be different," she said. She rose to her feet. "I must get your supper. You must be starved."

When she had left the room, Jacques leaned forward in his chair and put his face in his hands.

On her way to prepare their evening meal Marie paused and slipped something beneath the mattress of their bed.

"But is it working?" Marie asked Dédé, faint lines appearing between her eyebrows, the corners of her mouth twisted downward. "I am worried." She thought of the *gris-*

gris beneath the mattress—strands of her hair and his, plaited together, scrapings of drops of blood, his from a towel when he had cut himself while shaving, hers obtained deliberately by pricking her finger with a needle, a tiny heart of red wax with their names written on a piece of paper inside, a small vial of lover's oil, and other objects, all put together by Dédé in a chamois bag, with the proper ceremonies and the proper words.

The old woman in the bed sighed. She was still sick, no worse, no better. "Are you sure it is still there? He didn't find it and remove it?"

"I look every day. It is there." Marie gazed at the one dirty window in the bedroom of Dédé's shack. It was April now, and each week Jacques seemed more silent, further removed from her. She knew why. He was growing more upset because she continued to visit Dédé. She always came here in the daytime when he was at work, and they never mentioned it, but she made no secret of it. Dédé had promised her that the charm would overcome his objections, that it would so bind him to her that he would overlook anything she did.

"Someone is against us," Dédé croaked from the bed. "Has he another woman? Is he impotent with you?"

Marie shook her head. "Not that." Jacques was a passionate man. It was the way he looked at her in the early evenings and at breakfast, as if he didn't know what to say to her, as if they had nothing to talk about any more. "There is no other woman," she added. "I am sure of that."

"It may be my enemy sapping my strength," said Dédé. "As she weakens my body she weakens my work. But it is only for a time, my child. You will see. The *gris-gris* will hold your man to you, have no fear. He is helpless against it."

"I want him to love me, not to be helpless," Marie said. "I wanted the *gris-gris* so that he would love me even more—

33

and trust me, too. I wanted it so that we would not quarrel any more about this. Now we do not even quarrel about it; it is worse than that."

"Men are stubborn," said Dédé, "but he will change, dear. Leave me now. You must go."

"I'll come tomorrow," Marie told her. The old woman always dismissed her in this way, and she always obeyed. "I'll bring you something good to eat."

"Some sweet cakes of some kind," the voodooienne directed. "Lately I've longed for sweets."

"You shall have them."

Behind her Marie heard the old woman cackling shrilly, as she always did when she was pleased.

The smell of her washing filled the yard, the smell of red hot charcoal and boiling yellow soap. The bell on the front gate clanged noisily. Someone was pulling insistently upon the rope to which it was attached. Marie wiped the hot, strong suds from her hands and arms on her apron as best she could, and went around the narrow alley between her house and the side fence.

A small yellow woman stood outside the gate. As Marie opened it the woman lifted her hand to pull the rope again, and the hand remained in midair, making a kind of salute. Marie recognized her visitor; she had seen her in the streets many times, but they had never met before. "Marie Saloppé," Marie said, almost under her breath. Then louder, "Come in."

"Thank you." Saloppé stepped into the front yard and Marie closed and latched the gate behind her. She studied the small woman idly, but thoughtfully. Was this Dédé's enemy? The idea had not occurred to her before, but she knew Saloppé was a powerful voodooienne, that for years she and Dédé had ruled over separate cults, that there was rivalry and jealousy between them. "Come in the backyard," Marie invited. "I am washing, but we will have some coffee."

She stepped aside and let Saloppé go first. Following her down the alley she kept her gaze on Saloppé's straight back. Saloppé was wearing a white skirt and waist and a snowy white *tignon*. Both her arms were covered with gold bracelets and a heavy gold chain jangled about her throat and over her bosom. When she reached the yard in the rear she seated herself on the stoop leading into the house. She said nothing. Clouds of white smoke rose from the tub of boiling clothes on the furnace. "I will bring coffee," Marie told her, a little nervously. "It is always ready." She frowned as she crossed the yard to the brick kitchen.

When she returned, Saloppé was still sitting on the stoop. Her knees were drawn up before her, and her arms were crossed upon them. "I have come to invite you to St. John's Bayou on Saturday night," she said. "Will you come?"

Marie was pouring the coffee. As she proffered a cup to Saloppé her hand began trembling. "I have never been."

"I know," Saloppé said. "But it is time."

Marie sat down on the stoop beside her. "Why is it time?"

"Child, it is time," Saloppé repeated. "Saloppé has told you. Dédé will die soon."

Marie stared at her with immense eyes, but Saloppé did not meet her gaze. Now, thought Marie, I know she is the one: if such things be true, Saloppé is killing Dédé. She murmured only, "Dédé is very old and very ill, poor thing."

"She will die," Saloppé said again. She took a sip of her coffee, held it in her mouth for a moment and swallowed it with a gulp. Then she added, "Saloppé is going to die, too."

Marie could think of nothing to say. She did not even know what she thought or believed.

"You will come on Saturday night?" Saloppé asked. "You will see and then you will know." In a sort of sing-song way she said once more, "It is time. It is the hour."

Marie put her cup down and rose. She made herself look straight down at the woman. "What do I know of this?" she asked. "I am only a friend to poor Dédé. I go to see her because she is alone. I have never been to the bayou meetings. I am a good Catholic. Nearly every morning I go to church."

"I, too, am a good Catholic," Saloppé said quietly. "The saints work with me. I do no evil work, no matter what people say. Your mamma was one of us, Marie. At least she was once. I knew her all her life. I came with her on the sailing ship, with her and her mother. Your grandmother was a queen on the island, a great woman. That is why you have been chosen."

Marie was trembling visibly now. She knew the answer, but she asked the question. "*What* have I been chosen?" Suddenly it was as if she had known this a long time.

"Listen to me, child," said Saloppé, rising. "You have been chosen because I have selected you. You know a leader must select her successor." She sighed. "That was Dédé's sin. Long ago she should have made peace with me, and passed her power to me. You know that is true and how the line goes on. Surely your mother told you that."

"Mamma was no voodoo!" Marie cried. "She had nothing to do with it. She told me some things, yes! But she talked of it little. That is the truth!"

"It is sad," Saloppé said. "Yet in the end she sent for Dédé. I should have been the one to come, but that I have forgiven. It is you I have chosen. You will be with us Saturday night."

"No," said Marie firmly. "Besides everything else, my husband objects. We quarrel because I visit Dédé. I can't come to the bayou. It is impossible." She knew what went on at the bayou meetings. She had heard many stories, and there had even been times when she had been filled with curiosity to see one of the meetings. But it was out of the question now. Jacques would kill her, or at the very least despise her, if she were to so much as suggest attending one. It was one thing to believe a little in a harmless *gris-gris*, another to meet with

36

these people in the moonlight on the banks of St. John's Bayou.

Marie Saloppé was moving toward the alley. "I must go now," she said. "If you do not come this Saturday night you will come soon. Nothing can change that. You are the one, and you have much to learn before I die." She folded her arms over her breast, and opened her eyes wide at Marie. "Death comes," she added in a hoarse whisper. "It comes to Dédé and to Saloppé. It is strange that it comes to both of us in such a short time."

"How do you know you're going to die?" Marie asked her. "Why do you believe this?" She kept trying to think this was foolishness.

"You know how I know it." She began walking back toward Marie. "But death comes always in threes," she added, "so it has come to one other. It is already done."

Marie shuddered. "What do you mean?"

"I tell you this only because you will soon know, anyway," Saloppé said, "and because my telling you first may give you faith in me, and bring you to me sooner." She raised herself on her toes, placing a hand on Marie's shoulder, and whispered into her ear.

Marie felt for a moment as if she had been struck blind. When she could see again Saloppé was gone. In the distance she heard the gate close.

She finished her washing, working hard and deliberately, pouring into the work all her energy and all her attention. Otherwise she kept her mind blank. When everything was hung out on her lines she put away her tub, her scrubbing board, her brushes and soap, leaving the furnace to grow cold above the ashes, and went into the house and dressed herself for Jacques. Then she sat quietly in the parlor and began to work on her sewing, rocking back and forth in her chair, thinking of nothing but the christening dress she was making for her baby. But at last she dropped the dress and she ceased rocking. She sat there doing nothing, letting her hands lie idly in her lap, letting the thoughts come, the few memories.

She was still sitting there when Jacques came home from work. Without moving, and in a voice that was barely audible, she told him. "Jacques, my father has been dead for two days." It never occurred to her to wonder why she then repeated it, speaking as her mother might have. "Monsieur Charles is dead," she said. "He was killed in a fall from his horse two days ago."

It was nearly a week later before news of the death of her father reached Marie through other sources. He had died after being thrown from a horse. The report came through the grapevine that extended all along the Mississippi River country among the colored people.

"And that's how Saloppé knew it," Jacques insisted. "In no other way, Marie. It's just that it reached her sooner. Those women build up contacts in every way they can. It is a trick."

"Perhaps," she murmured. She had told Jacques only that Saloppé had come to tell her of her father's fate, nothing else. She did not dare tell him of the invitation to the rites at St. John's Bayou or any of the rest of it.

"There can be nothing else," Jacques said.

It was early in the morning, not daylight yet. They had heard about Charles Laveau the evening before. Now Marie was thinking that as soon as Jacques had gone to work she would attend Mass. There would still be time. It would do her good. It might stop her from feeling sorry she had not gone to Saloppé on Saturday night, at least to ask her questions.

"It is all trickery," Jacques said. "Trickery and boasting. That one is worse than Dédé."

"Dédé is dying," she told him.

38

Jacques' gray eyes flashed. "My God, you sound like a voodoo woman!"

"She is dying," Marie said.

"And will you go there today?"

"Yes, Jacques." She smiled faintly. "But first I'm going to church."

"I'll walk with you." Jacques put his arms around her, and she buried her eyes in his shoulder.

"Poor Papa!" It was the first time she had wept for him. Jacques held her tightly, and she did not weep long. When she raised her head, his hands were on her hair; they lingered there a moment; they touched the large hoop earrings Charles Laveau had given to her. "I'll pray for him this morning," she told Jacques.

He held her at arm's length, squeezing her shoulders gently. Even yet the child did not show much. She carried it well. Only another woman might have known. "I do not really mind your being kind to Dédé," he said. "But if the end comes for her you must forget those kind of people. If Saloppé comes here do not admit her."

"I don't like her, Jacques."

"Well, then," he said, "forget her. She can do you no good. You or our son."

She laughed, her eyes still wet. "You're so sure it'll be a son!"

"I hope it will be."

They walked through the streets in the pale light. There were already many people out. Neighbor women were scrubbing their stoops with red brick dust, for both cleanliness and luck, and gossiping with each other. Men were emerging from the small houses and setting out for work. Marie and Jacques spoke to nearly everyone, but did not stop; Jacques was already in danger of being late in arriving at Monsieur Mazereau's. They hurried on. As they reached the cathedral

39

there were even more people in the streets, and in the distance, across the Place d'Armes, there were the market noises. The city had awakened.

Jacques left her in front of the cathedral. When she emerged she walked out the narrow streets toward Dédé's house. She felt calmer now. Her prayers had warmed her heart, and the quiet in the church had comforted her. As she reached the trees that grew along the street where Dédé lived, Marie Saloppé came to meet her. "It was true, wasn't it?" Saloppé asked.

Marie nodded, wanting not to stop, but to walk straight past the woman. She had planned to visit only briefly with Dédé, then to go home and be alone, to try to preserve her inner quiet.

"You didn't come to the meeting," Saloppé said, not in a tone of accusation, but simply as a statement. "But you will come."

"I don't want to talk about it now," Marie told her. "I've just come from the cathedral. You've been to see Dédé?"

Saloppé smiled. "You know I could not go to see her. I've been waiting for you. I knew you would come this morning, as I knew you would go to church. The Church is good for you, Marie, but so am I. The Church can do certain things, but I can do many others."

Without saying a word, Marie turned and walked away, moving slowly away from Saloppé, her heartbeat rapid, but her head high, her eyes wide and unblinking. As she quickened her pace her earrings made a faint, jangling noise that only she could hear. Papa's earrings, she thought. My poor Monsieur Charles! Mamma's poor Monsieur Charles! She would wear the gold hoops always, she determined, until the very end of her life.

There were pattering, almost running feet behind her. "You will see! You will see!" chanted Saloppé in her ears.

Marie walked faster still, in long, graceful strides. Trying

40

to keep up with her, Saloppé was breathing hard as she tried
to talk. "Only for you I do this. Only because it must
be so, Laveau."

"Go and leave me in peace!" Marie frowned. No one had
ever called her "Laveau" before.

"I am peace."

Marie said nothing more. All the voodoo women she had
ever known talked this way. There had been moments when
she had thought it mere foolishness, yet beneath the foolishness something was concealed that frightened her.

"Now do you see?"

Marie halted and twisted her hands together in front of
her. They were in sight of Dédé's house. A large number of
people were gathered on the stoop. A woman released a loud,
long wail. Marie turned and walked away.

"Now I will be a great queen!" cried Saloppé, following
her. "I will be a great queen for a short time!"

Marie did not answer her, but Saloppé continued her chanting. "And then it will be you, dear one. It will be Laveau!"

Marie thought she felt her child move within her, and she
felt faintly ill. Passing a wooden picket fence before a cottage
along the street, she grasped it and stood there, swaying a
little, wanting to run, but unable to do so. Saloppé put a
hand on her arm. "You are sick, little one?" Marie thought
vaguely: It is all foolish talk. Little one! I am twice her size.

"I will take you home."

"No!" Marie wanted to turn and spit into the woman's
face. "If only you would go away!"

"Come." Saloppé's arm was about her waist. "You have
had too much grief."

Marie held fast to the picket. She shook her head. "I do
not grieve for Dédé. Please go!"

"Come."

Somehow there was nothing more Marie could do. It was
as if all her strength had left her and a film lay over her

41

brain. Was this as Dédé had felt, she wondered vaguely, and she grew cold in all her limbs. Then she knew her limbs were moving, and she was walking, Saloppé's arm about her, the small woman's head hardly reaching her shoulder.

Jacques sat on the edge of her bed and his hand was on her hair. But his face looked drawn and tired, and his gaze was withdrawn from hers. She raised the tiny, unfinished christening dress and held it against her cheek. Tears rolled from her great eyes. It was the first time she had cried. Jacques petted her, and she tried to speak. "Just rest," he said gently. "Don't try to talk now." Madame Laclotte, an old woman with pale yellow skin and clear and patrician features, came into the room with a bowl of steaming broth. "Ah, she weeps," whispered Madame Laclotte. "That is good. A woman must weep."

Marie rolled the little dress into a ball and thrust it at Jacques. "Take that away," she said, her voice breaking.

Jacques took it and left her. Madame Laclotte bent over her, spooning the broth as if to tempt her with its aroma. "You must eat, child. At least drink this." Marie turned her head and buried her face in her pillow.

"An empty stomach makes a sadder heart," sighed Madame Laclotte, setting the bowl down on a table. She pulled a rocking chair up to the bed and seated herself. "Listen, child," she said comfortingly, "you and Jacques are young and strong. You will have many children. You must get well now, for them and for Jacques." She reached out and took hold of the spoon in the soup again. "Let me feed you just a little."

Marie shook her head. Her voice came muffled from the pillow. "How long have you been here?"

"Almost a week."

So it had been almost a week now! It all seemed so vague, all the time since she had become ill before Dédé's house. She remembered some of it—the pain, Jacques being there,

Madame moving about, her mind clearing for moments, then the world fading away once more, day and night indistinguishable. "It was a boy?" she asked.

"It was a boy." Madame said it in a tone that indicated that she was repeating, that she had told her that many times.

"A boy." Marie rolled over on her back and gazed up at the ceiling.

Jacques came back into the room and Madame rose. "Try to get her to take the broth before it grows cold," she told him. "I will be back in the morning."

When Madame had gathered together her things and left, Marie let Jacques feed her a little. It almost choked her, but she was comforted by his arm supporting her head and the thought that it might please him if she ate. She got down nearly half the bowl and then could not continue. "I'll be better tomorrow," she promised, forcing herself to smile faintly.

He took the bowl out of the room and returned to the rocking chair. She put a hand on one of his and squeezed it until she imagined she must be hurting him. In that moment she wanted to hurt him, to make him feel something from her, for still he did not really look at her, but sat there withdrawn into himself.

"You must sleep."

"I have slept," she told him, "and I dreamed. I dreamed I was dead. I was floating on a dark river, and all about me other bodies were floating. Their eyes were closed and their faces were dead, but I could recognize some of them. I recognized Mamma and Monsieur Charles." She did not tell him Dédé had been in the river, too. "I recognized others, too," she went on. "And there were strangers—many, many strangers. I almost died, didn't I, Jacques?"

"You were very ill, Marie," he said tenderly. "But you must not think of that now."

"I know I was dying," she said. "Perhaps I was dead for a

while. I know Père Antoine was here. I could smell him, his good smell—incense and candle drippings." She looked away from Jacques and at the window. "It is dusk, isn't it?"

Jacques stroked her hair. "You are out of danger now. You must sleep and eat and get strong."

"I didn't care that I was dead," she told him. "Isn't that strange? Yet now I am very glad to be alive."

She thought his eyes narrowed a little as she glanced up at him. "Yes, Jacques," she said. "I am glad to be alive even now."

"Marie!" He flung himself toward her suddenly, his head pressing against her shoulder. Under the arm she put around him she felt his body tremble and shudder. But in a moment he broke from her and sat up, wiping his eyes. He rose. "Please sleep!" he cried, and went out of the room quickly.

She awakened in the night and stretched out an arm toward the other side of the bed and felt with longing in the cool sheets' emptiness, and remembered again, and knew he was on the sofa in the parlor.

Within a week she was up again, weak at first and hating being weak. But her strength came back rapidly. Madame Laclotte made her daily visits shorter and shorter, and then at last Marie found herself back at all her own tasks, and feeling well and strong, the blood running swift and hot in her veins. And Jacques returned to their bed, and at least when she awakened in the night he was beside her. But that was all. He still remained far from her. He was always gentle, always tender, yet it seemed that there was a barrier between them. There were questions unasked and unanswered, and she wondered what it was she didn't know, for she felt it must be that there was something she didn't know.

Then she awoke in the middle of a summer night and found she had been crying in her sleep. She lay on her back for a while trying to recall if she had dreamed. Suddenly she knew Jacques was awake, too.

"Why did it happen?" she asked, so softly it was almost to the darkness alone. That was the principal question.

He breathed hard. "I don't know."

Now she could be certain he was awake and with her. "I don't understand."

"It is better not to think of it."

"There was no reason for it," she said. "I had always felt well, Jacques. I did not hurt myself. I did nothing I should not have done."

He was silent a moment, then he said, "It happens to women. I don't know much about it, Marie. And this isn't the time to talk about it."

"Then when will be the time to talk about it?" She sat up in the bed, her feet pulled under her Turkish fashion. "We never talk about it. Is that what is between us, Jacques? Do you hate me for it?"

"I could never hate you."

"But you blame me."

"I do not blame you. Lie down, Marie."

"I know why you blame me," she said. "You know that Saloppé brought me home that day. Was she still here when you came home? You see, Jacques, I cannot remember."

Again he was silent. At last he said, "She was here." He made a choking sound in his throat. "She was doing all kinds of filthy things." He turned over on his side with a groan. "My God!" he whispered.

She put her hands on his shoulders, crouching over him in the bed. "Jacques! Jacques! *She* killed our baby!"

"I don't know!" He was almost whimpering. "I just don't know! I don't really believe that. She did nothing to you. I don't think she touched you. But she had put all sorts of things about the room, and in the bed, and under the bed. She said she was trying to save the baby, and you." He stopped, and then he said, "I beat her, Marie! Do you know that? I beat her and then I threw her out! She is the only woman I have ever struck in my life. Then I sent for Doctor Ducote and Madame Laclotte."

Her arms still about him, Marie began to shake and tremble, and he felt it. "Stop it!" he cried. "You believe she has power! That's what I have feared. Stop it, Marie!"

"I don't know," she muttered, her teeth chattering as if she were cold in the summer night. She would not tell him what she was thinking: Maybe you killed the baby, Jacques. Maybe you killed him when you dared lay hands on Saloppé. She said, "She wants power over me; that is all I know."

He pulled her down into his arms, gripping her fiercely in his arms, hurting her. "Listen to me, Marie," he whispered hoarsely, his mouth against her ear. "She has no power. Perhaps she would like to control you through fear, but that is the only way she could gain power over you. I was not afraid of her. If I had thought she had touched your body I would have killed her. Perhaps I should have killed her, anyway!"

"Hush, Jacques," she murmured. "Hush! Such talk is not good!"

He pushed her away from him so roughly that she fell back upon her own pillow and her hair tumbled over her face. She watched him cross the room and light a candle. The flame flickered wildly as he set it on the table beside the bed, and she knew his hand was trembling.

"What she did was all foolishness," he said, glaring down at her. "It was disgusting, but it was nonsense. It could do no good, but it could do no harm, except to make a person sick. I could have vomited!"

She was quiet, but she prayed he would stop.

"There was a dead female frog in your bed," he said, his tone lowered almost to a guttural whisper. "She said it was a mother frog she had sacrificed for you, to take your place, to appease the zombie. There was a kitten with its throat slashed under your bed, and the sheet covering you was sprinkled

46

with its blood. She explained to me, screaming at me, that the dead kitten represented our boy, Marie! There were rusty knives and scissors under the bed, too. For what? To ward off evil spirits, I think. There was a pot of water in each corner of the room, with stale bread floating in it. To soak up bad luck? Don't you see, Marie? It is all corruption, all utter filth!"

"Let us not take chances, Jacques," she begged. "Please be still!" Then she added, "I had to know what happened. I had to ask you."

His face was still angry, but he said only, "There'll be no more sleep this night."

"I am through with sleep."

"Marie, have you seen Saloppé?"

That startled her. "Never," she told him, and it was the truth. "Not since that day. I swear to you, Jacques!"

"I believe you."

"I never want to see her again," she vowed, although it frightened her to say the words. "Now, let us not talk of her any more."

He was staring at her. "Marie, do you believe she can know what we are saying?"

She didn't answer him.

"You do!" he cried. "You are frightened that she might know what we say to each other here in our own room!" He shook his head slowly from side to side. "My poor Marie!"

She put her hands over her face. "I just don't know, Jacques!"

"She can do nothing to you except what she causes you to do to yourself in your own mind," he told her. "Marie, come into the parlor with me. There is something else you must know, and perhaps it will convince you that Saloppé does not cause all our troubles—at least that."

She crawled from the bed and followed him, feeling still nervous, and now confused. "What is it, Jacques?" The clean,

47

polished boards of the bare floors felt cold beneath her bare feet.

He lighted candles on the table in the parlor and uncorked a decanter. "When we have a number of problems," he said slowly, "it is often easier than when we have but one. Drink some wine, Marie."

She raised to her lips the glass he handed her, and a few drops spilled on her thin nightgown. She watched as he took papers from the drawer of the table and spread them out on top of it. "It may be I should have waited until daylight," he said, "but what difference can it make? You must know about it. Marie, you have lost this house. It seems Monsieur Charles did not have the deed recorded when he died, and Madame Laveau has won the title to it in the court."

Marie stared at him, feeling numb, almost disbelieving.

"It is true," Jacques went on. "I knew of it first while you were sick, and Monsieur Mazereau tried to help us legally, but he failed. I thought it best not to tell you until you were better. And do not blame your father, Marie. I am sure he intended to put everything in order, but a man does not expect to die suddenly, by being thrown from a horse."

She drained her glass and put it down. "But this is my house!"

"According to the law it is not, Marie," he said gently. "But do not worry. You have the other one, the one in which you and your mother lived. That title is quite clear. Perhaps later we can move there. In the meantime we will find something to rent." He shuffled the papers. "Do you want to see these?"

"You know I read no English."

"We will get along, Marie," he assured her. "We will manage. Try not to be unhappy about it."

Her gaze was intense. "You had to tell me this way," she said. "You wanted to show me that misfortunes can come from others than Saloppé." She moved her head from side to

48

side. "My poor Jacques, you are a fool! For all my love of you, you are a fool, my dear!"

His eyes darkened.

"It is I who was the fool perhaps," she went on. "I should have taught you. Perhaps I would have if you would have listened. You and your Monsieur Mazereau! You listen only to him and to what is in his books! You want to be like a white man and learn a white man's ways, and his ignorance, too. You want to forget the knowledge of our people. You want to forget your blood. You think the power had nothing to do with this? Or that at least it might not have been prevented? If only I had known sooner! If only I had not been too ill for you to tell me!"

"And what would you have done, Marie?" He was almost shouting.

"I have not enough knowledge to have managed it myself," she said quietly. "But I could have found help."

"From Saloppé?"

"From someone," she replied.

"From voodoo!" he cried. "From Saloppé or some other like her!"

"To deny is to destroy yourself," she said. "We are being destroyed. Do you not see? This is only the beginning. You fool and child! Do you imagine all this is an accident, a series of accidents? Next perhaps it will be you, and I will be alone. Or it could be me. There is a curse against us. There is death at the door. I know. It is a great sin to deny."

"In God's name, shut up, Marie!"

She scarcely heard him. She dropped to the floor and sat there, drawing her naked feet up under her, her head lowered, a glazed look in her eyes. She was not really hearing anything, nor seeing anything.

Jacques poured out words at her.

"Do you know what voodoo is?" he shouted. "I will tell you! It is the worship of the snake, Marie. It is for jungle

49

savages! It is evil incarnate. It is cursing God! It is sin and abomination, Marie!"

She was not listening to him. "Madame Laveau could have been stopped," she said. "Even now perhaps she could be punished. I will see."

"What are you doing to us, Marie?" he cried. He was bending over her, his face twisted with pain and anger and colored a strange dark red. "You think me a fool? If I am a fool, you have become demented! You talk like a witch woman in the jungles!"

She trembled. "Hush, Jacques!"

"I cannot live this life!" he shouted. "I thought perhaps losing the baby would teach you, but you are still the same. You look like Saloppé now, like Dédé!" He seized the front of her gown and jerked her up roughly, until her face was inches from his own. "You are cursed!" he cried. "Cursed."

He let her drop back to the floor, and she buried her face against her knees. "God help you!" Jacques said. He clenched his fists, wanting in his heart to strike her.

When he left the room she paid little attention. She just sat there. He returned dressed for the street. She did not even look up at him. "Only the power can save us," she went on. "Nothing else. I will have the power and I will be the strong one. I will rule. The power is peace and you will see. Saloppé will teach me the wisdom. I will learn all she knows and then I will learn more than she has ever learned, and then I will be queen. I have always known this, and you will know it, too. The power was born in me."

In a thin, whining voice utterly unlike her own, she began to sing an ancient song Marguerite had sung to her as a child, a forbidden song so old that no one remembered the exact meaning of its words: *"He-ron mandé, tigui li papa, he-ron mandé, tigui li papa, he-ron mandé, do se dan do-go!"*

"I'm going out," Jacques said, sounding strangled and sick. "I'm going out and walk."

She stopped singing and dropped her face into her open palms, moaning like an animal in pain. "You must walk with me," she muttered. "You must walk in the power."

The door closed behind him and then in the distance there was the sharp squeaking sound of the gate to the garden. She kept sitting there, rocking back and forth and singing to herself: "*He-ron mandé, tigui li papa, he-ron mandé, tigui li papa, he-ron mandé, tigui li papa. . . .*" When the first morning light appeared at the windows the knowledge began to come to her that Jacques would never come back.

Chapter 3

IT WAS St. John's Eve and the moon was full. It blazed down through the gnarled branches of the live oak trees. It silvered the moss that hung from the branches, and it brightened the dark waters of St. John's Bayou. It fell brightly upon the naked flesh of gleaming dark skins. And beyond the moon the stars blazed, it seemed almost with anger.

At the head of the clearing at the bayou's edge Saloppé sat erect upon her throne, a plain wooden chair with a high back set upon a wooden platform. She wore a short garment made of scarlet kerchiefs sewn together. About her waist was a heavy blue cord, and about her shoulders a red shawl with a heavy, deep fringe. Her hair was bound in a red and blue *tignon*, its knots standing high above her head. Her feet were bare and on each leg was an anklet of tiny bells. Beads were wrapped in row after row about her scrawny yellow throat, and they hung to her waist. Bracelets of beads and of gold almost covered her thin arms from wrists to elbows, and she wore many huge rings on her fingers. She sat perfectly still, her eyes wide open and staring.

This was the most important night in the voodoo calendar, the twenty-third of June, as Marie had long known. Saloppé had explained to her further that the custom of celebrating this night was very ancient. It was older than Christianity; it had been celebrated in all countries long, long ago, before St. John himself had lived, although the date now bore his name. Their ancestors had brought the custom of this celebration with them from Africa to Santo Domingo, and from there to this country, to New Orleans, when they had come after the revolution in the island years ago. More than this Saloppé did not know. It was important only that the date be observed in the traditional way.

On a throne set somewhat lower than Saloppé's sat Doctor John, an old black man with red and blue lines, that curved and swayed when the firelight fell upon his face, tattooed on his forehead and his cheeks. Watching him Marie realized that the tattooed lines represented snakes, and she could have vowed that those that reached from his temples to the corners of his mouth really writhed and twisted. He was naked but for a red loincloth, a dirty white rag tied about his forehead and the thick blue cord about his waist that were the insignia of his position as Saloppé's king, a power far less than hers, but, nonetheless, second in importance. Bells were bound to his ankles, too, and a bracelet formed of human bone bound his left wrist. He was speaking now and they were all silent, although no one could hear what he said, for he mumbled and groaned, his eyes shut. He raised and lowered his arms, now and then jerked his body stiffly. Once he cried out so inhumanly that Marie felt a chill sweep through her body, and a young girl near her shrieked and fell to the ground, then rolled over and over. Most of the people paid the girl no attention at all. A few mumbled approval, looking down at her. Others laughed loudly.

Marie stood near the platform on which Saloppé and Doctor John sat. She was wearing only a white camisole that reached to her knees. Her hair was unbound, her feet bare; she had been instructed to remove even her hoop earrings. She was to dress thus and be quiet. Her time would come. Now she could feel herself shivering, despite the warmth of the June night; the earth was cold beneath her feet. She felt no fear, but there were moments when she was sorry she had come, although she had known she must come. She watched the king's lips move and waited. She knew he was calling upon the ancient gods and upon the saints who aided them.

Doctor John ceased his inaudible gibbering and his posturing. He opened his eyes and stared straight ahead. Slowly he raised both of his arms, and immediately from the darkness came two men clad in loincloths, carrying between them a large box with bars set across its front. Something like a great sigh went up from the people, and Marie felt a queer tingle pass through her body. It was the god, the Vodu, the holy snake, the zombie. Without a sound, Saloppé rose and stood stiff and still, her head thrown back a little, her arms rigid at her sides. The men set the box down in the center of the clearing and backed away from it for a few feet; there they dropped to the ground, their foreheads touching the earth, their buttocks in the air. Saloppé took a deep breath and stepped down from the platform. She crossed the clearing rapidly and stepped upon the cage containing the snake. A shout went up from her people.

Now Doctor John approached the cage, and slowly the others moved forward, forming a circle. Marie remained where she had been, for she was not a member yet, not worthy of the power, and she knew she still must wait. She forced her eyes to remain open, forced herself to watch.

Saloppé suddenly thrust out a hand, and Doctor John seized it. At once they both began jerking violently. Their hands remained grasped, but they writhed and twisted convulsively. Saloppé threw her head back and cried out wildly. Her head bobbed about, back and forth and from side to side, as she sent cry after cry up into the night.

At last a woman seized Doctor John's other hand, and at once she, too, began to shake and jerk as if she were receiving vibrations from him. A moment later someone grasped that woman's free hand, and then another worshiper his. Suddenly everyone was grasping a hand, and they were all

55

twisting and writhing. Even the girl who had fallen near Marie's feet sprang upward and ran across the clearing and joined the others, and still others came out of the darkness of the trees. The circle changed and became a chain, writhing like a snake in the moonlight, all its components shaking and jerking. Watching, Marie felt all the chill leave her. Suddenly she felt warm and excited. She wanted to plunge forward and join them. Once when screams went up, screams so loud in the night that they must have been heard for miles about, her mouth opened, too, and she restrained herself with effort from screaming also.

It all ceased as suddenly as it had begun. Saloppé withdrew her hand from Doctor John's, and the whole chain broke with it. Some of the people couldn't stop shaking, but stood where they were, still powerless to cease the vibrations. A few, also still shaking, fell to the ground; others appeared to be unconscious. Yet all were silent. Marie had to use effort to keep from falling herself.

Then Doctor John cried out: "Bomba hen! Bomba hen hen!"

"Eh! Eh!" chanted Saloppé.

"Eh! Eh! Bomba hen hen!"

Words began pouring from Saloppé. Her head twisted round and round on her shoulders as she wailed out the words. It was all in the ancient tongue, and Marie knew no one really understood their meaning, for they were secret, but they were invocations, blessings on the people, and curses on their enemies. The Vodu was speaking through Saloppé.

At last the queen was through. She dropped her head and was silent. Then the same men who had brought forward the snake approached the cage again. One carried several objects in his hands. The other dragged a young goat by a rope around its waist. While Saloppé continued to stand there, her head lowered, and seemingly paying no attention to what went on about her, Doctor John dropped to his knees beside the goat. Someone thrust a knife into his hand, and he jerked back the small animal's head and plunged the knife into its throat. A cup appeared, and Marie watched the blood pour into it. When it was brimming full Doctor John raised it toward Saloppé. She took it and drank, and then held it for the king. He drank, but did not take it from her hands. She pressed it to her body, and stood as still as a statue.

Somewhere in the shadows a drum began to beat. Then a tom-tom. Then another drum. It was like the music Marie had often heard in Congo Square. A man began a chant:

> *"Eh! Eh! Bomba hen hen!*
> *Canga bafie te*
> *Danga moune de te*
> *Canga do ki li!*
> *Canga li!"*

The people began to come forward with vessels to catch the blood from the sacrificed goat. Those who had no cup used their hands, when they could, to catch a few drops, licking greedily at the scarlet liquid with which they stained their fingers.

A black man seized Marie's wrist.

But before she was allowed to approach the Vodu and the queen, Doctor John stepped forward. With a gesture he dismissed the black man who had brought her forward, and Marie stopped before the witch doctor. "Do not move, my child," said Doctor John in French. Someone handed him a long stick with a sharpened point and he began walking around her, drawing a circle on the earth, so that she stood in its exact center. He encircled her seven times, chanting all the while in words Marie could not even hear, for her mind seemed blocked in some way, and she no longer was entirely conscious of what was taking place.

"Be blessed, my child, be blessed!" said Doctor John in French and stepped back. He took the cup of blood from

Saloppé and brought it to Marie. "Drink, my child, and be blessed!"

Marie took the cup and managed to get it to her lips and return it. She tasted nothing, and she felt nothing.

A cry went up about her. "*Li Grand Zombi! Li Grand Zombi!*"

"Come, my child!" It was Saloppé, her hands outstretched from where she still stood atop the cage. Half in a trance, Marie stepped out of the circle and received both her hands. Saloppé drew her up until she, too, stood on the cage.

"I am your Mamma!" chanted Saloppé. "I am your Mamma! You are my child!"

"Yes, Mamma," said Marie, hardly knowing what she was saying. "Yes, Mamma."

"Tonight you will sit at my feet," said Saloppé, and led her down again and across the clearing to the platform, still holding her hand.

Saloppé sat on her throne, and Marie on the platform at her feet. Saloppé placed a small black box shaped like a coffin in her hands, and Marie held it quietly in her lap. The dancing began.

A tall Negro sprang into the space between the platform and the Vodu's cage, and began the dance. He whirled with increasing speed as the tom-toms and drums beat faster, leaping into the air, his legs spread wide, dropping almost on his toes, it seemed, and springing up again, ever high and higher, until he looked to be almost his own height above the earth. Then someone tossed him a live black rooster, its legs bound. The dancer quickly broke its neck and flung it from him. It was a signal. Others began to join the dance until soon they were all part of it. They spun and gyrated and leaped upward, sometimes singly, sometimes two or three, or even more, joining hands. But always in the center was the first dancer, whirling faster than the others, leaping higher.

Now Marie's trance began to fade and she began to feel

excited again. She watched as the dance grew wilder and wilder. Some of the dancers fell back on the ground and lay there shaking violently, some clawed at each other with their nails, bit with their teeth. Clothes were in shreds. Blood glowed on skin. Saloppé sensed how Marie felt, and put a hand on her shoulder. "Not for you, my child," she whispered. "You will stay here with me."

Couples began disappearing into the shadows. Wild outcries came from the clumps of trees. A man approached the platform and reached for Marie. From his position nearby Doctor John struck his arm with his stick.

A cloud obscured the moon. "We will go now," said Saloppé. "We will go home."

One of Saloppé's helpers proffered Marie a cup. "Drink of it," said Saloppé. Marie took a sip. It was not the warm blood of the goat this time, but rum. Saloppé took the cup from her. "We will go home," Saloppé said again. "Come with me, my new child."

In the morning Marie awakened with a dull headache and a feeling as if she had been drugged. She was long in gathering her consciousness together, and then she first thought of Jacques, not of the night before. Each morning her first thoughts were of him, although it had now been more than a month since he had left her, but this morning they were different. She had an impulse to call out to him, aloud, as if he had only stepped into the next room for a moment.

Then she began remembering more clearly that he was gone, and, she was positive, forever. When she recalled the night before, the rites on the banks of the bayou, she told herself that she would never have gone there if he had remained with her. But would she? Was that really true? She wasn't sure. She knew she would never be sure.

Yet how wrong Jacques had been about it, or at least wrong in part. He had not been able to understand that voodoo was a religion, and that it was not so simple as snake worship. Perhaps it had been that once. To be sure, the snake was Vodu, he represented the old gods, and they spoke through him. He was a symbol. But was that so different from kneeling in prayer before the statues of saints in the cathedral? One did not pray to saints; one prayed for intercession. Were not the sacrifice, the ecstasy and the dancing but worship? God, she thought, had many names, and it was possible to worship him in many ways, even by the love-making with which some completed the rites.

Voodoo for her would never be evil. She would use only good *gris-gris*, good wanga. She would use the good candles —the blue for love and luck, the white for purity and salvation, the pink for peace, perhaps the green for money; she would never burn a black candle; that brought death and destruction; or even a brown one; that was nearly as evil. Her *gris-gris* would never hurt or destroy.

Then she smiled at herself, lying there in her bed, with her head still aching. Perhaps she would use none of it. Saloppé had talked her into becoming an initiate, but she was still a good Catholic. Then she remembered that Saloppé had told her that many Catholic saints aided those who had the power. St. John was their patron and friend. Did not they celebrate his date each year? St. Peter opened the door, and all voodoos asked the help of St. Michael and many others. If only Jacques had been able to understand all that!

Marie had washed herself, dressed, and had started outside to make her coffee in the kitchen when she recalled the box Saloppé had given to her. Then she retraced her steps, took it out from under the bed and carried it to the kitchen with her. While her coffee water boiled for the dripping she raised the lid and examined its contents. There were candles of a half dozen colors, and among them were black and brown. ("Black for Madame Laveau," Saloppé had advised. "She has stolen your house. You can have revenge upon her.") Marie shook her head from side to side, and put the dark candles at the bottom of the box, beneath the other paraphernalia. There was a tuft of gray chicken feathers inside the box—this to be put inside the pillow of an enemy over whom one sought victory. There was a pecan through which two needles had been thrust, making a cross—a powerful *gris-gris* for protection. Tiny bags of chamois skin held powders and dust from graves—simple charms to wear for good luck and protection, too. There was the dried scrotum of a goat. There was a tiny bit of bone; Saloppé had said it was human.

Marie's kettle sang and she closed the box and placed it on a shelf and drew the curtains over it. She thought much of Saloppé's *gris-gris* evil. Jacques had perhaps been right about her. The woman was evil. Yet what was evil? Had it not been so for Jacques to have left her as he had? Had she frightened him? Marie wondered. Could one you love be frightening?

On the third morning after Jacques had left she had gone to Monsieur Mazereau's office, which was located in the new Faubourg Ste. Marie, the American section of the city lying south of the old part she still thought of as being the real New Orleans.

Marie always felt strange when she crossed the wide commons that people were beginning to call Canal Street, and which divided the older part of the town from the new. In the American neighborhood most of the buildings were very ugly in her opinion, for nearly all of them were of red brick, instead of tinted and painted in delicate pastel shades of pink and blue and lavender, as were many in the Vieux Carré. There was little of the beautiful iron lacework one found in the old city, and the gardens seemed huge, but crude and sprawling, unlike the lovely courtyards in the old town. Few of the streets had cobblestones or proper *banquettes*, and in most places the passing wagons and carriages had to pull through mud and water, particularly if it had lately rained, and pedestrians often went ankle-deep in the slime. As always, Marie thought the Americans knew nothing about how to live. Some of the many who had poured into the city during the past few years were growing rich, already they possessed more money and property than the richest Creoles. But, as the Creoles said, all they cared for was the making of money. Some boasted that they did not intend to stay, but when they were rich enough to suit themselves they would go back to wherever they had lived before.

Marie picked her way through narrow, muddy Camp Street with growing disdain. She thought everyone she passed American, and most of the conversations were in English. She wondered why Monsieur Mazereau, himself a Creole, had chosen to establish himself in this quarter, although she knew some Creoles were moving up here now and were doing business with the Americans, a thing other Creoles considered shameful. Marie walked fast and with more than her usual hauteur, for she knew how Americans felt about colored people. They could not distinguish one from another, a quadroon from a Negro, a slave from a free man or woman. With the Creoles it was a different matter, and she was thankful that Monsieur Mazereau was a Creole, even though she held little love for him. Had he not been a witness at her wedding, though?

Monsieur Mazereau could not have been more polite. He ushered her into his office at once and offered her a chair. A stout and nervous little man, he paced the floor. He had thought Jacques sick, or perhaps that Marie herself might be ill again. But she must know something. Had they quarreled? A man did not walk off and vanish in a city the size of New Orleans in this day and age, in 1821! It was impossible! Had she notified the police?

She admitted to him that they had had what might be termed a quarrel. But he had said only that he was going for a walk. She went into none of the details. No, she had not notified the police yet. Monsieur Mazereau said he would do that for her. He expressed regret in regard to the matter of their house. "Perhaps the poor boy was distraught because of that," he said. "Do you think he is off getting drunk?" He spread his palms and shrugged. "Young men sometimes do that sort of thing."

"Not Jacques," she replied. "No, it is not that."

Monsieur Mazereau shook his head. "I am mystified. My poor child! We must not think of foul play, but I will do everything I can. I have good friends connected with the police."

"Thank you, monsieur." Marie rose. "I do not feel it is foul play," she told him. "Not yet, anyway."

Monsieur Mazereau raised his brows. "A woman's intuition?"

"Let us call it that, monsieur," said Marie, unwilling to tell him more. She had known the visit to Monsieur Mazereau would do no good, yet she had felt compelled to come. There had been moments when she wanted to believe that her conviction that Jacques was forever lost to her might be wrong.

The little man was fumbling in a metal box on his desk. He laid some bills and silver in her hand. "His last week's wages," he explained. "You may need the money. Go home and try not to worry. I am sure we will find your Jacques. Myself, I am lost without him. His services were most valuable to me."

"Thank you, monsieur," said Marie again, and went out quickly.

But neither Monsieur Mazereau nor the police found her Jacques, and she had known they would not from the beginning.

Madame Laveau sent patient notes through her lawyers, and by August Marie realized she had to vacate the cottage. She found some rooms above those occupied by Madame Laclotte in the Rue du Rampart and in the same block where her other house was located, and where she had lived all her life until her marriage. She felt herself fortunate to be with Madame Laclotte, whose kitchen she could share and whose company helped to ease her loneliness. So she moved at once, crowding her possessions into the two rooms that were hers.

And the first evening Saloppé visited her, and together they sanctified her new home, using mostly the contents of the chest that had been given her that night on St. John's Bayou. They sprinkled powders into the corners of all the rooms. They burned the white candle for purification, and the green one for money. They sewed pictures of certain saints into her mattress and pillow. All the time Madame Laclotte was there, looking on disapprovingly, but saying nothing.

However, after Saloppé left, Madame was silent for a moment, and then exploded. "I like none of it!" she cried. "It is all dangerous. The devil's work!"

Marie knew how Madame felt about voodoo practices. She took no part in them, yet she feared them. Marie smiled. "I will do no bad work," she said. "It is true I have written Madame Laveau's name on a piece of paper, and I was preparing to soak it in ginger and vinegar, but I had only planned to give her a severe headache. Is that so wicked?"

Madame rolled her eyes with distress. "From little evil grows great. In the name of your poor mamma, I beg you not to do that."

"Then I will not," promised Marie. "I will forget that woman. Perhaps she is not worth my trouble."

"You have been attending mass, Marie?" asked Madame anxiously.

"Of course, Madame!"

"Do God's work," said Madame, "not the devil's!"

"Perhaps the devil can be made to work for God," Marie told her. "Anyway, I must do the work, Madame. I have been called."

Madame sprang from the rocker in which she had been resting herself and flung her arms over her head with a passionate gesture. "It is blasphemy!" she cried. "You talk like a nun, but of evil!"

"Perhaps it is not too different," said Marie quietly.

"We will not quarrel," sighed Madame, crossing the room and placing a kiss on Marie's cheek. "I want to help you, my dear. I have been thinking. If your Jacques does not return you must make a living in some way."

"He will not return," said Marie, firmly, calmly.

"I am not so sure," said Madame. "But I know something of men, and he may not. I was thinking that perhaps you could learn my trade. I recall that you are clever with hair. You used to arrange your mother's with great skill. I often need an assistant, someone to go along with me at first, and then to take my place when I have too many calls, or when my backache is bad."

"Madame!" Marie hugged her with joy.

"Good," said Madame. "Then we will start within a few days. It is a good trade and there is a need for more hairdressers. It can at least earn one a living."

So Marie had two trades in prospect. She would be a voodooienne one day; she would be a hairdresser, too.

"You must wear a *tignon* when you go into the homes of the white ladies," Madame instructed. "Especially the American ladies. They do not enjoy being waited upon by a quadroon who has more beautiful hair than their own."

She helped Marie fashion her *tignons*, and they were bright and lovely, of brilliant colors—red and green, red and white, green and black, most of them of cotton, although in secret Marie made herself several in silk. With her head bound in any of them, her gold hoops dangling from her ears, her dark eyes enhanced by the colors of the *tignon*, her skin glowing in red and golden lights, Marie knew she was even more remarkable in appearance. Watching her try them on, Madame

65

Laclotte smiled. "The *tignon*," she said, "is a trick of our women—an old trick. It makes the whites more comfortable for some reason when they see us wear them, yet they make us look better than ever."

Marie veiled her eyes with her long lashes and raised her head arrogantly. "We must please the white ladies, I suppose," she said, curling her upper lip a little.

Marie knew the story of the *tignons* as well as did all the women of her race in New Orleans.

More than thirty years ago, before Marie had been born, when Louisiana had been ruled by the Spanish under Governor Miro, the white ladies of New Orleans had become violently incensed because of the appearance of the free women of color in the city. These quadroons and octoroons, most of them mistresses of wealthy white men, dressed with great elegance, and in elaborate exaggerations of the fashions of the time. They ornamented their petticoats and skirts with gold lace and heavy fringe, and affected trains of filmy gauze and silk. They wore slippers embroidered with gold thread and sometimes encrusted with jewels, and they wore many jewels about their necks, their wrists and fingers and upon their bosoms.

But what upset the ladies of New Orleans most had been their headdresses. They braided chains of gold and pearls into their thick black tresses, or fixed handkerchiefs of gold gauze, into which diamonds had been sewed, upon their hair. Others wore elaborate headdresses of jewels and towering plumes, even in the streets during the day, driving about in fine carriages driven by their own black slaves. Wherever they went, and especially at the theater and the opera, it was these women who were the cynosure of all male eyes, as they sat in the seats reserved for them, fanning themselves with their plumed fans, laughing haughtily, flashing their great dark eyes, and pretending not to notice the attention they were attracting from the men.

After many protests from the white ladies came Miro's ordinance. Henceforth, he decreed, a woman of color, no matter that she be free, could wear nothing upon her head but a *tignon*, a colored kerchief. She must always conduct herself humbly in the presence of a white lady, could not ride in a carriage within the city limits, or seat herself in the room with a white lady. The quadroons had had to comply with the law, but they had discovered that it did not prevent them from having their *tignons* made of fine silk, of adorning them with jewels if they chose, and so they had come to like the *tignon* and to wear it with pride as an emblem.

Of course this law no longer existed, Marie knew, and although until now she had never worn a *tignon*, she rather fancied herself doing so. "Do you think a *tignon* will make me look like a white woman need not be jealous of me?" she asked Madame.

Madame whooped with laughter. "The way you look," she said, "it might not work; I don't know. But I think it will. You have to act a bit stupid, too. You don't know anything much. It's funny how they are. They don't think you can hear or see or use your mind. They have an idea we're all deaf and blind. Child, the things I could tell you! You wouldn't believe some of them."

"I will be deaf and blind and stupid," promised Marie, twisting another brilliant length of cotton about her head, and arranging it on her forehead so that it parted exactly in the middle and flattered her eyes.

The old woman sank on the edge of Marie's bed and laughed again. "It pays off," she said. "Once they begin to see you as a human being you're out. All you do is follow orders, and say 'Yes, Madame' and 'No, Madame,' even if the way they want their hair done makes them look like freaks! It's just 'Yes, Madame,' and 'No, Madame.' You can laugh inside yourself, but not out loud, and you can't talk back to any of them if you want to work for them a second time. Of

67

course I don't mean to say you don't meet some nice ones. Most of them are nice, to tell you the truth. It's just that you remember the others."

Marie unwound the *tignon* and began brushing her hair up from her temples. "But one can learn a lot, perhaps?"

"You just keep still and listen, child, and you'll learn things you didn't even know there were to learn," Madame assured her. "They tell you all their troubles, a lot of them, only they don't really think you pay any attention. It's like they were talking to themselves."

So Marie began her journeys with Madame Laclotte. Several times a week she accompanied her into homes she had never dreamed she would enter—the fine town houses along Rue Royale, the mansions lining the Esplanade, and those of American ladies beyond Canal Street. She grew skilled in arranging curls and braids and buns, in curling hair that was straight, in straightening hair that was too curly and thus might start the dreaded New Orleans gossip that its possessor had a touch of *café au lait* in her veins—the delicate way Creoles referred to colored blood. There were ladies who required the artful use of transformations, false curls and other hairpieces. There was one, a middle-aged beauty who wore a full wig at the theater and at balls. There were others whose graying tresses must be stained with strong black coffee or by the ingenious use of a charcoal stick.

During all her training Marie obeyed Madame Laclotte's orders. She seldom spoke unless she was addressed, and then in a lowered voice, in soothing, acquiescent tones. She moved quietly through the houses and the boudoirs, her manner as meek as she could make it. She wore her *tignons*. As the weeks and then the months passed, customers increased. The social season was approaching its peak; there was the theater and the opera; there were balls and *soirées*. The ladies were in a frantic mood; their engagements were so many that each must have her hair done a number of times a week. There were other hairdressers in town, of course, but Madame La-clotte was demanded by all her customers. Appointments began to stretch from early morning until early evening.

At last Marie began filling some of them alone, while Madame took care of others. Soon some of them began to ask for Marie. A Madame Forshey complained that Madame Laclotte, for all her skill, had always hurt her tender scalp when she brushed her hair, and that Marie did not. Hence-forth no one would do but Marie. A Madame Rivard said Madame Laclotte's hands were old and rough, while Marie's were ever so soft. A Mrs. Westerley, an American, simply announced that she preferred a young person to an older one. Others also became Marie's own customers.

For a long time Marie was disappointed in Madame La-clotte's prediction that she would hear astounding and inter-esting gossip. It was true the women talked, both to her and to friends who might be present while Marie worked, but at first she found it difficult to concentrate upon it and her profession at the same time. Later, as her work became increasingly automatic, she became more conscious of their chatter, but none of it seemed of any consequence. The most vicious might concern the love affair of a friend's husband, the "truth" about the cause of some duel or other, or the expected bankruptcy of some acquaintance. After a while Marie ceased paying much attention to this and decided that after all Madame Laclotte was old and gossipy herself, and lonely, too, and so probably a bit given to exaggeration.

Most of her clients she found pleasant enough. There was an occasional harridan who screeched at her crossly, and several who tried to talk her into cutting her fee especially for them. The first sort Marie ignored, and to the second she was polite but adamant, as Madame Laclotte had warned her she must be. Middle-aged husbands and uncles, and young brothers and sons, lingering about the homes she visited, often looked at her with interest she could not ignore, but she pretended to do so, and froze them into inaction with her apparent disregard of their existence.

By spring she had so many clients that she was working almost entirely separately from Madame Laclotte. For the moment her work seemed to have become her whole life. Yet this was not really so. There was another life, and much of it was filled with almost nothing but fear of its being.

For almost every moment of her waking hours she was thinking of Jacques, remembering Jacques. There was never a word from him or of him. She still made inquiries of everyone she met who had ever known him. She wrote one note to Monsieur Mazereau, and received a kindly, gentle reply; he knew nothing. Sometimes she begged for help from Saloppé. The voodooienne had not been able to help her in this way yet. It was a strange and difficult affair, she explained. Jacques was alive, but he was far away. Marie was right in her feeling tht he would not return, but he was so far away that Saloppé's powers could not reach him, or so it seemed. Perhaps he had secured his own extremely powerful *gris-gris?* This Marie denied with vigor. Jacques would never use *gris-gris*. Of all people, he would have nothing to do with voodoo of any kind. Then it must be only the distance, Saloppé would say. She must cease grieving, Saloppé would say. Jacques had stood in her way. Once she even told Marie there would be another man for her. Never, never, Marie cried. There would never be anyone but Jacques!

She saw Saloppé often, and spent long hours talking to her, learning, learning. Three times she went to meetings on St. John's Bayou, but she took no active part. As Saloppé had said, that was not for her. But she watched. She learned. She also attended the small meetings Saloppé held in the back-yard of her home in Rue Dumaine. As yet she practiced nothing except small *gris-gris* to protect herself from harm and to increase her trade, and that was always growing.

She still hated Saloppé in her heart. Saloppé might have

killed her baby before its time to be born. She might have taken Jacques from her. Saloppé still said Jacques had been an impediment, and Marie listened to her and remembered everything, and wondered if the woman could know her thoughts. But now she had more courage. She believed that now her mind was becoming as strong as Saloppé's. Yet she would do her no evil, at least not at this time. She would wait. Saloppé no longer spoke of her own death, and Marie did not want her to die yet. But she wondered why Saloppé no longer spoke of it. Had she been lying from the beginning, a trick to tempt Marie to accept her tutelage? But if she were not going to die why should Saloppé want her? Perhaps Saloppé had learned some new way to preserve her life. Of one thing Marie was sure; Saloppé had killed Dédé. Is that the way it is, Marie wondered; do we kill each other? Is that the fate of queens?

It was on an afternoon at Madame Forshey's that Marie knew that Jacques was dead. Jeanne Céleste de Lisle Forshey was a tall thin woman with a long, proud throat and the face of a bird, immense eyes, large, hooked nose and almost no chin. Her hair was dark blonde, fine as silk, but as thin as the rest of her, and she added to the elaborate coiffure she preferred several false pieces and clusters of curls, attached on combs at her temples, which fell to her shoulders. "They fill out my face," she had explained to Marie. She was vain, but she was what Madame Laclotte called "a nice one," and she was nice to Marie, patient, quick with compliments when she was especially pleased, and generous of both purse and spirit. Her husband owned a sugar plantation some distance from New Orleans, and Marie had never seen him. It seemed to her that Madame Forshey spent all her time in town in the house in Rue Royale, alone but for her young daughter Delphine, her only child, and servants.

On the afternoon that Marie saw Jacques dead she was attaching the curls at one side of Madame Forshey's hair.

In her mind she saw Jacques, and it was exactly like the terrible dream she had once had. There was the water, the dark, cold water. Jacques was floating in it, his eyes closed, his face marble. Marie gasped and her hands tightened. Madame shrieked and leaped to her feet, a frantic arm sweeping Marie to one side. A drop of blood rolled from Madame Forshey's thin hair and down her cheek.

Marie was staring at her, but not seeing her. Then the picture of Jacques faded and was gone. There was only Madame standing there with blood on her face. "Are you ill?" Madame cried, and Marie knew her state must show in her face.

"Yes," whispered Marie.

"Sit down! Sit down!" Madame Forshey said insistently, pushing her toward the bed, which was the closest place there was to sit. Madame put a finger to the wet spot on her cheek, glared at her finger, and murmured, "Heavens!"

"I'm sorry," whispered Marie, sinking into the feather bed, a hand pressed to her forehead.

"It doesn't matter!" cried Madame, rattling the drawers of her dressing table. "Where are my salts? Girl, you looked about to faint!"

"I'll be all right," Marie said.

"I can never find anything when I want it," fumed Madame, slamming shut a drawer and, forsaking her search for her smelling salts, rushing back to the bed with a bottle of perfume in her hand. "Smell this. It may help. I'll get you some brandy. Nanette! Nanette!" she called for a servant at the door of the room.

She came back to the bed, a look of suspicion on her face. Marie had no trouble reading her mind. "You're not . . . ?" Madame began.

"No," said Marie bluntly, the irony of that suggestion giving her a fresh shock. "I'll get along now, Madame. My husband is dead." She scarcely knew what she was saying.

"Your husband?" Madame's big eyes softened with sympathy. "Oh, I'm so sorry, Marie. When did it happen?"

"I don't know," Marie murmured. "I don't know yet."

Nanette entered the room, but Marie refused the brandy. When the servant had gone Madame said, "I'm sending you home in my carriage. I insist upon it. But I don't understand, Marie. You seemed perfectly all right when you arrived. It is very wrong to hold anything like that in. You should not have come today at all."

"I didn't know it then," Marie admitted. "Only a moment ago I knew it. Forgive me, Madame. It is just that sometimes I do know things that way."

Madame stared, and her gaze covered Marie from head to foot and returned to her face. "I see," she said slowly. She paused and took a deep breath. Then she smiled faintly. "I'll go see about the carriage. I want you to go home and take a good rest."

For nearly a week Marie saw no one except Madame Laclotte. Locked in her rooms, she would have admitted no one else. Only Saloppé came, and Marie spoke to her through the closed door and told her she was too ill for company. She did not tell Saloppé of her vision. Did Saloppé know? Was Saloppé perhaps even responsible in some way? Marie could not decide, but she knew she did not want to see the woman now. She wanted to see no one.

It was impossible to keep Madame Laclotte out. Madame came and clucked over her, bringing food. For the first few days Marie told her nothing, then when the old woman found her in tears one morning Marie did tell her. Madame Laclotte gaped in wonderment, and went around after that shaking her head and sighing. Marie knew Madame did not know what to believe. Once she begged Marie to consider the possibility that she might be mistaken, and once when she awoke in the middle of the night Marie tried to tell herself that, but it was useless. She knew she was right as she knew the day of the week and the date of the month. Jacques was gone. Jacques! Jacques! She ate little, and she slept only when she was exhausted. She hardly bothered to change her clothes or to wash. She walked the floor barefooted day and night, her long hair streaming wildly over her shoulders, uncombed and matted. When she ventured to glance into a mirror she told herself that a stranger seeing her would have thought her mad.

Then one evening at sunset Madame Laclotte knocked on her door and told her she had a visitor. Marie protested, but Madame whispered through the door, "He brings news of Jacques!"

"Wait! Wait!" Marie cried. She slipped on a kimono, wrapped her tangled hair hastily in a *tignon*, shoved her feet into slippers, and unbolted her door. With Madame stood a large and heavy-set man of about fifty, with grizzled, graying hair and skin about the color of her own.

"This is Captain Glapion," said Madame, and fluttered away down the stairs, glancing back over her shoulder with an expression on her face that told Marie that now Madame believed that Jacques was dead.

"Christophe Dumíny Glapion," said the captain, bowing courteously. "I was named for the Emperor." When Marie looked puzzled, he added, "In Santo Domingo. Madame, I bring very sad news to you." He cleared his throat. "It is difficult to have to tell you."

Marie closed her eyes for a moment. "I already know, Captain," she whispered. "Please sit down."

"I didn't realize you had heard already," he said, seating himself stiffly on a chair, holding his hat in his lap. He was well dressed and prosperous-looking, as much so as any white gentleman.

"What happened, Captain?" asked Marie. "How did Jacques die? Please tell me that."

74

The captain sighed. "My young brother was on the ship with him," he explained. "They had been together throughout two trips to Marseille."

"A ship?"

He raised his eyebrows. "Didn't you even know he was working aboard a ship?" he asked. "I'm so sorry. Perhaps I had better get to the point, Madame. They were nearing the Balize, almost home, which I know makes it seem almost all the more tragic, when a storm arose in the Gulf. Your husband, poor lad, was swept overboard. It occurred almost a week ago, but the ship was badly damaged, although no other lives were lost, and it arrived at New Orleans only this morning."

Marie had remained standing. "I know when it happened," she sighed. "I know. I know." It was strange to her that she felt less shock now than she had that day at Madame Forshey's. She felt no pain now, only the swelling of her grief in her.

"My brother is not well," the captain said, rising. "That is why I came. Please accept my deepest sympathies. My brother says your husband was a fine young man and spoke often of you. His effects will be sent to you as soon as certain technicalities can be arranged."

Marie bowed her head. "Thank you, Captain."

He paused in the door, scrutinizing her closely, although there was nothing impolite in his concentration upon her. "Madame," he asked suddenly, "may I ask a question? Perhaps it is not the time to ask, but how did you know? The boat just docked, and you did not even know he was aboard a ship. Forgive me if you consider such a question rude."

Marie raised her eyes to meet his, and was startled to discover that his eyes were the same gray Jacques' had been. "I knew, Captain," she said. "That is all I can tell you. No one brought me news of Jacques' death. I knew."

The captain bowed. "I think I understand," he said. "Good evening, Madame Paris."

In the morning Marie bathed herself and put on fresh clothing. She combed and brushed her hair and did it up in a huge knot. Before noon she was glad she had done so, for there was a rap on her door, and when she opened it Madame Forshey was standing there, carrying a large basket of fruit.

Madame sat down and unloosened the strings of her bonnet. "I won't stay a moment," she promised, "but I had to know how you were, and there was no other way but to come."

Marie set the fruit down on the table. "You are more than kind, Madame." She took a deep breath. "I am quite all right now, and I can come back to you any time you wish."

"My poor girl," sighed Madame. "Do you want to tell me about your husband? You have had more news?"

"A confirmation," said Marie quietly. "He was aboard a ship, and fell into the sea."

Madame was silent a moment, then she asked, "Marie, how did you know?"

"I knew," said Marie, remembering how Captain Glapion had asked the same question the evening before.

"I believe in second sight," Madame told her. "I have seen many instances." She rose. "But I'm so sorry that you were right this time. It seems to me it would be terrifying to be so gifted." She crossed to the door quickly. "If there is anything I can do?"

"There is nothing, Madame."

Madame stood still for a moment, holding the door ajar. Then she suddenly closed it. "Marie?" She walked back across the room, and said again, "Marie?" Her face had turned bright red.

"Yes, Madame?" asked Marie, startled at the change in the woman's expression.

"Marie," Madame Forshey asked quickly, "can you do other things? I know there are people who claim they can, although I've had no experience with them. One hears of so much of that sort of thing in New Orleans—especially among colored people." She dropped back into a chair and pressed both hands to her cheeks. She blurted out, "Marie, I am in trouble. Can you help me?"

Marie studied her for a moment, her mind racing, her heart beating quickly. "It depends what it is, Madame," she said slowly. "Perhaps."

To her astonishment Madame Forshey began to cry. Tears rolled out of her eyes and down her cheeks and a muffled sob broke from her lips.

"What is it, Madame?" asked Marie, sinking to a stooping position beside her.

Madame found a handkerchief and blew her nose. "I suppose I have to tell you now," she said, "or you can't possibly help. But I am so ashamed!" She gave a vigorous tug at her large nose. "Marie, the other day when you told me your husband had died, I almost wished I had been in your place." She bowed her head, and repeated, "I am so ashamed! Oh, I don't really mean it, Marie. I love Henri, but it would be easier for me to know he was dead than to know that he wanted another woman! I suppose I'm a vain, selfish woman, but that's the way I feel!"

Marie rose and made herself tall. "I do no bad work, Madame!"

"Oh, I don't want him to die!" squealed Madame Forshey. "I just want him to come back to me. I want the other woman—she's a mere child, really, and Henri can't mean to her what he does to Delphine and me, and, besides, she's my third cousin—I want her to go away . . . or *something*. I don't care what; all I want is to get Henri back."

"Let us start from the beginning, Madame," said Marie.

"I knew you could help me," cried Madame. "I felt it!

77

I said to myself that if you had second sight to such a degree as I was inclined to suspect the other day, then you would know about other things."

"I warn you I am a novice," Marie said calmly, "but perhaps I can help you."

Madame talked rapidly and the story was actually simple and trite. Henri de Lisle Forshey was in love with Madame's seventeen-year-old cousin, Annette, who had come to visit them the Christmas before on their plantation. Since then Monsieur Forshey had behaved like a schoolboy, and, indeed, Annette seemed infatuated, too. They had seen each other on every opportunity, although Annette lived on her parents' plantation nearly fifty miles away. Now Henri refused to come to the city even for a visit, and he used every excuse to keep Madame from returning to his plantation. Gossip was flowing up and down the river, and a scandal was brewing. The gossip had not reached Annette's parents yet. If it did, her father would kill Henri, Madame was sure. But suppose they ran away together? Annette was impetuous and bold for such a young girl, and Henri seemed deprived both of his senses and his decency. Even Delphine was suspicious and she grieved that her papa no longer seemed interested in her existence.

"Marie, can you aid me?" gasped Madame Forshey at the conclusion of her tale. "I will pay you one hundred dollars."

Marie concealed her elation. "Only if I succeed, Madame. I will prepare what I need and come to you tomorrow."

"I am so afraid they will run away!" exclaimed Madame, as she departed. "It has happened, you know. One of my closest friend's husband went off to Paris with a woman just last year. I could not bear losing Henri, and then there is the scandal! A shadow cast upon the future of my poor Delphine!"

As soon as she had gone, Marie went to work. She never

considered going to Saloppé for advice or aid in this matter. She would do it herself, alone; she would try her own power.

When Marie arrived at Madame Forshey's the following day she had everything ready. Madame watched while Marie prepared her charms. Marie placed a blue candle with seven notches cut into one side on the mantel in Madame's bedroom. "You are to burn it down to one notch each night for seven nights," Marie instructed. "As you light it each night you are to say these words, 'Liba, help me! Dani, help me!' Do not be afraid, Madame. Liba is a secret name for St. Peter, Dani is one for St. Michael. Now I want you to write your name, your husband's and that of the girl who is your rival on separate bits of paper."

When Madame Forshey had done so, Marie filled a saucer with vinegar and sprinkled salt and pepper into it. Into this she put the bit of paper on which was written the name of Madame's rival, Annette. Then Marie filled a saucer with brandy and carefully lighted the brandy with a match. As the blue flames rose she dropped the other two pieces of paper containing Madame's name and that of her husband into it. "As you burn together so will your lives be together," Marie told her. "Fire is life. You will keep the name of your rival in the vinegar for seven days." She paused, and then asked, "Madame, have you a slave you can trust without reservation?"

Her eyes widening, Madame said, "Nanette. I would trust Nanette with my life. She's belonged to my family since she was born, and her parents before her. She took care of me when I was a baby."

"Write your name and that of the girl on separate pieces of paper again, Madame," said Marie.

When this was done Marie cored an apple she had brought, and inserted the two scraps of paper into the hollow. "Nanette must go to where your husband is living," she said. "Use any excuse. She must place the apple somewhere in the house where he will not find it, or smell it. As the days pass and the apple shrivels, so will their love."

"I think it will work, Marie!" cried Madame. "I have great faith in you!"

Marie smiled faintly. "Send me a message when you know, Madame."

In less than three weeks the message came. As Marie opened the envelope which a young male slave belonging to Madame Forshey brought her, a crisp one-hundred-dollar bill fell into her lap. The note accompanying it said that Annette's parents were sending her abroad for the grand tour and that Monsieur Forshey had written Madame that he was most anxious that she rejoin him in the country. Madame expressed her joy and her gratitude to Marie.

That same afternoon Marie received a bouquet of violets with Captain Glapion's card attached. She put them in a vase on a table near her bed. That night she dreamed of Jacques and awoke with a start to find the room sweet with the faint fragrance of the violets, and somehow it comforted her in her loneliness, and she was warmed.

Chapter 4

YET IT WAS a long time before Marie saw Christophe Glapion again. Then on a Sunday in October as she took an afternoon walk, the sounds of the drums drew her to Congo Square, and he was standing outside, leaning upon the picket fence, watching the dancers. She remained some feet away, watching, too, but feeling oddly shy as she glanced at Glapion now and then, unwilling to approach him. At last their eyes met and he came over, staring hard. "The Widow Paris," he said, sounding surprised.

Marie did not wonder at his uncertainty, for she knew she looked like a very different woman from the one he had seen when he had come to tell her of Jacques' drowning. Her dress was a simple one of the blue calico she now almost always wore, but over it she had tossed a beautiful woolen shawl that had belonged to Marguerite, and she was wearing a handsome *tignon* of scarlet and yellow silk. She was also adorned with a heavy string of jet beads, gold bracelets and the earrings Monsieur Charles had given her, which she almost never removed.

"It is good to see you, Captain Glapion," she said politely.

Standing together, they both returned their attention to the dancers. The square was jammed with celebrants, and in the center stood Saloppé, not dancing now, although Marie knew that she often did, but standing almost like a statue while the others whirled about her. Crouched on the ground were the ancient musicians with their weird instruments, and among them was Doctor John, beating with the heels of his hands upon cowhide stretched over an immense gourd.

"This is foolishness," Glapion remarked suddenly.

Marie shrugged. "It gives them pleasure. It is an amusement."

"Do you attend often?"

"I have never danced in Congo Square," she answered haughtily. Saloppé had often invited her to attend, but she had always refused. She saw little of Saloppé now, and the woman had been cool to her on the streets. Perhaps Saloppé knew of the clients who had been coming to her rooms. Madame Forshey had whispered to her friends, and they to other friends. There had not been many as yet, by no means enough to rival Saloppé's pre-eminence in the work, but enough to worry her. Marie gazed again at the dancers, moving at a slower pace now, undulating, swaying, forming the snake. "The drums give me a headache," she told Glapion. "I am happy to have met you again, Captain."

But as she moved away he was at her elbow. "May I walk with you?" he asked.

"If you like."

"It is foolishness," he said after a moment, "yet these people are voodooists, aren't they? I have heard much about the woman, Marie Saloppé."

"I know her well," said Marie, not answering his question, and wondering what he had heard of the Widow Paris. She asked a question of her own. "What do you know of voodooists, Captain?"

"I am from Santo Domingo," he replied.

They had turned out of Rue d'Orleans and come to the Théâtre d'Orleans, its front plastered with posters advertising the plays to be presented during the season that had just begun. The captain changed the subject and began talking of the theater, to which he said he was devoted. He attended every play, he told her. The theater was a great solace for a lonely man, a middle-aged widower who had no one in the world. Marie said that she had been to the theater but seldom, and not at all, of course, since Jacques had died. She did not wear mourning for him, but she kept it in other ways. Before her marriage she had gone rarely because of her mother's ill-health, and, too, because Marguerite's pride had made her resent sitting in the loges reserved for colored people.

Glapion smiled at this last. Did she not know that their people were advancing to high places in the theater nowadays, as well as in all the arts? he asked. The great actress, Cecilie, was due to appear at the Théâtre d'Orleans this winter, and, although it was not generally known, Cecilie was a quadroon who had come originally from Santo Domingo, and had enjoyed triumph after triumph in Europe. Also, several New Orleans quadroon playwrights had enjoyed enormous success in Paris.

"Captain, I have heard of such things, but I am a simple woman of little education," answered Marie.

"You do not look simple, Madame," said Glapion with a wry glance. He gestured toward the towers of St. Louis Cathedral rising against the sky at the end of the short street. "Are you religious?"

"I believe I am a good Catholic, Monsieur," Marie told him. "Perhaps you have heard otherwise?"

The captain shrugged. "I pay little attention to gossip," he replied. "Also, Madame, I believe God can be served in many ways. Do you wish to preside at the Congo Square dancing?"

Now Marie knew he had heard everything about her. She did not lie to him. "When I take part, I will preside," she said frankly.

As Glapion walked home with her, dusk came quickly as it does in New Orleans, and a lamp lighter was busy in Marie's street lighting the lamps that swung from ropes at the corners. Marie, a bit shaken by her discovery that he knew of her activities as a voodooienne, tried to bid him a hasty goodbye at the gate before Madame Laclotte's house, but Glapion put a gentle hand on her arm. "We are lonely people," he said honestly. "I do not know why you should be with your beauty, yet I feel you are as much so as I am, Marie. I must see you again."

"It will be a pleasure, Monsieur," Marie told him, and fled.

Evidently Madame Laclotte had watched them through her shutters, for Marie had barely reached her rooms when the old woman came up the stairs. "He is a fine man," she told Marie. "I have heard much about him lately. He was at Chalmette with General Jackson. He is one of the heroes who saved the city from the British in 1815. Also, he is a man of splendid character and reputation."

Marie was amused, and she laughed. "I know exactly what your hints mean," she said. "You are incurably romantic."

"Why not?" asked Madame Laclotte. "You are too young to live alone, my child. You should have a husband and children."

"Children?" Marie sighed and shook her head violently. "No, Madame. There will never be anyone but Jacques. Never."

"Nonsense," clucked Madame. "You need a man. A good man like the captain, middle-aged and sensible but young enough to give you children, is what you need."

Aristide Broutin was a small, wiry man, who kept pacing Marie's floor talking nervously but seemingly unable to reveal to her the purpose of his visit. Marie rocked patiently, knowing that in time she would discover whatever it was that had brought him to her rooms. Patiently, she prompted him. "You are a friend of Madame Deslonde's, Monsieur?"

"A very old friend," said Monsieur Broutin. "She vows you helped her."

"I believe I did." Madame Deslonde's problem had been to prevent the marriage of her eldest daughter to a young man of whom she had not approved. The marriage had not taken place. Instead, the young man had married another.

"I have never had any belief in this," said Monsieur Broutin. "Only the extremity of my circumstances has driven me to come here."

"You do not flatter me."

"Pardon. I intended no insult."

"It is nothing, Monsieur. You are upset."

Monsieur Broutin closed his eyes. "I am distraught. Do you not read the newspapers?"

Marie smiled. "Almost never," she said. "I do not read very well, and all I need to know is gossiped about in the streets these days."

The little man sank into a chair and covered his eyes with his hands. When he took his hands away his eyes were wet. "It is my son Jacques who is being tried for murder tomorrow," he blurted out. "Have you not heard *that* in the streets? He is innocent. It was in self-defense. The other man was a blackguard. Jacques would not harm a fly."

Marie rocked slowly. "His name is Jacques," she said. "It is a name dear to me."

"He is my only son!" cried Monsieur Broutin. "I have the best attorneys, but they have little hope for him. I have done everything! If you can help I will reward you well." He sprang to his feet and began walking up and down again. "You live here in crowded rooms. I own a cottage in the Rue Ste. Anne, just around the corner from here. I have little money in cash at the moment, but I will give you the cottage if you can help save my son."

"Calm yourself and tell me what happened, Monsieur," said Marie. "I must know the details so that I will know what to do for your Jacques."

The tale Monsieur Broutin told was rather ordinary. The

killing had occurred in a café. There had been a quarrel over a lady. According to Monsieur Broutin the other man, a Spaniard, had made an insulting remark about the lady in his son's presence, whereupon Jacques Broutin had challenged the Spaniard. But the Spaniard had not been a gentleman, and had not waited for the necessary and proper arrangements to be made for a duel. Instead he had drawn a knife on the spot and attacked Jacques Broutin. Jacques had had no choice but to fight the ruffian in his own fashion. Tossed a knife by a friend, he used it to defend himself. The men rolled on the floor. When Jacques arose the Spaniard lay prone, a knife buried in his chest to the hilt. At the end of his story Monsieur Broutin blew his nose vigorously.

Marie gave him a searching look. "Perhaps Monsieur has nothing to worry about," she said. "It would seem that the court would free your son. Witnesses will testify that he acted to defend his life."

"They would but for one thing," Monsieur Broutin said. "The devil Jacques eliminated from decent society was of a rich and prominent family. A black sheep! The café in which the affair occurred was a place of low reputation. I do not know what Jacques was doing there, except that he is young, and young men are not discreet. So, because of the class of those present, bribes were distributed widely. I am told that Jacques cannot hold any certainty that anyone there will speak the truth at the trial. The name of the Spaniard was Antonio Morales y Boaz."

Marie nodded. "I know of the family. It could be true." They were people of wealth. If they chose to bribe they could well afford to do so.

"Antonio's father is a man of no character," cried Monsieur Broutin, "but I did not dream he would stoop to persecuting my son, when surely he knows his own was the guilty one!"

"Monsieur, what is the name of the café?"

"It is the Café of the Angels," Monsieur Broutin said with a shudder. "What a name they chose for the cesspool that it is!"

Marie repressed a smile. She was familiar with the establishment by hearsay, and she knew a Negro who was employed there, a man called Saiya, who came to the meetings and who knew of her growing reputation. "Monsieur," she said serenely, "I think that your Jacques will be home tomorrow night."

The little man sprang to his feet. "Can you be sure? I swear the cottage I promised will be yours!"

"It will be mine," replied Marie, closing her eyes. "Go now. Go in peace."

At dusk Marie entered the St. Louis Cemetery and strolled idly among the tombs until she found that in which was buried Antonio Morales y Boaz. She knelt as if to pray and buried in the earth before the tomb an egg and a small cassava stick. "You will let the truth be known, Antonio," she whispered, and then hurried from the walled place of the dead.

A few minutes later she inquired for Saiya at a rear door to the Café of the Angels, a shack of a building near the levee and the marketplace. When Saiya emerged, his eyes bulged at sight of her. Marie spoke to him gently, but without a smile. "You've been summoned as a witness at the murder trial tomorrow?" she asked.

Saiya shuffled about uneasily. "I couldn't help that," he told her. "The police came after me. They came to my home."

"And other men came and gave you money," she said. "I know. I know all things. They want you to lie. When you go to court you will say that Monsieur Jacques Broutin was defending his life, that you saw it all. After the trial you will return the money given to you."

"Those men will kill me!" cried Saiya, his eyes getting bigger and bigger.

"They will not kill you," Marie promised. "They will not even touch you. For you will also tell the court of the bribe. Then if any harm should come to you the police will know where to place the blame. The bribers would not take that chance. You must do as I say, Saiya. You know I am a powerful woman."

He bowed his head. "I'll do what you say."

"Monsieur Broutin's father will give you the same amount of money the others gave you," she promised. "I will arrange that. He will be glad to reward you for your honesty and truthfulness, Saiya."

In the morning she went to the cathedral with three Guinea peppers in her mouth and prayed a long time, most of her devotion spent in asking St. Peter for intercession. When she left she entered the Cabildo next door, where the trial was to be held within a few hours, and found a cleaning woman she knew. After some words with this woman Marie was admitted to the bare and empty room where the trial was to be held. She spat the Guinea peppers into her hand and concealed them beneath the judge's chair.

All day she lingered in the neighborhood, and she was in the Place d'Armes, watching, when the elder Monsieur Broutin emerged from the Cabildo, his arm around the shoulders of a youth. Marie felt her pulses pounding in her ears as she hurried away. This was the greatest of her successes until now, and there was little doubt in her mind but that her own power had freed the young man. It had been cautious of her to guard against mishap by contacting Saiya, but she felt that even without that Jacques Broutin would have been freed. And she had done nothing wrong. She had not even threatened Saiya, although he might have feared she would.

As she walked swiftly toward home, she thought she heard people she passed whisper to each other, "It is she! It is the

Widow Paris!" She lifted her head high and made her skirts swirl about her ankles.

The next morning she went to look at the cottage. She knew it well, but she wanted to see it again, now that it was to be hers. It was on Rue Ste. Anne just a few steps off Rue du Rampart, a low structure set almost flat on the ground, with a sloping roof of red tiles. It was only a few years old and the white paint was still fresh on its wooden walls. There was a fine garden at one side, a large one that gave the house some degree of privacy, for in it were tall bamboo and banana trees and a fig tree or two. There was a wild, almost jungle-like growth of red roses, and the walk was bordered with purple violets. Behind the cottage was a small brick building containing the kitchen and a room for a servant. If she could make enough money she might be able to afford a slave! Studying all of it, Marie already felt this to be her home. She would be contented here. Across the front of it she would build a high wooden fence to shield herself against the peering eyes of passers-by in the street. Then, she decided, this would be the only home she would ever want. She could live here the rest of her life.

During the months that followed she saw Glapion constantly. Usually he spent several evenings a week visiting her. She would cook him supper, and frequently he brought delicacies—a brawling sack of live crabs, a bucket of crawfish, a pair of wild ducks, a brace of the tiny birds she loved best of all fowl, called papabotes. He brought strawberries and wild rice and great brown and purple figs, bursting with juice.

He took her to the theater, to the Théâtre d'Orléans, which they had discussed that Sunday afternoon when they had met at Congo Square. She had been only a few times in her life, as she had told him, and with Glapion she found it exciting for the first time. To her the theater seemed immense, and Glapion said it held nearly a thousand persons. The curtain seemed spun of pure gold, and gigantic chandeliers hung from its roof. The curfew had been moderated, and now night performances could be held, so that they would sit in their third-floor gallery seats from six o'clock until long past midnight. She loved looking down upon the white people in their boxes and in the orchestra, and watching the young men wander about between the various short presentations—the singers, the dancers, the performers with trained animals—and again between the acts of the play that closed the evening. Often she recognized people she knew, some of them women in all their finery and plumes who were her clients.

And often when they emerged into the street she found a moment more exciting than any theatrical performance. Carriages lined the streets, the horses that drew them sweating impatiently and making music with their hoofs upon the cobblestones. When people began pouring from the theater she would sometimes make Glapion wait. Slaves would appear with glowing lanterns and lead the way home for those who were on foot; the ladies would cling to their escorting husbands and disappear with them into the darkness; fathers would lead their young daughters past leering young men with an air of determination and sometimes of desperation.

Often when Marie and Glapion emerged from the Théâtre d'Orleans the Orleans Ballroom next door was also emptying. This was the place where the largest of the Quadroon Balls in the city were held, and they would see these people, too, the young men strolling away, gay and laughing, or sometimes climbing into carriages; the girls going slowly down the street, well chaperoned by their mothers or some other woman of proper age.

"You love it, don't you?" Glapion asked Marie, after one evening at the theater.

"I have not had much fun, Captain," she replied. "Perhaps I never realized that before. I have been content with much of my life."

"Have you, Marie?" he asked.

Yet he was long in making love to her, and it worried her that he was. It was not, she told herself, exactly that she wanted him to do so, but that she wanted his companionship. If he did not make love to her he might tire of her. Then she would wonder if the end might come if he did so. Did she know her own mind?

She was coming to like him more and more, and certainly to need him more and more. But she still thought of Jacques nearly every moment, even when she was with Glapion. There was no similarity in her feeling for Jacques and Glapion; she felt toward Glapion as she had once felt for Monsieur Charles. She could not imagine that Glapion could ever be much more to her than the kind friend of those first months of their friendship.

During those months the rest of her life went on, too. She was learning much about New Orleans, about her world. Until she had been alone, without Marguerite, then without Jacques, she had really known little about it. She had led her life within the confines of a small group; for through the long years of Marguerite's illness she had known only her neighbors, a few people she had met in the streets, and those she had come to know at church. With Jacques this had changed little. He had had no close friends. Her days and most of her evenings had been spent at home.

It was different now. As a hairdresser she met all kinds of people in the white world. In her growing activities as a voodooienne she met as many in the colored one. How involved it all was, she often thought. The whites—Creole and American—were not all of one kind. In every important sense the Creoles and Americans lived separate lives, and among themselves each group divided and subdivided. There were the rich and the grand, the poorer and less elegant, the strivers, the ambitious. Her own world was no less complicated. Here shades of color, of income and ways of life, occasionally of education, of anything that gave illusions of power and superiority, made even more difference than did similar conditions among the whites. Indeed, there was a closer bond between the higher class quadroon or octoroon and the aristocratic Creole than there was between any free quadroon or octoroon and a Negro slave. They spoke the same language; their customs were the same, and their loves and hates and preferences and prejudices. Figuratively speaking, sometimes literally, they were cousins.

The Negroes whom she met in the white households she visited treated her with respect. At first it was only the outward respect most Negro slaves displayed toward free people of color, at best superficial, often veiling deep resentment, even hatred. Gradually, however, as word of her power spread, this changed. If resentment or hatred or envy was there it was entirely concealed by fear. There were exceptions, but to most servants a word from Marie, even a look, was important, either desired or dreaded, as the case might be. She became more and more conscious of her control, of her power over the slaves. She had long known that between the household servants in New Orleans there was a kind of grapevine, unknown and undetected ways of communication. In the world of servants the whites had no secrets, and, therefore, with only a few exceptions did the whites hold any secrets from Marie. Sometimes she exulted in this; sometimes, in these early days, a kind of fear possessed her. What could one not do with this kind of power? It could be used at her will, as she had used Saiya and the cleaning woman at the Cabildo, for any purpose she chose, for good, for evil. One could grow rich; without their knowledge one could change the lives of many people, even white people.

In these days she rarely saw Saloppé, and she was certain now that Saloppé was avoiding her. The woman would not die! Marie felt no shame in feeling anger at this. If Saloppé did not intend to die, why had she brought Marie into the old religion? It was a broken promise, and Marie did not forget all she had paid for what she now possessed, and paid because of Saloppé. It pleased Marie to know that the woman must be chilled with envy these days, for she would have learned of Marie's growing pre-eminence through the same grapevine that brought Marie other kinds of knowledge.

"Why doesn't she die?" Marie would cry to Glapion. "Why did she want me if she was not going to do so?"

When she asked him this Glapion would shrug in his stoic way. "Perhaps to make you serve her. To rule you."

"To rule me?" Marie laughed rarely, but when he would say this she would roar. "*I* will rule, Glapion." Yet when she answered that way she would think she sounded like Saloppé herself, like Dédé.

Once Marie found a loaf of bread, covered with green mold, into which had been stuffed some rags and a piece of black candle. It had been tossed over the high wooden fence she had built before her new house. She decided then that Saloppé was working evil *gris-gris* against her. That night she crept out and concealed it beneath Saloppé's house, and returned home smiling to herself. When salt appeared on the walk before her gate she simply washed it off and worried about it not at all. Saloppé could not hurt her any more. Marie Laveau, the Widow Paris, was too strong for Saloppé. Glapion agreed with this. He practiced voodoo not at all, but he believed, and he had faith in Marie.

Yet Marie was not completely happy. She was lonely. Even now she had few friends. There was only Glapion and Madame Laclotte who counted. It was not possible to have friends in either of the worlds in which she moved. She served the whites; the colored world stood in awe of her. Even Madame Laclotte seldom came to see her. Marie knew Madame feared voodoo as she feared the yellow fever. As the Widow Paris walked through the streets of her neighborhood the people greeted her politely; they smiled and paid her compliments. They came to her with their troubles and their problems. But there it ended. On many evenings she would have been alone in her empty house if Glapion had not come. She had heard stories that queens were always lonely.

And of course there were two kinds of voodoo clients. The whites and some of the more prosperous colored paid her fees for her oils and powders and little bags, even for her advice. But there were also the poor, who paid at best with favors, mostly in the form of gossip which might be of use to her some day. To these she gave as much time as to those who could pay, as much good *gris-gris* to keep them from harm, to help with their troubles. Now and then she even gave them money or food. "She is good," the people whispered as she passed along the *banquettes*. "The Widow Paris is a good woman. She is kind to the poor."

Aside from this there was only Glapion. He admired her with his eyes and flattered her with his constant attention, and sometimes she wondered what it would be like if he ceased to come to see her. She knew he was lonely, too, but she reasoned that life was different for a man. He did not have to be lonely, for she thought him a fine-looking man. Many women would be pleased with his company. So she worried at certain moments before he pulled the rope bell on her gate that he might stop coming. He might find someone else with whom he could pass his evenings. As he had not made love to her there was not that to hold him, and he might find it with another woman. Then she would lose him. Yet it was still not that she wanted Glapion to make love to her; she simply continued to worry why he did not do so. When she looked into her mirrors she was sure she was as beautiful as ever. And Glapion was a widower.

When it happened it frightened her at first. She had often imagined how it would be, yet the reality was as new and strange as if she had never considered the idea.

It was a cold night, and Glapion had brought in wood from the backyard and piled it high on the fire in her parlor. The flames sprang up and the room blazed with a light so bright that as she stood before the grate with her hands outstretched she was blinded for a moment and could see nothing. It was then that Glapion came behind her and put his arms about her beneath her own outstretched arms, his hands resting gently on her breasts, his mouth finding the side of her throat. When he moved his mouth away he said nothing for a moment.

The fire was too hot, too dazzling, and she swung around, still encircled in his arms. It seemed to him that she was struggling to release herself, and he asked, "Shouldn't I have done that, Marie?"

"It's the fire," she said. "It's so hot." He dropped his arms and she moved away.

He followed her, and she found herself meeting him halfway. He kissed her and it was different from being kissed by Jacques, an older man's kiss, his lips rougher, his beard a little scratchy, his breath sour-sweet with wine and tobacco. Yet it was not unpleasant. There was fright in her which she didn't understand, but beneath it was relief, even a feeling of comfort.

"I was afraid to do that before," he said.

"Afraid?" She stared at him. Of all people, she had never thought Glapion afraid of her.

"There is something about you," he said.

"Glapion." She moved to him and he began kissing her again. "I'm so lonely," she said when she could breathe.

They made plans in the morning. "There must be no lies

95

between us," he said. "I have told you only one, but it is an important one."

She had made spoon bread for their breakfast, and a veal hash. It was a fine breakfast, like a wedding breakfast, the table in the parlor spread with Marguerite's nicest linen and her best silver, and the fig preserves set out in a crystal bowl. Marie put down the plate of spoon bread and smoothed her braids with both hands, smiling down at him, feeling indeed almost a bride again, warmed and happier than she had been for a long time. "You told me a lie, Glapion?" she chided. "Aren't you afraid of me now? I might do terrible things to you. You're not going to marry me as you said last night? If that is it, my friend, take care! I forgot the butter. I must get the butter."

As she swung toward the door, running like a girl, he called behind her, "Wait, Marie!"

"Glapion?" She whirled about at the door, startled at the seriousness of his tone of voice. She frowned. He was sitting at the table, his head bowed slightly, his gaze upon the empty plate before him.

"We cannot be married in the church," he said quietly, moving not a muscle, only his lips. "The lie I told you was that my wife was dead. I told you that long ago when I didn't think it mattered. I tell everyone that. She went off with another man many years ago, but she is alive." His lips stopped moving and he just sat there.

She came back into the room, walking slowly to the fireplace. This morning their fire was low, and she stood gazing down at the smoldering coals. I have power over others, she thought, but none I can use for myself. I cannot make my own life go right. It is always wrong.

Glapion rose and came and stood behind her. "I will be a good husband to you, Marie," he said gently. "I've dreamed of it for a long time. You will see that I will be a good husband to you. Do some words in church make good husbands?"

She leaned against him and rested her head on his shoulder, moving it about a little until she was comforted and the warmth came back to her body. "I will marry us, Glapion," she said, "if you want me to do so." She took her head from his shoulder and stood straight and tall. "You are not bound," she added. "You do not have to do this."

"Marry us, Marie."

She married them that afternoon. She prepared the altar by spreading a small table in the parlor with a clean linen cloth, and upon it placing a framed, brightly colored picture of St. Joseph. Before this she placed a bowl filled to the top with white sand. She wrote their full names on bits of paper and carefully buried these in the sand. Then in the sand she placed two blue candles, thick ones that would burn for a long time. She fetched two small dolls, one male and the other female, and bound their tiny hands together with white satin ribbon and set them on the altar before the bowl containing the sand with their names in it and the blue candles.

"Glapion," she said, "build up the fire."

Until then he had been watching, looking pleased and happy. Now he did as she directed, and the fire in the grate flamed upward.

She fetched a dish of salt and a bottle of brandy. "You must light the candles," she said.

He lit the thick blue candles.

"Kneel with me."

They knelt before the altar, the dish of salt between them on the floor, the brandy to one side.

"St. Joseph, pray for us!" she cried in a loud voice.

Glapion trembled a bit, and she was conscious of it.

"St. Michael, pray for us!" she said loudly. "Dani! Dani! Blanc Dani!" She took a deep breath. "St. Peter, help us! Liba! Liba! *L'a commande!*"

Glapion shifted nervously.

"Until death?" she asked him. "Until death? Say it!"

"Until death!"

"Until death!" she answered.

Still kneeling, she uncorked the bottle of brandy and passed it to him. "Drink."

He took a great gulp and then she drank. She rose, giving his shoulder a push as she did so. They went to the fire, to which she carried the salt. Each tossed in a handful. Blue flames rose. "It is good," she said, sighing.

Then she went out to the kitchen and brought back the small black snake she had cooked, divided on two saucers. When he retched at the first taste of it she bent and kissed his hand closest to her.

At midnight they went out together and placed a bowl of cooked macaroni sprinkled with parsley beneath a sycamore tree in Congo Square, and walked home together in the cold winter moonlight.

The food was a sacrifice to the old gods and to the saints. It would bring them good luck and long lives, perhaps even children. It would appease their enemies, those who were not living.

Chapter 5

WHEN their child was born Marie was calling him "Jacques" even before they took him to the cathedral to be christened. The name did not annoy Glapion. He knew how she felt about that other Jacques and he was not a jealous man. Also, Marie added his own. The baby would be Jacques Christophe Duminy Glapion. Although she had cooled as a friend, Madame Laclotte accepted their invitation to be the godmother, and Glapion asked an old friend, another veteran of Chalmette, Baptiste Coquille, to be godfather.

At the cathedral the baby was christened with due ceremony by Père Antoine. Throughout the ritual Marie was nervous, and she could not look the priest in the face. To be sure she still came to Mass on Sundays, and occasionally she came to pray on other mornings, but no longer as often as before, and it had been over a year since she had come to confession and as long since she had held a conversation with her old friend. She knew, too, that the father was perfectly aware of her activities. Little went on in New Orleans without his knowledge.

So she was not surprised when he called her aside on the *banquette* outside the church and laid a long, almost transparent hand first upon the warm, blanketed bundle that was little Jacques, then upon her arm. She looked down at his hand. It was withered and thin and covered with brown splotches, for he was very old now, almost eighty, people said. "Are you all right, my child?"

She forced a smile. "Yes, Father."

"I don't see you often." He directed his attention to Glapion, who was standing a few feet away. "I have known Marie all her life," he said. "I baptized her, too, you know. She aided me when the wounded returned from the battle with the British, and she helped me when the yellow fever was so bad in the year after that. She is a fine nurse."

She patted the baby. "Thank you, Father."

"A good daughter to her mother," Père Antoine said. "A good wife." But he was frowning sternly when he gazed at her again. "And now she saddens me. I can only hope the rumors are exaggerated."

"I do no evil work, Father," she murmured. "If that is said, it is a lie." Her eyes were directed to his at that moment, large but gentle.

"All work is evil that is not God's work," he told her, still scowling with all the fire in his eyes that had been there, she knew, when he had been a younger man. "Do not judge what is evil and what is not, Marie. Your practices come from the jungle, from pagan savages."

"The saints aid me, Father."

"Nonsense," he said. "You defile the names of the saints!"

There was a pain under her heart, but it did not show in her face. "I only help people, Father," she said, keeping her voice as strong as possible. "Do not dislike me for it. I want your love."

"I dislike no one," Père Antoine said. "I will pray for you, Marie." He turned and strode back into the cathedral, his head high, his withered hands clasped together behind him.

They walked home slowly and almost silently, Marie carrying the infant, Glapion beside her. Behind them Coquille assisted Madame Laclotte along the narrow *banquettes*, which were in a bad state of repair, and across the bridges that crossed the open, water-filled ditches.

"I thought he would complain that our marriage was not in the Church," Glapion said at last. "He said nothing of that."

"He disapproves, I'm sure," Marie told him, "but after sixty years of living in New Orleans he has become used to such things. He hates voodoo worse. Our marriage saddens him some, but the other is worse. He sees the devil in it." She was thoughtful a moment. "Once I did, too, Glapion. Do you think I have become evil? I know I am not. The saints do aid me in my work, and I am still a Catholic. I will always be a Catholic."

Glapion laughed. "He is a fanatic," he told her. Glapion had little religion. "He has always been a fanatic. You must forget it."

"I will go to Mass always," Marie said. "No one can keep me away. I hope he will forgive me, too." She turned her head in time to see Madame Laclotte cross herself hurriedly. "Do you think me evil, Madame?"

Madame Laclotte swished herself nervously and lowered her head. "It is not for me to judge you, Marie," she said. They were at an intersection and she turned from them. "I must stop and see a friend," she added. "You will excuse me?"

"But you must come home for some wine," Marie protested, narrowing her eyes. "A celebration!"

"I will come over soon," Madame said hesitantly. "This is important, and I had forgotten."

When Coquille had left them a few hours later, and the baby was asleep, Marie sat on the floor in the parlor, her head resting against Glapion's knee, just as she had used to sit at Jacques' feet. Glapion took the decanter from the table beside his chair and refilled her glass. He stroked her hair fondly. "Do not let the priest make you unhappy, Marie."

"I cannot help it," Marie told him solemnly. "I wish he could understand. And Madame Laclotte. She ran from us like a pigeon! It is all right for some to fear me, but not my old friends." She set the glass down on the floor, and sighed. "But no one can stop me, Glapion. I will be powerful. I will be rich. It is not wrong to be powerful and rich if one does no harm to good people."

"Good people?" he muttered, still caressing her hair. "What of bad people?"

"I will harm no one," she vowed. "Of course, sometimes the good must be protected from the bad. If the bad ones suffer because of their wickedness it is no fault of mine. They destroy themselves. That is not evil work. It is so difficult to make people understand."

She raised her glass and sipped her wine. Her blood was warmed. "I have been lazy, Glapion," she said. "Not enough people come to me. I must do many things, and you can help me. I must set aside a room here for meetings, and have an altar. I must have a snake. Saiya can get me one from the swamps, and you must build me a cage for it. I must have a cat, a black one, and I must make much *gris-gris* to sell. I will need roots and herbs, bones and dried creatures—frogs, lizards, bats."

"Witch!" It was the same thing Jacques had called her once, but Glapion's tone was different. She knew he was laughing at her a little.

"Of course some of it is foolishness," she told him. "But it impresses people. I must take them away from Saloppé." She tasted her wine again, then handed the half-filled glass back to him. No more wine. She must think clearly. "You must help me, Glapion," she added.

"I will help you."

She knew he would. He had little to do, for his income was a small pension and he had no regular occupation, although sometimes he took odd jobs of sorts—as a roofer, as a blacksmith's helper, the kind of work most quadroon men did. "Help me," she promised him, "and we will be rich."

Her second child, a girl, she called Marguerite, and the next, at Glapion's insistence, Marie. The fourth, another boy at last, she called Jean. Père Antoine christened them all, and never again did he refer to her voodoo work. In fact he spoke to her scarcely at all. It grieved her deeply, but she did not know what to do, so she did nothing. Each Sunday she went to early Mass, and sat in the rear of the church, and she comforted herself by bringing more and more of the saints into her work. They are with me, she told herself constantly. They work through me. The good Father is mistaken, that is all.

Then one day it was whispered through her neighborhood that Père Antoine was dying. At first she could not believe it, for he seemed imperishable, and she almost felt that the whole world she knew must go with him. In all her life she had never talked with anyone who could remember a time when Père Antoine had not been alive. On the evening of the day she heard the gossip she could bear it no longer. Leaving Glapion with the children, she fled the house, knowing she must see him again.

She had been to his hut before, a crude cabin thatched with palmetto leaves, about two blocks behind the cathedral. He had always lived here, since he had first come to New Orleans, and had refused to move to more comfortable quarters. Now, as she approached the cabin, she saw that there was a crowd of people outside—people of every class and color—and beyond them the date palm, planted by Père Antoine himself from, it was said, a date seed brought from Spain. Marie walked swiftly through the crowd, some of them stepping aside to let her pass as they recognized her, past the date palm and into the cabin.

He lay on a cot in a corner of the first of the two rooms,

still clad in his serge cassock, his face yellow wax, his lips invisible, his closed eyes buried in deep wrinkles. A stout priest came out of the shadows beyond the candlelight, and Marie recognized him as one of the two new fathers she had noticed at the cathedral. "You should not be in here, my daughter. There are orders that there are to be no visitors."

"May I speak to him?" she asked. The man did not know her! It astonished her now when anyone did not know her.

"He cannot," the priest told her. "He is not conscious."

She swept to the cot and put the back of one hand against a cold cheek. "It is not the fever," she said. "He is like ice." Yet he was not dead. She could hear the rasping fight for breath, and she could see the faint rise and fall of the sunken chest.

"You must go, woman."

"I will pray, Father," she murmured, and fell to her knees.

The fat priest sighed heavily. "Of course. Then you must go."

When she rose she asked, "May I stay with him, Father? I am a good nurse. I think I could help."

"We have a Negress," he said coldly.

She repressed her temper, and examined the room for the first time. In the darkness on one side a black woman sat crouched on a box. "Please, Father," she begged. "Père Antoine was an old friend." She kept her expression humble, but she was studying him, deciding he was either an American or a German. His accent was strange, although his French was not bad.

The priest belched. "I have not had my supper," he said irritably. "Stay until I return."

"Widow Paris," said the black woman, coming out of the darkness when the priest had gone. "What can we do? Can you help him?"

"Not in the way you think," Marie told her. "I wanted to be with him for a while; that is all. Let me see if I can speak with him." She bent over the small man on the cot. "Father? Father?"

There was no answer.

"The kitchen is there?" Marie asked, indicating the door to the other room. The woman nodded. It was not really a kitchen at all. Marie found only a bare room with an open fireplace, unlighted because it was summer. A wooden table and some chairs, a scanty assortment of pots and pans were the only furnishings.

Marie sat down on a chair. There was nothing she could do. After a while she went back into the room. The crouching woman looked up at her. "There is no food here," she said. "The other fathers brought it to him when he could eat. I made soup for him myself."

"He will not want food again," Marie said. "I only wanted to see the other room. I will sit here until the priest returns and then I will go."

The Negress grunted. "Father Scheffler is a pig." She moved closer to Marie and to the man on the cot. "Can you not do work for Père Antoine?"

"Not for him," Marie told her. "He would not want it. If his mind hears us now he is angry that we even discuss it."

The woman looked startled. "You think he can hear us?"

"Perhaps," said Marie. "Often the dying do, and often even the dead linger before they depart. He knew of these things, for he was not like others."

"We must be careful what we say!" the woman whispered, her eyes wide with sudden fear. She fluttered about the room. "I have said nothing but good things about him. No one could say anything else."

When Father Scheffler returned, Marie said to the woman, "I will come back in the morning." She bowed to the priest and left. As she passed through the crowd outside, the colored people began whispering, "That's Marie Laveau! It's the Widow Paris!"

She awoke before dawn with the knowledge that Père Antoine was gone, and when she reached the street outside the cabin the crowd was much larger than it had been the night before. She watched as Father Scheffler and another priest came out and began, each in turn, to make short talks, begging the crowd to disperse and go home.

"It was terrible," a woman told Marie. "They broke into his room and began cutting pieces of his cassock from his poor body. They would have left him naked if the fathers had not threatened them with excommunication from the Church! Some of them wanted clippings of his hair and his fingernails!"

As she walked toward home Marie saw that already some people were nailing black crepe on their front doors. The whole city would be in mourning. She would not need to display mourning, she decided. The mourning was in her heart. Too, another cord binding her was gone.

The twins, Noemi and Felice, were prematurely born and rather sickly, so it was several months after their birth before Marie held her first meeting in her own home. With great care and Glapion's help she made the plans. She thought of the danger of a visit from the police, for lately there had been gossip that the police planned to break up voodoo gatherings, but she determined to take that risk. The meeting must be a grand one, impressive, and designed to make Saloppé's meetings look poor in comparison. The room in which she had constructed her altar would not hold enough people. It would have to be held in her yard, behind her high board fence.

She chose a Friday night. Saloppé's meetings were always held on Saturday nights, and Marie decided that since many of Saloppé's friends would come to hers, too, they might, after the night was done, decide not to go to Saloppé's on the following night. This amused Glapion, when she told him of her idea, as her shrewd thinking always amused him. "You will see," she told him. "After mine they will either be too tired to attend hers or they will find hers dull and stupid."

She felt her greatest triumph was in getting Doctor John to come to her meeting. She went boldly to his cottage and asked him. The wily black man blinked at her, the wrinkles deepening about his old eyes. "You grow proud, Widow," he told her bluntly.

Marie glanced about her. The room into which the old man had led her was dark and smelly. On shelves there were human skulls, melted candles and weird small bundles covered with rags. "Do not call me 'Widow,' " she told him. "I am remarried and I have six children."

"A Vodu marriage," he murmured. "It is good. What do you call yourself now?"

"Most people call me Marie Laveau," she said. "But I am not concerned with that. Come tonight to my meeting and I will give you half the collection." She paused. "Bring your drum and help me. Do you have love for Saloppé?"

He spat on the floor. "I am old and tired," he said, "and I need the money. I will come. I love none of you. I hate brown people. You are all mules. I am black." Then he saw the resentment in her face. "Be as angry as you like," he added. "You can do no harm to me and I have no fear of you. I will come tonight, but I'll tell you again, I do not like your kind. I spit on all of you." Again his saliva marked the floor.

Her anger left her as she walked home. He was coming, and his mere presence would enhance her prestige. That was all that mattered.

Glapion moved the cage containing her own snake, her Vodu, consecrated by herself soon after Saiya had brought it to her, into a prominent place in the yard, and tied the rooster she had decided to sacrifice to a stake nearby. They bordered the yard with candles, and spread a white sheet in the middle. When all the preparations were completed she dressed herself carefully in blue calico and tied her *tignon* about her head in a new fashion she had lately adopted, doing it with seven knots for luck, with the points jutting straight upward. Her gold earrings were polished and glittering, and upon each arm she wore a thick gold bracelet. Before dusk she fed the snake, a black moccasin whose poison had been removed, talking to it affectionately, for it had become a pet. Then Glapion helped her feed the children. Glapion would remain in the house tonight and take no part in the meeting, for it was getting so they had trouble coaxing the older children to go to sleep early.

The people began to come as soon as it was dark, and as she watched them arrive she was pleased. Word had been spreading for days through the grapevine, but she had had moments when she had wondered as to how many people would appear; but soon after night had come there seemed to be a great many. She let them wait, let the hours pass. She wanted them worked to a pitch of impatience. She knew, too, that there were many, especially house servants, who would be late in getting away from their work; there would be slaves who have to sneak off after their owners had gone out for the evening or had retired. Doctor John was late, but as he entered the yard a murmur ran through the crowd. As he had been instructed, Saiya brought Doctor John into the house, and Marie sat him in the kitchen and gave him a tumbler of rum. The children ran about the room and the old man grumbled, but soon the rum worked and his temper improved.

Soon after this the yard was crowded and it was easy to see that the people were becoming more and more restless. They sat on the ground and talked or walked about impatiently. Marie watched for a while from behind the shutters of a window, listening to their talk. What she heard of herself was mixed. Some were saying that she was too new and inexperienced, others that she was already the greatest of all the voodooiennes. These said they would swear by Marie

Laveau, and they would tell tales of what she had done, some of them exaggerations. She listened, pleased. Then she decided it was time to begin. There was a limit as to how long she should make them wait. She fetched Doctor John and sent him out. He crouched on the ground and began the steady beat on his weird drum with the palms of both his hands. The crowd quieted so she imagined she heard their breathing, steady and in tune with the rhythmic beating of the hands of Doctor John. As the beat increased, then reached a certain pitch, she stepped into the yard. A loud outcry of approval poured from numerous throats.

She stood in the center of the white sheet, the caged Vodu just behind her, the rooster to one side, with no one else touching the white sheet, and let herself grow tall and rigid. Doctor John ceased his beat and there was complete silence. For more than a minute she let the silence remain. It became agony. A woman far in the back cried out. Marie clapped her hands quickly together. Again there was silence. Then Marie suddenly screamed: "Papa LaBas!"

Answers came immediately. "Yé, yé!"

She screamed that name again: "Papa LaBas!"

She could almost feel them shudder. "Yé, yé!"

It even frightened her a little, for not even Saloppé had dared to call that name in an open meeting. Papa LaBas was the voodoo name for the devil. It was dangerous to use, but she had known nothing would cause greater excitement than to do this at her first big meeting, and she had protected herself with strong *gris-gris* and many prayers. She called the name once more, in a stronger voice than ever, as if she really wanted to summon him.

"Papa LaBas!"

Murmurs and groans passed through the crowd. Some women sobbed, evidently in terror. She watched carefully. No one left. She had thought a few might flee.

Until now the yard had been almost dark. Now Saiya went

about lighting the candles. The glow spread and increased. The faces staring at her were tense and filled with fear. She smiled.

"Have no fear, my children! Have no fear, my little ones!"

"Yes, Mamma!" The response came from more and more of them. "Yes, Mamma!"

"I will protect you from harm! My power is strong! Papa LaBas, my power is strong!"

"Yes, Mamma!"

She clapped her hands toward Doctor John, and he sprang to his feet as if he were a young boy instead of an old man. He brought bottles of rum and set them up around her on the sheet in a twisting pattern. Marie seized one bottle from him, jerked out the cork and threw it away. She raised the bottle to her mouth and drank, almost choking as the fiery liquor poured down her throat. She handed the bottle to Doctor John, and he drank and returned it. This time she filled her mouth and spat the rum full into the faces of those nearest her. "My power is strong!" she cried.

"Oh!" they shrieked. "Oh! Oh! Oh! Yé! Yé!"

Saiya came with more candles and set them up between the bottles forming the pattern on the sheet. When he had lighted these the yard glowed almost as brightly as daylight.

"Yé!" they cried. "Oh! Oh! Oh!"

Marie sprang on top of the cage containing the snake. She felt elation so strongly that her body began to quiver and tremble. She swung from side to side, raising her hands above her head. Like them, she cried, "Oh! Oh! Oh! Yé! Yé!"

Saiya appeared and fell to his knees before the cage. He lifted its gate and brought out the snake and handed it to Marie. She lifted it high. Women screamed.

They began the dance. A woman sprang forward to lead it and others followed quickly. The woman strutted around the first candle on the sheet, the others behind her. They wove in and out, about two dozen of them taking part. The rest of the crowd hung back at the edges of the sheet. Some closed their eyes and clapped their hands. Doctor John returned to his tom-tom beating. The dancers bowed low as they passed Marie, who was still standing on the cage, passing the snake back and forth over their heads. "Papa LaBas!" they cried. "Papa LaBas! Yé! Yé!"

On their seventh time around, the first ones picked up the bottles of rum, uncorked them and drank. They passed the bottles to the rear, and others drank. They spat rum upon the sheet. "Papa LaBas! Yé! Yé!"

Those not taking part in the dancing howled and moaned.

Marie wrapped the snake around her shoulders, and began to twist and writhe. Now she scarcely knew what she was doing, at least for the moment. The drum affected her as well as the people. Then a man sprang into view before her, a black man wearing only a loincloth, and she realized he was a slave she knew, named Daniel, whom she had instructed to appear at this moment. In his hands he held the fluttering, struggling black form of the rooster. She opened her eyes more widely and pointed a rigid finger. Daniel seized the rooster's head, swung the creature over and over his head, and the fowl's neck snapped. He then held the creature before him and tore its neck with his teeth. Blood gushed down his chin and his black chest. Marie heard the screams, heard her own voice rising above the others. Her legs felt like rubber, and she thought for a moment she would collapse in ecstasy, yet she remained upright as the vibrations of her body increased and increased, and the drum beat and beat and beat.

It stopped, and she seemed to return from a place far distant. She lifted the Vodu and Saiya took it and returned it to its cage. She heard the sounds—the wails and moans, the tearing of garments, the heavy breathing. Some of the people were on the ground, prostrate before her. She felt high above them, exalted and alone, far removed. She felt the power, yet she felt exhausted, too, drained of strength. "Rest, children!" she cried down to them as they groveled. "Peace, children!"

"Yé, Mamma!"

"Peace, children!" She was only breathing the words, and she wondered that they heard. "The rooster's blood!" she cried.

Doctor John brought the cup, and she drank of the hot, rancid blood. When Doctor John had sipped from the cup, she poured the rest of the thick red liquid upon the ground before her. The Negro who had torn the rooster's throat with his teeth lifted his face from where he lay on the earth before her and the blood splashed upon his forehead and eyes, and he moaned and sank down again, his face buried.

Doctor John brought the pewter bowl and placed it at her feet upon the Vodu's cage, and they came forward and placed silver coins and paper money in the bowl until it was filled to the brim. Once she put a bare foot in it and pressed the money down, and still they came with more. All were standing now. All gave.

"It is over, children!" she cried at last. "It is over! Go now in peace!"

They drifted out slowly, talking among themselves, still shaken with emotion, some of the women crying. She slipped down from the box and stood, still trembling and shaking. When Doctor John came to her, she said, "Come back in the morning. Do not worry. I will not cheat you. Marie Laveau has never cheated anyone." He scowled a moment, but he picked up his drum and left. When she was alone she slipped to the earth and sat there, staring into the cage. Many of the candles had burned out now, and the rest were low, but she could see into the cage. The snake uncoiled itself and moved toward her. "Yes, my dear," she whispered, hardly conscious of what she was saying. "Yes, my dear."

Glapion came out of the house and helped her inside. Then he returned and put out the candles that still burned and brought inside the bowl of money. She lay stretched across the bed, too exhausted to undress. He untied her *tignon* and slipped the heavy bracelets from her arms. He was kind enough not to speak to her, and almost instantly she fell asleep.

She could not rise the next morning, and Glapion brought her coffee and took care of the children. For a long time they talked only of trivialities, not mentioning the meeting. Then, as he was leaving the room, she said, "I did not know how it was until last night. Glapion, it was the first time I really knew."

"Try to rest, my dear," he said, and nothing more.

And a little later when Doctor John came he entered her room and gazed at her with a respect that she had never seen in his face before. "You are great, Marie Laveau," he said.

"You are kind," she told him.

Still dressed as she had been the night before, her hair tumbling about her shoulders, she rose and led him into the parlor. They sat at a table and she divided the money carefully, watching his greedy eyes as she counted it out.

"Will you work with me again?" she asked, when she was through.

"I will work with you," he said. "If you wish, only with you."

"Only with me," she said. "And the next time your share of the offering will be a third. That is enough for you. A half is too much!"

He nodded his woolly head, as white and as light in texture as if his cranium were covered with soapsuds. Then he lifted it. His face twisted into a grimace made horrifying by his wrinkles and tattooed lines.

"Then we understand each other," Marie told him, her huge eyes as cold as she could make them.

"Marie Laveau is great," said Doctor John. He blinked and

113

dropped his head. Suddenly he became in appearance an old, decrepit man, harmless and almost helpless. Then he asked, "But what do you know? What have you learned from the great Saloppé?"

"You despise Saloppé," Marie told him evenly. "Do not pretend with me!"

"That is true, Laveau," he said. "But what have you learned, woman?"

She found it hard to breathe for a moment. Then she said, "I have learned much. And not all of it is from Saloppé! There are things I have always known. Can you believe that?"

"Yes," he murmured. "I can believe that."

"We address our God through the spirit that dwells in our Vodu," she told him coldly. "You know that? Do you intend to speak to me as a schoolchild? Or shall I deal with you as such? I know what the powders mean, and the candles, and what all the *gris-gris* are to do, or most of it! But why should I answer you, old man? I have had enough of you for today." She sank back and closed her eyes. She had never been so tired in all her life. "I do no evil."

"Already they are saying you keep the skeletons of babies in your *armoire*," Doctor John told her, leering across at her. "It is to be expected."

"The only babies' skeletons I have are those of my children," Marie said, "enclosed in their own flesh."

"Marie Laveau is great," said Doctor John.

The next morning she felt strong. She went about the house singing after she returned from Mass, and as she gave the older children breakfast. She rocked the twins and crooned to them, and Glapion, watching her, smiled. "One would think you had been drinking wine all morning," he remarked.

"Glapion!" she cried out suddenly. "I think it is very much

like drinking wine in the morning—the way I feel! This afternoon I am going to Congo Square."

"Are you sure you want to go?" He looked only faintly startled.

"Glapion, I know!"

Outside the square the crowd was thick, and many of the people were white. The sun was hot, and there were carriages everywhere. "The whites have come to watch today," she told Glapion. "They like to watch their slaves dance and to see the great Saloppé. The great Saloppé! We shall see who is great! They will have a show!"

As she turned at the corner and crossed the wide street, all the colored people stepped aside, whispering among themselves. Most of the white ones stared at her curiously. She walked very swiftly, with long, bold strides, her head raised high in her usual way. She towered over nearly everyone she passed.

The dancers in the square were performing a calinda, the men whirling about the women with slow grace, the women never moving their feet, but twisting their hips and shoulders to the rhythm of the drums. In the center stood Marie Saloppé, a circle of men about her. The red and blue handkerchiefs the dancers held above their heads or moved behind their hips made bright colors in the scene. The drums and the tom-toms beat steadily; the high-pitched wind instruments whined.

Marie pushed open the gate in the wooden picket fence and walked straight into the dancing crowd, never slowing her pace, her gaze straight ahead. As she walked through the gates the dancing stopped. Whispers came first, then louder comments. They all recognized her. "It is Marie Laveau! Marie Laveau!"

She spoke to them, but without looking into anyone's face. "Peace, my children! Peace!"

115

The music ceased. She was facing Saloppé.

"What do you want?" Saloppé narrowed her eyes. She stretched the blue and red kerchief she still held tautly before her. "What do you want here, Laveau?"

Marie did not answer at once.

"Let there be music!" Saloppé shouted to her musicians.

But the music did not begin. The dancers drew back until Marie and Saloppé were alone, face to face, in a circle of emptiness. There was more whispering beyond it.

"I have come," Marie said, in deliberately dramatic tones. "It is my time."

"You grow bold, Laveau!" Saloppé cried shrilly.

"I came first to ask a question," Marie said. "Why did you promise me to die? But it does not matter, Saloppé. I know the answer. And I have the answer for the question you might ask. You did not believe I had so much power. You did not know me! Now go, Saloppé! I will do you no harm. I bring death to no one!"

All about her Marie heard the people murmuring. There were those that were for Saloppé, but there were those that were for her. She quieted herself, for she felt she was beginning to tremble. She was gambling, but she knew she must gamble now.

Saloppé was shrieking at her. "What could you do to me? I taught you all you know. Now I curse you! My curse is upon you, Laveau!"

Some members of the crowd were saying there would be a fight, but Marie did not fear that. She was twice Saloppé's size, twice her weight. She would have enjoyed beating her. Once Jacques had beaten Saloppé, she remembered. Suddenly this idea became intriguing. It also seemed useful. "I will not use the power I have against you," Marie said. "I do not do bad work. But I will beat you, Saloppé. I will beat you here for all to see."

She watched Saloppé quail. The woman stepped back, but she cried again, "My curse on you!"

"Keep your curses," Marie said serenely, "and go! Go work them elsewhere, or I will beat you now." She stepped forward. "I will beat you with my fists!"

Saloppé made her decision in a hurry. "Come, my children!" she called in a loud but hoarse voice. "The dance is over. Let us go!" She turned quickly and walked away.

As some of the dancers began to follow her and others gaped about the square hesitantly, unable to make up their minds, Marie cried, "Stay, my children!"

When she had reached the gate Saloppé again called to them. "Do you want the police to come here?" she asked. "We have had little trouble with the laws. We have had peace. Follow me!"

Marie spread her arms wide. She gazed from face to face with her great eyes. "Stay, my children!"

Suddenly someone began a chant and others took it up, until the words filled the square. A drum began beating an accompaniment. It was an old song they had sung to Saloppé, and they sang it in the patois which was the language most of them spoke.

> Eh, yé, yé, Mamzelle Marie
> Ya, yé, yé, li konin tou, gris-gris;
> Li té kouri lekal, aver vieux kokodril;
> Oh, ouai, yé Mamzelle Marie. . . .

Marie knew that it was for her now. Saloppé's name was "Marie" too, but scarcely a dozen from the crowd were following her. The rest remained. They were singing for Marie Laveau. It was a gay and childish song, but it said of her that she was wise and that she had gone to school with the crocodiles, and it went on to praise her as a great voodooienne and a proper consort of the Grand Zombie. She knew now that

117

all she had said to Saloppé had not been mere bragging. It was her time.

Filled with exaltation, she snatched a handkerchief from a man standing nearby and, holding it stretched out above her head, she cried, "Peace, my children! Peace!"

The song went on:

> Oh, tingouar, yé hén hén,
> Oh, tingouar, yé éh éh,
> Li appé vini, li Grand Zombi,
> Li appé vini, pol fé mouri!
> Oh, ouai, yé Mamzelle Marie!

Chapter 6

IT WAS August 1832. Everyone in New Orleans was saying it was the hottest month of the hottest summer that they could remember. It was known that there had been several cases of yellow fever in the city, and people talked with fear in their voices of other years when the fever had come at about this time, and, as fall approached, had become epidemic. Marie had borne her twelfth child in July, and this time her strength had not returned as rapidly as before. The children had come fast. Only eleven months before there had been another set of twins, a boy and a girl. The twelfth child was a girl, and one with amazingly flaxen fuzz on her tiny pink head.

Marie was nursing the baby out on the gallery, holding the infant to her breast with one arm and fanning herself and it with a large palmetto fan at the same time, when one of her neighbors, a woman who attended her meetings, pushed open the gate and came in. The yard was filled with the children, and the older ones ran toward the front when the gate opened, yelling, "Hello, Delia! Delia, come play with us! Have you seen the new baby, Delia?"

Marie moved the baby gently, and it screamed. Delia came toward the gallery, the children clustering about her. "It is bad," she kept muttering. "It has started worse than the other years. Already people are frightened."

"The fever?" Marie asked. "Sit down, Delia."

Delia sat on the stoop near Marie's feet. "Even old women cannot remember when it was so bad."

"You are wearing the little bag I gave you?" Marie asked.

"I wear it." Delia touched her bosom, and Marie knew she had pinned the bag there as she had been instructed. The bag contained a lump of camphor, some herbs, a tiny picture of St. Joseph; it would protect its wearer from yellow fever. "It is not that I lack faith. I cannot help my fears."

"Fear not and you will not be harmed," Marie told her. She wore the same kind of bag herself, as did all her children. One was even pinned to the tiny undershirt of the infant in her arms.

"It is not just the fever," Delia said. "Perhaps you have not heard of what happened yesterday. A man dropped on the levee. He was a seaman, poor creature. People say that he turned black in a few moments, and within an hour he was dead." She shook her head woefully. "People are saying it was the cholera!"

Marie shuddered. "The cholera!"

"Old people are saying they can remember when it came before, Marie Laveau," said Delia. "It came with the fever. It was very bad, but the city was much smaller then. Now that the city is big it will be terrible!"

Marie shuddered inwardly, but concealed her feelings from Delia and the children. Marie Laveau must never show such feelings. She was above fear. She must never allow her followers to suspect that she, too, could be touched by terror. But it was said that New Orleans now had a population of more than 100,000 persons, for the city had grown rapidly during the past ten years, and Marie wondered what an epidemic would mean. She glanced anxiously at her children—her tall, slim Jacques, now nearly ten years old, Marguerite and Marie, almost as tall, all the giggling, happy little ones. She patted the baby, and returned her gaze to Delia. "Will you stay this evening with the children? I have an engagement with Madame Riviere. It will be only for an hour or two."

"I will stay," said Delia, her face still twisted with worry.

Glapion was not well these days and he was unable to cope with all the children in the evenings, so often Delia or one of the other neighborhood women kept the children when Marie had an appointment to dress the hair of one of her clients. Marie still kept all the appointments she could, although her childbearing kept her from obtaining much work. Madame Laclotte was very old now, almost ninety, and so she had retired. Marie might have had all her business, had she had time, for although there were many other hairdressers in the city, none possessed Marie's reputation in the art.

"You are so calm," Delia said suddenly. "I shake with fright when people talk of the plague. Next week will be September and it is at this time of year that the fever begins."

"You must have faith, child," Marie said serenely, although she felt not at all serene. "It is true no one is perfectly safe, but I have given you powerful protection. We must all have faith. We must pray."

Marie tried to be still serene as she entered Madame Riviere's mansion on the Esplanade. It was dusk, and when a slave woman admitted her, the wide center hall was already beautifully lighted with candles. The big boards of the floor gleamed with polishing at the edges of the gently faded old rugs, and upon the walls family portraits showed their rich colors in the reflected light. Through open doors leading from the hall Marie caught glimpses of shining mahogany furniture, of brilliant mirrors in gold leaf frames, of crystal and silver, and of vases filled with flowers. Madame was entertaining at a *soirée* this evening, and the house was filled with the festive scents of roses and jasmine, of wax and polish, of the tallow of the burning candles.

"She is not well, I can tell you that," remarked the fat, black servant, as she led Marie inside. "Still, she won't give in to not having company this evening. She's waiting for you up there now, poor darling, worrying about how her hair looks, as if it matters when you're sick. I wish I could talk some sense into her." She indicated the curving staircase. "It's the storm that brought on the sickness," she added. "I've never seen it fail."

Marie smiled faintly as she ascended the graceful stairs. There had been a mild tornado during the week before. There had been some damage in the city. The angry river had washed over the levee in some places; the wind had uprooted great live oaks and cypresses; roofs had gone. Many people, especially Negroes, believed that the yellow fever always followed the tornadoes and hurricanes that so often attacked New Orleans at this time of year. Marie did not believe this, nor was she worried about the pessimism of Madame Riviere's servant, for at the moment Marie felt particularly cheerful. She always loved to enter these beautiful old houses, and, as devoted as she was to her family, it was good to escape her own crowded home and the constant noise of her brood, at least for a short time.

But when she entered Madame Riviere's boudoir she was shocked at the woman's appearance. Madame, a young girl of only nineteen, a bride of but a year, was sitting at her dressing table, her hands pressed to her temples, her dark hair streaming down her back. In the reflection in the mirror her face was flushed, her lips pale and withered-looking, her eyes feverish. Marie felt a chill envelop her heart. She knew well the symptoms, although they could of course also indicate only an attack of malaria or even a more minor ailment.

Madame Riviere turned, startled at Marie's quick entrance, and cried, "Oh, Marie! I've been waiting for you. I'm giving a most important party!" Her voice sounded strained and thin.

"Yes, Madame." Marie went over to her and met her gaze

in the mirror. "Are you ill? Arthemise told me you were not feeling well."

"Oh, bother Arthemise!" The girl lifted her hair from the back and lifted it as if its weight oppressed her. "I have a headache, that is all. And this dreadful heat! I will be all right as soon as I am dressed. I need some excitement!"

Marie began dressing her hair, working slowly and gently. When her hands touched the girl's temples and forehead they burned like fire. "You have a fever," Marie said at last.

Madame Riviere forced a laugh. "You are as bad as that Arthemise. Don't worry. Just fix my hair and I will feel fine." She paused a moment and touched one of Marie's strong hands with one of her own fragile ones. Marie had been coming to her for a year, and they were friends. "It is true I don't feel well, Marie, but I am going to the country with my husband next week. He will hunt and I will rest. It is just that I must get through this one evening." She added, "Perhaps you should have brought me a *gris-gris?*"

"I will send you something tomorrow," Marie promised solemnly.

"I was only joking," Madame said. "No voodoo, Marie! Just your skill with my hair so that I will be beautiful for my guests."

Marie sighed. "You would be more beautiful if you would go to bed," she told her. "Forgive me, but you should rest."

Less than two weeks later Marie learned of Madame Riviere's death from yellow fever. The news brought tears to her eyes. Madame had been so young and so pretty. Marie had sent her one of the little bags she prepared, but Arthemise reported that Madame had thrown it away.

In September the deaths increased. There was no rain and the weather was sultry and oppressive. It was reported that the Charity Hospital was crowded with the sick. Victims lay two to a bed and on the floors of the rooms and the corridors. The boarding houses along the levee closed their doors, and the hotels received no more guests. In the last week of the month the health authorities set up cannons in both the Place d'Armes and Congo Square. All day and night these fired blasts of powder into the still and heat-glazed atmosphere, for the authorities believed this would alleviate the epidemic by dispelling the evil air that brought the disease.

The rich fled to the country, to their plantations or to the homes of friends. The rest of the population remained indoors as much as possible. Windows were sealed with tar paper and doors kept shut, and families huddled together in dreadful heat and discomfort in preference to admitting air that might bring with it the fetid vapors from the swamps that they considered to be infectious.

Marie's second-born, Marguerite, was the first of her family to become ill. Then her first pair of twins, Noemi and Felice. In the first week in October Marguerite died. Marie and Glapion buried her quietly, only a few neighbors attending the funeral, for no one had big funerals now. Noemi and Felice, although they had always been thought delicate, rallied quickly. Then the boy Jean was struck down. He lived less than a week from the day he first complained of a headache. Within another week the other twins died.

Fortunately there was little time for grief. Marie wept, and sometimes in the night she and Glapion lay awake and talked of their children who were gone and of those who were ill. Another boy, Georges, died. He was only three and he suffered extreme agony. Marie did not think she could bear burying him. When she returned from the tiny, pathetic funeral, her six-year-old, a girl she had christened Minette, was in convulsions and dying.

It was the same with everyone she knew. Madame Laclotte died, and so busy was Marie that she scarcely could hold any thought for her old friend. All about her she saw it happening. People, young and old, vanished. It became not like death any longer, but just a disappearance. Someone would be missing, and that was all. In the night there were screams as women noted the passing of another.

In October, too, another man died on the levee. He and a companion had just disembarked from a ship when he collapsed, and the blackness came into his face. His friend was feeling ill, also, and he was left on the levee beside the dead body. During the following night he expired. The bodies remained there three days, for no one would approach them, until at last the rotting, fly-covered corpses were dragged away with hooks and ropes by slaves belonging to the city.

"Six of our children are gone," Marie wept to Glapion in the night.

Glapion, growing old, his sturdy body wracked with rheumatism, embraced her. "The others are well," he whispered. "We must be grateful. Even the baby."

The baby thrived. It was unchristened, unnamed as yet, for there had not been time for that.

She laid her head on his shoulder. "Glapion, I love you."

He chuckled. "Have you discovered that?"

"I have known it long," she told him.

"I have known it long."

She was thinking of him and of Jacques, of the brief part of her life with Jacques, and of all the years with Glapion, of the children who were also his children, of all the life she had lived with Glapion as compared to the short time with Jacques. Time had a way of folding like a fan, its painted scenes vanishing, its very importance seemingly lessened. There would always be Jacques in her memory. Not even Glapion could erase him. Yet, in his way, had not Glapion been more important as measured in the whole of her life? Then this thinking depressed her. It was a time of death, a time when such thoughts came, when life *was* measured this way.

She said suddenly, "Glapion, I have failed my people. Many of them are dying, and I thought I could save them. *They* are my children, too."

He moved an arm that had been around her, but only to draw her closer to him. "You have done all you could," he whispered. "It isn't only the fever. It is the Asiatic cholera, too, and some people have both at the same time. Not even the doctors can do anything."

"The doctors!"

She had called no doctors for her children, but she had heard of their treatments for the plague, and she believed the doctors killed more people than the yellow fever itself. Some recommended strong purges daily. Others, despite the intense, lingering heat, put their patients to bed under innumerable heavy blankets, with hot bricks at their feet and under their armpits, so that the fever might be sweated out. Still others, holding to the theory that the fever should be driven inward, packed their patients in ice, and sprayed them with ice water from time to time. Many doctors refused to give their tortured victims any water, while a few held fast to a belief in a diet of champagne. Some bled their patients until the poor creatures died of hemorrhage, others recommended the raising of blisters over the kidneys, the burning of a small amount of pitch in the patient's room, and huge doses of opium.

Marie had no faith in any of these methods, and she had used none in treating her children. It was true she had lost many, but Noemi and Felice had lived. When Jacques contracted the fever in the first week in November she treated him as she had the others. She gave him cool baths with an alkali in the water; she fed him when he could eat and let him have all the liquids he desired; she kept lump camphor wrapped in muslin pinned to his bed linen. She placed a bowl of sliced onions beneath his bed. She prayed. Jacques quickly recovered. By the time he was up and around again she was

126

thin and haggard. Somehow her fear of losing Jacques, her eldest, had been the worst ordeal of all.

As the weeks passed New Orleans itself seemed dead. The streets were deserted, and doors and windows remained closed. Every post and tree and, or so it seemed, almost every door bore the hideous death notices—the terrible black words on the simple black-bordered rectangles of white paper. The whole town reeked of the carbolic acid the City Council ordered poured into the open gutters. In almost every yard burned the tar fires the city had ordered set, and clouds of black smoke rose to hang like a frightful pall over the town, blotting out the sun, making the nights blacker than night's own black. All business closed its doors.

The only movement in the streets was motivated by the burying of the dead. Each dawn wagons rumbled through the cobblestone streets, stopping at the corners, where the drivers would cry out, "Bring out yo' dead!" A door would open and the relatives would appear with the corpse, wrapped only in a sheet, which the Negroes in charge of the grisly collection would seize and dump roughly into the cart on top of other bodies. There were very few pretenses at funerals. Shallow ditches were dug behind the graveyards, and the bodies were piled in, sprinkled with quicklime, and the earth shoveled over it all in a haphazard fashion. Sometimes bodies, without coffins, lay stacked like cord wood for days before being dumped into the trenches. There were no religious services, no prayers, no attendance by relatives. The survivors remained at home, constantly tormenting themselves by searching their own bodies for a symptom that would mean they had caught the pestilence. There were, of course, a few exceptions. Now and then a father could be seen trudging through the streets, a crude coffin he had made himself upon his shoulder, determined to give his child as decent a burial as possible. A few families buried their dead secretly in their gardens. Others, preferring the river to the horror of the quicklime trenches, weighted the bodies of loved ones with bricks and stones and sank them in the Mississippi at night.

Many tales of horror reached Marie and Glapion. After the illness of Jacques their family remained well, but they kept the children inside and remained there themselves as much as possible. But soon Marie discovered she could do so no longer. All over the neighborhood people were ill, often whole families, so she began going out to help them, filled with fright at first that she might bring more contagion home to her own family. But soon she grew braver. She must have more faith, she told herself. Perhaps by the very act of helping others she might be blessed by being spared further grief.

In every house there was illness, and those she nursed she treated as she had her own. No doctors, she would advise sternly, although by now there were few doctors to be had. Many were themselves ill, or had died. She used her alkali baths, her camphor, her liquids, her bowls of onions. Many of her patients recovered, and they looked at her with more faith than ever. She had feared that the deaths of her children had cost her much prestige, although at the times of those deaths it had not seemed important, but now she saw that her power was increasing, as patient after patient that she treated got well.

In these houses she heard the stories of many happenings during the epidemic. A family of nine persons had eaten supper together, all feeling well. Twenty-four hours later eight were dead. A small hospital had been entered by a group of men after no movement had been observed near it for several days. Everyone within was found dead—patients, doctors, and all hired help. Bodies lay in beds and upon floors, even in the halls. The stench of death was everywhere. A young couple who had not wanted to postpone their wedding were found dead a few hours after the ceremony. The dead were often found in the street—a priest on his way to visit the sick, a baker in his cart, some carpenters who had been brave enough to go on building a house. Once Marie passed the St. Louis Cemetery. Men were unloading corpses from carts and carrying them into the graveyard. They handled them roughly and without dignity, screaming obscenities at each other, perhaps, she thought, to bolster their own courage. Yet she wanted to run shrieking from the scene. It seemed the end of the world.

Then there came a morning when somehow she knew it was over, at least for a time. There was nothing especially different about the morning, and she did not know why she knew this. She had come out into the yard. In the rear Glapion was lighting a tar fire as usual. From within the house came the sound of the children's impatient voices. Marie looked about her yard. Her flowers looked dead, and her fig tree. Her chickens were gone. Only her snake, her Vodu, writhed in his cage. The black pitch smoke had not harmed him. Marie spoke to him and then walked restlessly about. Then she paused and gazed up at the sky. The black clouds seemed to touch the roofs. Not a bird showed against the darkness.

"Glapion," she said suddenly, "it is going to storm. Then it will be over."

He came toward her, looking old, looking thin and very tired. "If you're right," he said. "Oh, my God, if only you're right!" He put an arm around her. "I've been worried about the baby."

"Hush!" she told him. "The baby will be all right now."

She thought quickly, as she did every hour of every day, as she did almost every minute, it seemed, of the children left to them—Jacques, Marie, Noemi and Felice, Christophe, and the unnamed baby, whom she had decided to have christened "Marguerite" in place of the Marguerite she had lost—and of all those they *had* lost. Half were alive, half gone. She must try to think mostly of the living!

The storm came after midnight. They wakened to hear the heavy wooden shutters banging. They still kept the shutters closed even now that the weather was cooler. But the shutters did not close tightly at any time, and wind always sent them into a riotous clamor. Now Marie lay thinking this was the worst she had ever heard. The baby cried and Marie sprang from the bed and went to her crib at the other side of the room. "Quiet, little Marguerite," she whispered, as she picked up the baby. "Quiet, new little Marguerite!"

Glapion yawned loudly, pulled a handkerchief from beneath his pillow and blew his nose. "It is your storm," he grunted.

"Yes," Marie said. "Yes! I knew it would come."

The lightning flashed through the break in the shutters. In the next room the twins, Noemi and Felice, set up a howl. The door swung open and Jacques was standing there, his nightshirt flapping about his legs. "Try to quiet them, Jacques," Marie pleaded.

Glapion sat up in the bed with a groan, and swung his hairy legs over the side. "I'll see to them," he said, inching his bare feet toward the floor.

But first he struggled with the blinds, trying to tighten a rope that bound one pair. The rope broke in his hands, the shutters slammed back against the outside of the house and lightning crashed through the room again. "This is it, Marie," he remarked, and staggered through the darkness toward the room where the children waited in terror.

Marie changed the baby, snuggled her for a few moments, and, when she was asleep, laid her down gently. She looked into the children's room, and saw that all was quiet; Glapion sat on the edge of the twins' bed, talking to them softly. She closed the door and went out through the kitchen into the yard. "Vodu! Vodu!" she coaxed. She stooped and whispered to him. The cage was heavy, but she lifted it and bore

130

it back to the house. Thunder roared; the lightning came again. Still holding the cage, she gazed upward. The sky was bright with light and a blue almost as clear as on a good day. The air was sweet. It was like another world. "It is over, Vodu," she whispered. She carried him into the kitchen and set the cage down.

Glapion came in. "They are all right," he said, staring down at the cage.

"I brought him in." She smiled. "Glapion, listen to the storm!"

The sound of it was wonderful. The lightning was fire and flame, burning the world clean, purifying it.

She took a candle and went into the room where she had her altar and where she received most of her clients. She lighted candles there, then she returned across the yard to the kitchen. Glapion was making coffee. "I am taking him into the house," she said simply, lifting the cage containing the snake again. As she crossed the yard again large drops of rain fell.

She set the Vodu down before the altar and fetched more candles. Soon the room was blazing with light. It was a small room and it contained no furnishings but the altar and a plain wooden table and two chairs. But shelves along the wall held all the necessities of her work. There were jars and bottles and boxes, all filled with her oils and powders, her dusts, her scraps of bone, her dog and cat hairs, all collected over the years and hoarded for future usage. There were stacks of candles of every color, and some of curious shapes—owls, snake, skulls. There were real human skulls on the shelves, and there was a skull of a cow and one of a cat. Her own cat, her sleek and black Minou, came from beneath the white linen cloth covering the altar and rubbed against her ankles, purring softly.

She rearranged the candles now, all white candles, for peace, for purification. Seven she set in a semicircle on the altar before the colored pictures of St. Joseph, St. Peter and St. Michael. Seven others she lined up on the shelves. She placed a candle in each corner of the room, and two others on the floor before the altar. She set down another on the floor in the very center of the room. Twenty-one candles. Two and one were three—a good number. She prayed. Liba! Dani! Great Father Joseph! She could hear the rain now. The wind swept it in a torrent like a fierce wave against the side of the house. Thunder crashed and lightning flashed beyond the window. Vaguely, she heard Glapion slam a door as he ran into the house. She prayed on. Liba! Dani! Somehow wind penetrated the room and the candles flickered. But none went out.

When she was finished praying she crouched on the floor before the cage and talked to the snake in a whisper: "Vodu! Vodu! Papa LaBas, let it pass from us! Let is pass from the people. I will make a sacrifice at the crossroads! I will give you roast chicken and green peas! Vodu, you shall have a present! You shall have a new home—a beautiful box of alabaster! I will buy it for you and you will be proud, my Vodu, my pet, my love!"

The storm lasted nearly all the next day. There was damage and tragedy in the city. Great trees fell, roofs were carried away, a drunken man fell into an overflowing ditch and was drowned. But toward evening the rain ceased and the wind quieted. At dusk Marie and Glapion stepped out into the garden. The sky was clear now and no black clouds lowered above them. All the tar fires were out. No cannons sounded. The air smelled clean. "It is over," Marie said. At midnight she took a plate of roast chicken and green peas and set it down beneath a tree where two streets met behind Congo Square.

And it was really over. There was little sickness in the days that followed, few deaths. Windows and doors were opened. Business was resumed, and people walked freely in the streets of New Orleans again. But for months the town had a sad and weary look, for soon after the storm there was a counting of the toll. Thirty-five thousand persons had remained in the city throughout the epidemic. Of these, six thousand had died.

Before Christmas Marie held a small meeting one night. The weather was chilly so she called only for those to come who were the most devout of her followers, for the meeting had to be held in her secret room where she kept her altar. It was too cold to gather out in the yard. Many of those attending were people she had nursed during the plague, and they brought offerings of thanks—money, live chickens, bowls of eggs, fresh vegetables from their small gardens. Marie accepted the money and the chickens with gratitude —the chickens would replace those she had lost. The other gifts she redistributed, giving them to those who were very poor and so had been unable to bring anything.

They thanked her. "Bless you! Bless you, Mamma Marie! You are good!"

Even Doctor John came. People said he was more than a hundred years old now, but he was unchanged. Neither cholera nor yellow fever had touched him. "I am too old and tough," he told Marie. "And you are strong. You were not sick."

She made her eyes large and peered down into his. "I am strong, it is true," she said. "But I could not save my children."

"You still have much to learn," he said. "You are wise for a mule—for one who is neither black nor white—but do not grow vain, Marie Laveau. You will learn more when you are done with childbearing. The apprenticeship is long, and one must give it all one's life. Unless your power grows it shrinks, and you can be displaced, even as you displaced Saloppé."

She had not thought of Saloppé for a long time. "Where is Saloppé?" she asked him. "Did she die in the plague?"

Doctor John lowered his wrinkled eyelids. "She is not dead," he told her. "But she has vanished. She is nothing. You must be warned by her. I will tell you this, Marie Laveau. You think the pestilence is passed, but it will come again."

She felt as if someone had doused her with cold water, but she laughed at him. "Get to your drums, old man!" she said lightly. "My people must dance. They are happy and they must dance and sing."

"When the pestilence returns," said Doctor John, "burn no pitch. Let the cannon's foolish noises go unnoticed. Kill a rat and bury it beneath your doorstep. Surround your house with salt. Let there be no space between the grains. Let one grain touch another. Give some money to the poor. You will have no death in your house."

Marie thought little of his advice as the winter passed. The city grew more and more normal in its habits. Those who had fled to the country had returned. Dimmed by the widespread grief, life was quieter, yet there were balls and *soirées*, and the theater flourished. Delia, who had survived the epidemic, stayed often with the children, while Marie went about her calls as a hairdresser. More and more clients came to talk with her in the altar room and to carry away a little bag, a vial of ointment, a tiny box. More and more money went into her account at the bank. "We are not rich yet," she told Glapion, "but we need not fear the lack of money."

Early in the spring she increased her wealth in still another way. Receiving a good offer for the house where she had lived with her mother, she sold it. She was tired of being irritated by tenants. Some had moved owing her rent, others had been disagreeable. Glapion protested this, for he thought it wiser to keep the house. "Money is the thing, Glapion," she said. "I want money. I want cash that I can use whenever

I so choose." And she spent money that spring. She bought fine new mahogany furniture for the house, giving away the old pieces, replacing almost everything. She bought carpets and curtains and silver candlesticks until she thought her cottage looked almost as handsome as some of the mansions she visited as a hairdresser. She bought more gold bracelets to wear upon her arms.

Then, in June, several cases of yellow fever were reported by the Charity Hospital, and a woman fell into convulsions while shopping in the marketplace. The cry went up again, especially in regard to the woman. Cholera had returned!

The scene of the summer and fall before was repeated—the flights to the country, the closing of business, the bolting of doors and windows. Soon the cannon boomed again, and the tar fires were lighted. Glapion caught a rat and killed it and buried the body beneath their doorstep, and Marie poured a circle of salt three inches high all around the house. This time they did not close their windows against the heat nor stay indoors all the time. Marie went nursing every day, carrying baskets of food on her arm. She was careful to give away money, too, to those who needed it, although most of her patients preferred the food she brought to money, her rich broths, her custards and puddings. During the weeks that both cholera and yellow fever again raged she learned that she was once more pregnant, but she went on with her nursing. To all families of patients that she nursed she also gave the advice of Doctor John—the buried rat, the circle of salt. Some obeyed her and it seemed effective, others refused. When it did not work she told herself it was because it was too late. The patient was already ill.

Late in the summer this second epidemic ended, this time quietly and without a storm, but just as suddenly. Again the city returned to life. Another four thousand persons had died, but now death seemed almost a commonplace matter. When there were no more tales of sickness to be heard Marie swept away the salt she had kept around her cottage. No member of her family had been ill during this terrible summer.

In the winter she had another boy, and she named him Jean, and she almost felt that the Jean she had lost had returned.

Chapter 7

SHE HAD HAD enough sorrow, she often thought, but it was not over. The following year she bore a stillborn child, and early in 1835 her young Marie died suddenly in convulsions. Marie could not understand the cause of this, for the girl had seemed healthy that very day. During the night the whole family was aroused by her screaming, and in a few minutes she was gone. Marie wondered about this, and thought it might have been done by an enemy. She had enemies, other voodooists, but she could think of none who would attack her with such cruelty. That spring she gave birth again. It was a girl and she called her Marie Philome.

Marie was past forty now, and she hoped she was through with childbearing. She had borne fifteen children to Glapion, and of these she had lost eight. It was true she knew people who had lost as many or more. Whole families had perished of yellow fever and cholera, but knowing this made it no easier. "I can spare no more pieces of my heart," she told Glapion. "If we have no more children we have no more to lose." She felt that she could protect these. She made them all carry protection from evil, powerful *gris-gris*. She saw to it that defenses against harm were in their mattresses and pillows, even in those of the babies.

Yet, despite her fear for the children, that for Glapion grew even more intense that spring. Glapion was aging, and she knew he was ill. He complained little, but he had become very stout again and he suffered with difficulty in breathing. Sometimes she awakened in the night and found him sitting up in a chair panting audibly. When she would speak to him he would make light of it. So her worry for him grew. She was constantly brewing him concoctions she heard were good for his breathing problem, but nothing seemed to work, and she had to admit to herself that there were limitations to her power over his physical being.

It was in May that she found the conjure ball in her yard. It was a commonplace one, of a kind she had made often enough herself, a sphere of black wax with feathers stuck in it and a cross made with blood upon its surface. One brought bad luck to an enemy by rolling it across his property. She buried it quickly, but that afternoon she went to see Doctor John. Since the birth of her last baby she had been out little, and although she knew there were several women who had set themselves up as her rivals, she thought Doctor John might be better informed as to who this particular rival was.

"There are two," Doctor John told her. "Rosalie and Margaret—the one they call Hoodoo Mag. Rosalie has more power. You have not been to Congo Square for months, Marie Laveau. I am told she was there."

Marie's temper flared. "She dared!" She knew both these women. They were black women who had been coming to the meetings for years. She had heard through her grapevine that they had been selling some *gris-gris*, and that Rosalie told fortunes, but until now she had placed no importance upon this. "No one dares preside at Congo Square but I!"

"The people need a leader," said Doctor John quietly. "You are always having babies—always babies. You have neglected your people. They will not wait forever."

Marie sighed. "It is true."

"The woman Rosalie has a great figure carved of wood," Doctor John told her. "There are those who say it is from Africa and that it is a powerful god. I am telling you only what has been told to me, for I do not know what it is, and I have never seen it. But there are those who believe in it and it has given them faith in Rosalie."

"She is a liar and a faker!" said Marie. "We will see how much power she possesses!" She turned and strode out of Doctor John's dark and grimy room, her blue calico skirts swirling furiously.

She knew Rosalie's address. Rosalie lived in a small, mean house, scarcely better than a cabin, on Rue Dumaine, not far from where Dédé had lived. Marie hurried there, and rapped noisily on the front door. When there was no answer she pushed the door, and, finding it unlocked, entered. On an altar in the front room stood the statue. It was a crudely carved figure of a woman, black as soot, with a distended belly and a hideously painted face. Marie snatched it up, put it under her arm and stalked out of the house. Rosalie's neighbors stared at her from where they sat on their stoops. They whispered to each other, "That is Marie Laveau! It is Laveau herself!" Marie made no effort to conceal the statue, but walked past them boldly, smiling faintly and bowing to those she knew.

That afternoon the police came and placed her under arrest. Rosalie was in court, and at the sight of Marie and of the statue a policeman now carried gingerly in his arms, she began shouting curses and threats. Marie widened her tremendous eyes and said quietly, "I will cause all your teeth to fall out, and the hairs on your head. I will fill your belly with maggots and turn your blood to green slime."

Recorder Dabézies squirmed anxiously and threatened them both with jail sentences, and they became silent. In the end he fined Marie fifteen dollars, gave her a severe warning, and returned the idol to Rosalie.

The next morning Recorder Dabézies appeared at Marie's door. He entered her house timidly, not looking her in the face, and Marie concealed a smile. With a hand that trembled a bit, he laid fifteen dollars on a table. "I have heard much about you," he said, "and I thought you could help me. Of course I trust you to keep this matter in confidence."

"All that happens between us will be secret, my child," said Marie. "How can I help you?"

"I have been courting a young lady for nearly two years," said Recorder Dabézies. "Perhaps with your aid I can win her."

"That is not impossible," Marie told him. "And when you win her you will be my friend?"

The muscles in the young man's cheeks quivered. "How can I be your friend?"

Marie shrugged. "The woman Rosalie is a cheat. She has no real power. Her ugly statue only frightens people. The police should destroy it before it does more harm. There are laws about such things."

"What do you know of the law?"

"You are not the only gentleman connected with the law who has come to me, Monsieur." She was boasting a little, although a policeman or two had been her clients and she had aided them with minor problems. As a matter of fact, she was not even sure there was a law concerning such articles as Rosalie's statue, although there were certain, although rarely enforced, regulations against the practice of voodoo. "They have taught me much," she continued. "Among other things, they have taught me that it is almost always possible to find a law against anything one dislikes. I do not like Rosalie's statue, Monsieur."

"It is an ugly thing," admitted Recorder Dabézies, "and no doubt does harm to those who believe in its evil power."

Dabézies did not bother to come to tell her about it himself, but a week later she learned through her grapevine that he and his young lady were formally betrothed. A little later she heard through another part of the grapevine that Rosalie's statue had been confiscated by the police. The following Sunday there was a dance in Congo Square, and Rosalie did not appear.

Neither did Rosalie attend the St. John's Eve rites in the secret place on the bayou, and Marie knew then that Rosalie's influence over her people was gone, for otherwise she would have come in defiance. Standing on the new alabaster box, its marble bands gleaming in the firelight, the Vodu writhing inside, Marie gazed out over the huge crowd of celebrants with satisfaction. No one would take her place while she lived, she thought firmly. A rival could not be tolerated. A queen must keep strong, and her vigilance must never be allowed to relax. She had been weak and careless in many ways until now. She would continue to be a good wife to Glapion, a good mother, but she must tend her work, too. And there must be no more children.

There were to be no more children. A few days after that St. John's Eve Glapion died in his sleep. She awoke just before dawn and touched him because he was so quiet, and he was gone. She gave him a large and expensive funeral, and hundreds followed him to the grave. For three days she scarcely stopped weeping, and she tried to seem resigned only when the children were present. She had loved Glapion.

New Orleans was changing. It had spread far beyond its original limits. It had grown rich. The streets were crowded with people and the river with commerce. The steamboats continued to come in such numbers that the wharves seemed always filled. The Americans had brought prosperity and a changing of old ways. There were new hotels, and theaters where plays were performed in English. English was becoming the language most often heard. Even the streets were often referred to by the English forms of their names. People were calling Rue Ste. Anne, Marie's own street, "St. Ann Street." Marie did not like English; she spoke it poorly, and only when forced to do so. She continued to dislike all Anglo-

Saxons. She hated even their new gaslight that was being installed in all the new buildings and at some street corners. She despised, in general, the newcomers who built their new and fine homes beyond Canal Street. For their wider streets she had only scorn, and for their paving, and their sprawling gardens, open to the streets but for iron picket fences, and not walled for privacy as were most of those in the Vieux Carré, which, to her, was still the real New Orleans. "It is a circus," she would say. "They live like fish in a fishbowl. It is not decent."

Yet she carefully concealed her dislike for Americans from Americans, except when she was among friends who thought as she did. Many Americans were her clients in both her professions. And there were Americans whom she liked as individuals. It was the English-speaking people as a whole for whom she had contempt. When she had to go uptown she wanted to spit through the picket fences into the gardens. She thought the newcomers crude, bold, indelicate in speech, and, excluding exceptions which only proved the rule, bad-mannered.

Yet there was no denying their influence in the city. They had brought prosperity; she thought they cared more for money than for anything else, and although she liked money, too, in them she considered it an evil trait. "They put on a show," she was apt to say. She put on no show. She lived as she had always lived. The Americans were different. They must have big houses, which were covered with gingerbread trim and topped with turrets and towers. They loved stained glass windows and white columns. They built Gothic castles or Greek temples, and sometimes combined features of each in their homes. Of course these were the rich Americans. Like all the other New Orleanians who thought of themselves as old residents, Marie ignored the poor Americans. They were riffraff—"poor, white trash." The rich ones were bad enough. Fortunately most of the poor were transients, rough riverboatmen, temporary workers, people who left the city quickly to take up land outside to farm. With these the older citizens of New Orleans usually included the Irish and Germans. They were as bad as the Americans. They did not speak French. They were different.

Where the Americans lived there had been great plantations, but these had been subdivided long ago. Now streets stretched far above Canal Street. There was wide Nayades Avenue and streets named after the Muses, just above Tivoli Place. Those streets running south near the river curved with the river. Mansions rose along the Rue du Colisée, or Coliseum Street, and the Rue du Prytanée, or Prytania Street. There was constant talk of building both a Coliseum and Prytaneum in this section, for the Americans talked much of culture, although the Creoles did not consider they possessed it. Above Felicity Street, in what was still called the Village of Lafayette, lived even wealthier Americans in more costly homes with larger gardens and more display of wealth.

The Americans lived almost in a separate world from the Creoles now, but, as a hairdresser, Marie entered both. If she was happier among Creoles, the Americans paid her better. They were free with money, extravagant, she thought with scorn, but their money was the same as any other, as good to spend and as good in the bank. And let them pay! She began raising her prices to the American ladies.

After Glapion died she worked harder. It was true that for the most part she had always been the provider in her family. But now work served a further purpose, one that she had not needed for years; it distracted her and gave her less time to grieve for Glapion, especially during the first year after he was gone. During that year she bought a slave, an intelligent black woman named Rose. She hated spending the money for the woman, but in a short time she was glad she had done so, for Rose took over almost all the necessary work at home and the care of the children, and Marie found herself free to accept more and more clients. Also, Rose helped her in another way. She had belonged to an American family who had left the city, and she had many friends among slaves in American households, and because Marie was good to her and treated her as a member of the family, and allowed her to visit her friends on occasion, she brought back information of many kinds and often of great value.

Mrs. Hobley was troubled, Marie knew, and she knew why. Also, Mrs. Hobley was cross and there was a deep line between her brows the entire time Marie spent in arranging her coiffure.

"You French colored people drive me crazy!" she cried at Marie, as the final comb was set in place in her graying hair. "It seems odd to me that in a city this size there is not a single white hairdresser to be found!"

"You got nerves bad, Madame," said Marie gently, speaking in English for Mrs. Hobley understood no French. "You not feel well today, no?"

Mrs. Hobley pushed her palms against her temples. "No, I don't," she said. "I don't know if I can stand this city. The heat! The mosquitoes!" Mrs. Hobley had come from Philadelphia less than a year before. She sighed. "Excuse me, Marie. I didn't mean to raise my voice to you."

Marie shrugged. "I don't min'." Then she murmured in French, "You old fool, I know what is the matter with you. Your young lover left you, and your husband's no good any more, and you want a man." One of Mrs. Hobley's servants had reported this to Rose, who had in turn given Marie the bit of gossip and with glee.

"Please speak English, Marie," Mrs. Hobley said. "You know I don't understand a *word* of that gibberish."

"I forget, Madame," Marie told her. "Almost always I speak French, and my thoughts just jump out in French. It is like that with me some time. I only say Madame's hair look pretty."

Mrs. Hobley gazed into her mirror irritably. "It's getting so terribly gray. Sometimes I think I'll let you tint it." They had discussed this before. "You say strong coffee is good?"

"I be glad to," Marie told her. "Madame is too young for gray hair." She thought Mrs. Hobley past fifty, but she knew Mrs. Hobley did not like to believe she looked that. "I make it nice and dark for you, very natural. No one would ever guess it not that way."

"Well, perhaps next time you come," Mrs. Hobley said, carefully counting money into Marie's hand; she was not the most generous of Marie's American customers. "I must think about it."

Marie gazed down, widening her eyes. "Madame is unhappy," she said softly. "Maybe I could help, no?"

Mrs. Hobley stared up at her. "How do you know I'm unhappy?" she snapped. "Are you a mind reader or something?"

Marie smiled gently. "I read your min'. You in love, yes?"

It took Mrs. Hobley a full minute to collect her composure. She dropped her head and stared at the floor. She paled a little. "I don't think that's any of your concern, Marie."

"I apologize," Marie murmured, rolled the money Mrs. Hobley had paid her into her fist and went quickly toward the door.

"Wait, Marie!" Mrs. Hobley rose, drawing her wrapper about her. "Come back here and tell me how you knew that. Have my servants been gossiping to you?"

"I read your min'," Marie repeated, and assumed an innocent expression. "Nobody have to tell me."

Mrs. Hobley folded her arms and scowled. "Tell me what else you know!"

Marie stepped to one side and closed the door. "If Madame wish."

"Madame wish!"

"You have lover," Marie told her, lowering her voice. "He younger than you, very handsome." Of course Mrs. Hobley would be sure to think her lover handsome. "He go away. That's all. But it make you unhappy. All women unhappy when a young and handsome lover go away. You no be ashame' of that, Madame. That is natural, yes?"

Mrs. Hobley collapsed into the seat before her dressing table and buried her eyes in a handkerchief. She did not appear to be crying. She just sat there as if she were frozen, hiding her face. Marie waited a few seconds, then walked over and put a hand lightly upon her shoulders. "Maybe I can help Madame?"

Mrs. Hobley took the handkerchief away. Her eyes were dry, but her face looked old. "How could *you* help?" she asked bitterly. "It's over, that's all. Besides, I have a husband." She paused. "That's what frightened him away—the man I love. Oh, I don't know why I'm telling you this!"

"You never hear of me, Madame?" Marie's expression changed and another woman stood before Mrs. Hobley, a haughty and commanding woman, with uplifted and proud chin and intensely darkened eyes. "I am Marie Laveau."

"Oh, of course I know your name," said Mrs. Hobley wearily. "No, but wait a minute!" She was gaping. "Marie, you are *that* woman? I've heard the servants chatter, and even some of my friends, but it never occurred to me that it was you!" Mrs. Hobley suddenly looked frightened. "A voodoo or something! Why, Marie! Of course I don't believe in anything like that, but I had no idea that was *you!*"

"I can help you," said Marie, her face unchanged. "It make no difference if you doubt the power. I believe in it. That is all that count." She let this sink into Mrs. Hobley's mind. Then she added, "Your husband, he is old. You need to be loved. That is not strange. You come by my house at two o'clock tomorrow. I fix you. I wait for you at that time." Then she turned and left the room, walking slowly, not looking back, and leaving the door open behind her. Mrs. Hobley did not call her back.

Marie was waiting at two o'clock the next afternoon when Mrs. Hobley's carriage stopped before the house. Rose, as she had been instructed to do, showed Mrs. Hobley into the room where Marie received her clients, and left her there. All was prepared within the room. The shutters, tightly drawn, eliminated almost all outside light, candles glowed on the altar and on the shelves, the soft light reflecting on the skulls and the other objects that were kept there; a tiny amount of burning incense filled the room with fragrance. But there was light enough to make visible the snake, and the Vodu moved slowly but restlessly about in his beautiful alabaster box. Marie allowed Mrs. Hobley to wait alone in the room for more than five minutes before she entered it, and when she did so she did not apologize. She entered without speaking and seated herself in the rocking chair she kept near the altar. She glanced once at Mrs. Hobley and saw that the wait had had its effect. Mrs. Hobley was walking about nervously and there were beads of perspiration on her face. Marie closed her eyes and rocked.

Mrs. Hobley began to mutter. "I don't know why I'm here. I don't know why I'm here at *all*. Marie, for heaven's sake! How I detest snakes! They make me shiver!"

"My little pet?" murmured Marie. "You hate my little pet? Why?" She opened her eyes. "But he is much more than a pet, Madame. And that is the truth." She smiled. "Maybe your good luck, it is up to him."

Mrs. Hobley stood before her. She wrung her hands impatiently. She said, "Marie, I am willing to try this. I am willing to pay you well. I know almost nothing about it, but can't we get on with whatever it is you do?"

147

"I do much, Madame." Marie rocked herself some more. "We must not hurry. Your trouble is not easy to cure, but we will try." She gestured to a small straight chair before her. "Sit down, and do not be nervous."

Mrs. Hobley sat down, clenching her hands together again. It was obvious that she was forcing herself to appear calm.

"Your young man, you want him back?" Marie stared full into Mrs. Hobley's face. "Or do you want another one?"

"I think you're insulting me!" gasped Mrs. Hobley in sheer amazement.

Marie ceased rocking and leaned forward in her chair, grasping the arms. "I am not insulting you," she said. "All I ask is what you want. I think I know, so it is polite of me to ask, eh? But let us talk about my price. I do not want money from you, Madame. From you not one cent!"

The line between Mrs. Hobley's brows deepened. "What do you want, Marie? I had thought you did this for money."

"If I help you you must help me," Marie told her evenly. "You understand? I need more Americans to come to me. You know many people. That is how you can help me. That I want instead of money." She shook her head as Mrs. Hobley began to protest. "You need not tell them why you came to me, or even that you did. All you tell them is that you know about me, and that you have heard of what I do. That is enough, Madame. We make a bargain, us. You do that for me, I do much for you, and no one will have to know what I do for you here in this room."

Mrs. Hobley nodded. "All *right*, Marie." She sighed.

Marie allowed herself the faintest of smiles. "Good. We understand. We have no more worry." She rose and went to the altar and lighted a blue candle. "Blue is for love, Madame," she explained. She picked up a scrap of yellow brocade with scalloped edges and a small design of embossed flowers, and, turning, gave it to Mrs. Hobley. "You are to keep this in your prayer book," she instructed.

"But I am a Protestant!" said Mrs. Hobley, accepting the bit of material gingerly.

"Then you must keep it in your Bible," Marie told her.

Next Marie gave her a small bag of rose-colored flannel. It was about an inch square, but its contents bulged. Mrs. Hobley took it and began squeezing it, as if to ascertain its contents. Marie glared at her with some disdain. "It is not good to feel a *gris-gris* so much," she said. "You must not even look at it unless it is at the times instructed. I will tell you what it contains, Madame. It is not a secret, and you will not understand after I have told you. There are fifty seeds of black pepper, Madame, some spice and herbs, a little crushed lead, crumbs of bread, some hair, a half of a white bean and a brass medal of St. Benedict that is tarnished. That is for your love, Madame, and you must do this to make it work for you. You must put the bag in a secret place and each Friday sprinkle upon it three drops of rum. And do not stop when it works for you, no. Keep doing it every Friday, but not on Good Friday. That would bring you bad luck. Every Friday but Good Friday. Put it in your purse, Madame."

Mrs. Hobley did so, but she was gaping, and she looked for a moment almost as if she were about to laugh.

"Do not laugh," said Marie crossly, for this American, this Protestant, irritated her as much as any client who had ever come to her. "Good day, Madame!"

"Is that *all?*" cried Mrs. Hobley.

"That is a great deal," Marie said. "But I must warn you to keep our bargain. If you do not you will be sorry. I know bad work as well as I know good." She returned to her rocker, seated herself and pretended to close her eyes. She watched Mrs. Hobley, however, from beneath her lowered lids. Mrs. Hobley hesitated a moment, stared down at her, and then glided out of the door, with just one nervous, backward glance.

As soon as she was sure the woman was gone Marie rose,

blew out the candles and hurried out of the room, too, going toward the rear of the house, from whence she had been hearing the older children wrangling for some minutes. If only Rose would learn to keep them quiet when clients were there!

It was about a month before Marie heard news of Mrs. Hobley's good fortune. Then Rose told her that Mrs. Hobley's servants said that their mistress had a new young man, whom she had met at a *soirée*. Mrs. Hobley did not send for Marie to arrange her hair again, but Marie understood that. She did believe, however, that Mrs. Hobley had kept her bargain, for more and more American women came to ring the bell on the gate of her cottage.

More Americans came, more Creoles, and more colored people of every shade of skin and mixture of bloods—Negroes, mulattoes, quadroons, octoroons. More money came in, too, and Marie continued to charge as she had from the beginning, which was in accordance with what she thought her clients could or would pay, and which ranged from a bowl of fresh eggs to hundreds of dollars for a single charm. And all the time she was creating new charms, new *gris-gris,* and it seemed to her that the knowledge to do this came to her from some great inward power, for no matter what she prescribed to a client there were few failures, and if there was a failure she had only to invent a new and more powerful *gris-gris,* and for a higher price, providing her client could pay it.

She learned to use moss and horsehair, which she shaped into a nest held together by two crossed herbs. Sewed into the hem of a dress, it protected its wearer from bad luck as long as it held together. She used many kinds of love powders and oils, but she discovered the most powerful was the one she brewed from a quart of vinegar, a quart of rain water caught from the first rain in May, a teaspoonful of graveyard dirt and nine used nails. These she would boil down together until half the liquid was gone, let the rest stand for nine days, then fill to its former quantity with equal parts of May rain water and vinegar. After another nine days it was ready to sell, and the buyer was instructed to go to the home of his or her beloved and sprinkle some of it where the loved one must walk. This must be repeated nine days later. Marie never saw it fail from the day she began to prescribe it, and her clients begged for it. She learned to make and sell all kinds of charms to gamblers—lodestones and twisted roots, rabbit's feet, and steel filings wrapped in red flannel.

She learned of more evil *gris-gris*, too, but she refused to use them. A mixture of Jimson weed and the powdered head of a snake could cause blindness. Small black caskets containing a tiny doll stuck with pins left on a doorstep with a black candle burning at the head and foot of the coffin would bring death to the household within. Bags containing dog and cat hair, and salt and pepper, left where a person would not find them, but secreted in his room, preferably among his clothes, were nearly as bad. These might also be scattered in a person's path, and misfortune would surely befall him. There were many others of this evil sort, but she continued to avoid them. "I do not need to use evil *gris-gris*," she told Rose once. "The good is enough. It is giving me power and money. I need no more." So when clients asked for such things she sent them elsewhere. There were other women and a few men who sold to those who were wicked, who wanted to destroy.

For a year after Glapion's death her good luck increased, and she came to believe this was perhaps due to the fact that she did no wicked work. The saints had rewarded her, she told herself.

The attendance at her meetings grew, too. She held them once a month now, which date she established as the third Friday in each month. Her yard was filled to overflowing then, and many who came to take part could not get in. Every Sunday that it did not rain she presided in Congo

Square, and attendance here grew, too. The square was always packed with dancers, and hordes of white people came to watch. Their carriages lined the streets for blocks around and they pressed against the picket fences to see the dances and hear the music and the singing. So much noise was raised on these Sundays, however, that Marie sometimes thought, not without amusement, that they might well have stayed home and listened there. The din must have penetrated far to the outskirts of the town.

It was this that brought misfortune. Quite suddenly Congo Square was closed by the police. Padlocks were put on the gates and signs were posted forbidding colored people to enter the premises or for anyone to enter them on Sunday. The news reached Marie through her neighbors, and she went to read the sign herself. She left in a fury and walked straight to the office of her friend Recorder Dabézies. Standing before his desk, she lashed out at him. What was the meaning of this? They were old friends. He could help if he chose!

"I can do nothing, Marie," he told her. "It is the mayor himself, the aldermen, the officials. I have no influence with them. I cannot help what they do. You know I would help you if I could, Marie."

"Then I will go to the mayor and the officials!" she cried.

"It will do no good," he said pessimistically. "You have your meetings at home, and the place on the bayou."

"We meet on the bayou only on St. John's Eve now," she said. Then she tried another tactic. "We practice no voodoo in Congo Square. It is only dancing and singing. It is the only diversion some of the poor people have, especially the poor blacks—the slaves. Why do they deprive them of this?"

"They consider it dangerous for there to be such a large congregation of the black people," he told her bluntly, but gently. "There is nothing you can do about it, Marie—nothing I can do. It is a law they have made. We cannot change the law."

"I will put a curse on them," she threatened. "I will put on them such a curse as they have never known!"

Recorder Dabézies looked nervous. "Don't talk that way, Marie. Nothing you can do will help." He wiped sweat from his red face.

As she departed she felt that she really did want to put a curse on whoever was responsible for this outrage, at least a small curse—balls of colored feathers in the pillows of all these fine gentlemen would give them such headaches they would wish they were dead! Of course she could do much worse than that. But she had promised not to do evil work. She had promised herself, and the saints. She had promised people who had loved her.

Yet to give a man a headache was not so wicked, she reflected, and to avenge herself against even one of those men would be a satisfaction. So the next day she dyed chicken feathers bright green and red, rolled them into a tight ball, and sent them by Rose to be delivered to a servant she knew within the household of the mayor. The ball would be sewed into his pillow.

Within two weeks a report reached her. The mayor was not well, he was suffering severely from migraine. Marie laughed. "He should come to me," she told Rose. "Only Marie Laveau could remove his headache. Only removing the cause can cure." She considered having the mayor's servants hint of this to him, but she changed her mind. To have the mayor as a client would be a triumph, but he did not deserve her ministrations.

A year had passed before she had cause to wonder if she might be punished for the mayor's migraine. But, quickly, she decided she was not. For the trouble that befell her in 1837 was far from being hers alone.

What happened that year she was never able to understand. Suddenly the bank where she kept her money closed its doors. She learned in time that thirteen other New Orleans banks had also shut down. People whispered one word: Panic! And fear did sweep the city. Some people told her that it was the same all over the country, but this did not interest Marie. She rarely gave a thought to the world outside of New Orleans. Indeed, she gave few thoughts to any world but that in which she lived her life. If it had not been necessary she would never have crossed Canal Street into the neighborhoods where the Americans lived; she would never have left the Vieux Carré, many of whose residents boasted that they had never set foot in the American section, and would never do so as long as they lived; and Marie admired and envied those who could say that.

Not a dollar could be taken from the bank for food, but Marie did not go hungry. It was true her hairdressing dropped off, but her other business increased. People came to her for advice, for *gris-gris* to save their constantly dwindling incomes, and they paid her well out of whatever money they could raise. She hid the money in the house and spent it as discreetly as possible, although prices soared and money became increasingly less valuable. Finally private companies and even private individuals issued their own money. Money. It was almost worthless, but Marie accepted it and used it as best she could.

By the next year money was so valueless that it took huge sums even to buy food. Once her young Jacques came in from the street to report that he saw people carrying sacks of money to the shops to buy a supply of groceries; Marie began to observe this herself, and, finally, to witness Rose staggering out of the house under a great load which looked like a great bag of potatoes and was actually money for the merchants in the market. A neighbor whispered to Marie that a pair of shoes was priced at a thousand dollars. Marie smiled tightly. When her family's shoes wore out they would go barefooted. She was depressed and the city had an air almost as funereal as it had worn during the last great yellow fever epidemic, but she kept telling herself she had been poor before. She would make money again. Nothing lasted. Remembering that could make life bearable. She had her chickens and eggs. She and Rose and the older children planted beans and potatoes where flowers had been in her garden; they planted even a watermelon vine. It did not help much, and not at all right away, but in time it did a little. All her neighbors were doing the same; people traded and gave away any surplus; not that any had much surplus, but anything helped a bit. So Marie's family did not starve. Many of her clients gave her food, sometimes so much that she shared it with those of her neighbors who needed it most. Rich white clients sometimes brought her old clothing, broken shoes that could be mended. This was more valuable as payment than was money, even when it was gold.

At last, toward the beginning of the third year after it had begun, the period of depression ended. Change came slowly at first, but finally people started to think of printed paper money as of some use again. Marie gathered together her thoughts and started to make plans once more. The money she had was gone, and she must start again, but her family had survived, and she felt stronger than she ever had before—stronger and proud. She could do anything, she told herself. She could bear nearly anything. She would get more money. She had the power. She was Marie Laveau, and she would have more money and more power.

What depressed her most that winter was that old Doctor John finally died. She had been helping him for years now, taking him food, seeing that he had fuel and was as comfortable as possible, but he caught a cold which went into pneumonia, and there was no way to save him. She took care of his funeral and buried him decently. But she was saddened. One more was gone who had helped to shape her life.

Chapter 8

ONE MORNING Jacques came to the open door of her bedroom as she finished dressing for the day. She turned at the
sound of his footsteps, staring as if she had not really looked
at him for a long time. He was taller than she was now, and
almost twenty; she wondered with sudden astonishment what
had happened to the years. Jacques called himself "John"
these days, of which she disapproved, although she had
never mentioned it to him; and he had a girl.

Marie went to him quickly and kissed him. "Come in,
Jacques, come in." He seemed shy with her. Her own son
shy with her! She thought of her children. Had she been a
good mother to them? Was she always too busy? At times she
had reflected that perhaps they were more at home with each
other, even with Rose, than with her. She took the boy's hand
and led him to the bed, and they sat down on the edge of it
together. She glanced up at him. He was very handsome; and
he was like her. He had her great eyes and the same golden
tones in his skin, and his black hair curled softly behind his
small ears. "We don't talk enough lately," she said. "What
have you been doing, son? How do you like your new
work?"

Jacques had been working at various kinds of employment
for some years. He was intelligent, but he had never been
scholarly. He could read and write French, and he spoke
English better than his parents had ever spoken it, but Marie

knew he would work always with his hands, as did most of the men of his race. Lately he had been driving a dray for a quadroon named Legendre, who was prospering in the wagon business. Perhaps he would be like Legendre, Marie thought hopefully, and would some day grow rich in a business of his own. She wanted good lives for her children.

"Mamma, I want to go to sea!" Jacques spoke suddenly, sharply.

This startled her so much that she withdrew her hand from his and leaped to her feet. The other Jacques sprang instantly into her mind. But this was not Jacques' son. He was Glapion's, and she saw Glapion in him, too, as well as herself. He had Glapion's powerful shoulders and arms.

He was grinning. "You look scared, Mamma."

She was. "But I thought you were happy with Legendre," she told him. "And you have a girl, Jacques!"

"Tinette will wait," he said. "Legendre will wait, too, and give me work again when I come back. I want to see the world a little. I can get a berth on a ship. In six months or a year I will be back. I can save money."

"I can give you money."

A stubborn line formed between his black brows. "That is not the same."

"It is dangerous. Where will you go?"

"To France if I can. There is a man I am going to see today. I've already told Legendre. It is not so dangerous, Mamma. Everything is dangerous. A man can have his throat cut in the streets of New Orleans. He can be stomped to death while shoeing a horse for Legendre."

Marie sighed. "You seem to have made up your mind already. It seems I have nothing to say."

"Yes, I am going, Mamma," he said. "I want to see something before I marry and settle down. Once a man has a wife and children he can never go anywhere. It will just be for a little while. You will have all the other children."

Marie crossed the room and began putting on her gold bracelets. "Let us have breakfast, Jacques," she said. "There is nothing more to say about this. I will give you powerful protection from harm and I will pray for you until you come home again."

It was at breakfast each morning that she was alone with all her children, and somehow this morning seemed more important than any for a long time. Jacques had made her think of her children in a way she had not for years. There was even shame in the way she felt. Suddenly they all seemed so big. Even the baby; little Marie was six, and so like her, she realized—more like her than any but Jacques. When she looked full into Marie's face she saw a small reproduction of her own. The features were duplicated, even the unusual eyes with the white iris showing beneath the black pupils, and there was her expression in them already, as if the child always had secrets. And she was a quiet child, who talked little, but seemed to prefer to listen to others. There was an attitude of waiting. Yes, she is the one most like me, Marie thought, and could not decide whether this made her happy or sad.

The others all seemed different. Noemi and Felice were young women now—sixteen. Young men courted them, and she hoped they would marry soon and not wait until they were twenty-five, as she had done, for it was dangerous for a young girl to wait so long for a husband. She must pay more attention to her twins' beaux. She must be careful. They were a little dark, her Noemi and Felice, but they must marry men no darker, and the men must be both substantial and kind—kind like Jacques, she thought, kind like Glapion, kind like Monsieur Charles. What sort of mother am I? she wondered. I arrange the loves of strangers, but I have neglected to help my daughters to find love!

Quickly she scanned the faces of her other children. Christophe was a big and husky boy, at an age, Marie thought, when she had to worry neither about his leaving her nor about caring for him as if he were a baby. He was the studious one. Already he had more schooling than Jacques had ever acquired. He loved reading and talking. He looked like Glapion, and his nature was quiet, like his father's. She hoped he would go on studying. She had always felt there was little use for their race to acquire much learning, but she felt it would do Christophe no harm. Some men of their race had profited from it. Some owned large businesses, others large plantations. A few wrote books or plays or had gained fame as composers and musicians. When a quadroon or an octoroon became wealthy or cultured or famous he was accepted, at least to a limited extent, by white men these days. Certainly they did business with white men on an almost equal footing and between them there was a certain amount of social mingling and carefully observed politeness, although the women of the two races never mixed in any way. If Christophe could rise so high, Marie knew it would make her very proud. She did not expect it, but she could hope.

Jean was only eight, a playful and lighthearted child, who resembled Christophe in appearance but, Marie thought, only in that way. He is still a baby, she reflected, watching him at that moment; something Marguerite had said sent him into such a fit of giggles that he collapsed in his chair at the table and buried his face in his arms. His disposition seemed to her to be more like Jacques' than any of the others.

It was Marguerite, she knew, who might in time be her greatest problem, for Marguerite was blonde, and strangers were sometimes amazed at the sight of her among the other, darker children. Her eyes were blue—the eyes of Monsieur Charles—her hair a mass of flaxen curls, and her skin too fair. There had been moments when Marie had prayed she would darken, but she did not. She was only a year older than Jean, but already her appearance was causing comment and attracting attention, not all of it kind. Neighborhood children called her a "white roach," especially when there was a childish quarrel ensuing, and some of Marie's white clients, glimpsing Marguerite at play in the house or in the yard, had blurted out hints not too veiled. Marie knew very well what they thought: that Marguerite was her child by a white man. This shocked neither them nor Marie, yet Marie did not like it. She considered herself a woman of high morals, and of that she was proud.

But what would become of Marguerite when she was grown? She was still a child, and happy, except when she was taunted by her playmates, but what of her future as a young woman? Marie felt she must work hard with this one. Most girls like her, and many not nearly so fair, scorned the men of their own race. Some formed alliances with young white blades. Marie still felt as she had always felt about that. Besides, the Quadroon Balls were becoming less respectable each year now. No child of hers would ever take part in them if she could help it; that she knew. Yet she did not want Marguerite to remain unwed, as did some of her kind, and grow frustrated within the shell of her pride, to become, as some people called that sort, a "bleached turtle," too good for her own people, not accepted by others. There were others like Marguerite who "passed" into the white world, but this was a difficult and rarely happy transition.

She was still absorbed in her thoughts when her bell rang. It jangled loudly over the gate, and she left the table, her food almost untouched, crying out over her shoulder, "I will answer it, Rose!" As she crossed the garden she lifted her head high, quieted her face with her will. Who at this hour?

Marie felt a sharp pain under her heart when she opened the gate. How had this happened? Why did this woman have to come now, just as she had been thinking of her own Marguerite?

For the woman standing outside was Madame Lefebrve. Madame Lefebrve was in her fifties, and very stout, but the hair beneath the lace scarf she wore over it was still golden and her eyes were a piercing blue. No stranger would have guessed she was not quite white. "Marie, I must talk with you," she said.

Marie forced herself to say calmly, "Of course."

She led the way through the garden.

Madame seated herself in the altar room. "I have trouble," she murmured.

Marie rocked herself. "Tell me." They were old acquaintances. Madame Lefebrve had come to Marie often. She was wealthy, for her husband owned a great amount of property in the Faubourg Marigny below the old quarter of the city, but she had suffered much because of her small percentage of colored blood, and her husband was like her. Marie kept remembering her thoughts about Marguerite. Yet she wondered why the Lefebrves should feel as they did. They had the respect of everyone. They were rich.

"I will be brief," Madame Lefebrve told her. "There is no point in making a long story of this. Marie, could you come and visit us for a few days? It is most necessary."

Marie stopped rocking. "That is almost impossible."

"You have Rose," Madame said, "and the children grow large. We will pay you well. I will give you two hundred dollars if you will come to us for two days. A hundred dollars a day, Marie. It is good pay."

"It is fine pay." Marie smiled. "But you have not yet told me why it is so important that I do this."

Madame pushed back her scarf and let it drop from her bright hair to her shoulders. "We have been fixed," she said. "At least I think so, and my husband agrees with me. Someone has laid a curse on us, and it must be removed, yet we can find nothing about the house. Of course our home is large, and it would be difficult to find a *gris-gris* that might be hidden anywhere within it. Only you can find it, Marie. That is why I want you to come and visit. We will pay you for the two days even if you find it sooner. I promise you that."

"What has been happening?" Marie asked. "Why do you think an enemy has fixed you?" She paused. "And who do you think your enemy might be? Have you any idea?"

"A slave I had," Madame told her. "I cannot be sure, but I suspect her. She is a lazy and dirty creature, sullen and vicious. Some weeks ago I gave her to a cousin of mine in the country, who is using her as field hand. Her name is Peggy, and she is good for nothing but work in the fields. I think that she concealed a *gris-gris* in my house before she left. She had some knowledge of such matters, and I had had some reason to feel she was plotting against us before. She hated me because I reprimanded her often because of her slovenly ways. Now everything has happened to us, Marie."

Madame began to recount their misfortunes. Monsieur Lefebvre was losing tenants in his properties and he could not find others. Two of their servants were ill, so that there was no one to take care of their house properly. Even when Madame cooked it herself, their food had a strange and bitter taste. She feared it would poison them eventually. And last night the worst calamity of all had befallen them. Monsieur Lefebrve had slipped on the stairs and had a fall. His leg was badly bruised and might easily have been broken. They now felt themselves to be in danger of death, and that only Marie Laveau could save them.

"I will come," Marie said wearily. "It will be difficult for me to do so, but I cannot refuse you." She thought for a moment. "It may as well be this evening. I will come after dinner."

"Bless you," said Madame. "May the saints bless and guide you. We will be waiting."

There were few houses belonging to white residents of the city that were more handsome than the home of Madame and Monsieur Lefebrve. The tall white mansion in the Faubourg Marigny had generous gardens in front of it and on both sides. The high picket fence that surrounded it held an iron gate of intricate design and polished brass knobs. White columns supported the porches, which had more graceful black ironwork as railings, and the long French windows were hung with draperies of rich damask, their colors brilliant even at dusk.

Madame admitted Marie herself and led her down the wide center hall over thick carpets and into the front parlor. Glancing about, Marie noticed tall, gold-framed mirrors that stretched from floor to ceiling, gleaming mahogany tables, sofas and chairs of beautiful design. Madame lighted candles under great glass hurricane lamps and the room glowed. Marie saw that the ceiling above was exquisitely carved and that an oil portrait of Madame, done some years ago, hung above the white marble mantel. She seated herself, trying not to appear too impressed, for she did not consider that dignified to her position.

"It is a big house," she said. "Yes, you are right. It may not be easy to locate a *gris-gris* with so many hiding places available." She set down the cloth bag she had brought.

"That is our problem," Madame said. "My husband will be down in a minute. He has been soaking his leg."

Presently Monsieur Lefebrve limped in. He had gray hair and was almost as fair in complexion as his wife. "Thank God you have come," he said, sinking onto a sofa. "I hope you can do something to help us."

"If there is evil here I will find it," Marie replied serenely. "I will go to work at once. I have brought most of what I need. If there are other things, you will have them in the house. First, you must take me into every room in the house. Fetch me some salt and I will begin a purification of your home."

As Madame guided her through the rooms, each as richly furnished as the next one, Marie sprinkled salt in the corners of each one, and in the corner of each she stood silently for a moment, her head bowed, and said a prayer, varying the saints to whom the prayers were addressed, asking for power to rid the house of the evil that lurked somewhere in it. When she had completed this exorcism in each room, Marie took a small paper sack she had brought, went out on the galleries, lower and upper, front and rear, and sprinkled grains of red brick dust on all these porches. Then, returning to the couple, she asked, "You have whiskey?"

When Monsieur Lefebvre limped back with a bottle of whiskey, Marie proceeded upon another tour of the house, the others following her. In each room she would pour a few drops of whiskey in the palm of her right hand and toss them upon the walls. "I hope it does no damage," she apologized. "Your house is so beautiful it would be a pity to harm it."

"I am not concerned with the beauty of my home," replied Monsieur. "Do what you must, Marie Laveau."

"I am weakening the power of whatever may be troubling you," Marie explained, "and I have defended you from any outside evil. If wicked thoughts are directed against you from without they cannot cross your galleries or pierce your walls."

When they were again seated in the front parlor, Marie said almost at once, "Now I will retire. I will rest and you can sleep peacefully. I will rise early and find whatever has been put upon you by your enemy."

"First we must have gumbo," said Madame. "Just a small bowl, if you like. I prepared it for you myself."

After Marie tasted her gumbo, she said, "It is good. It is very good."

"Do you see, André?" cried Madame. "Already she is helping us! My gumbo does not taste bitter at all!"

"Each of you light one of these when you retire," Marie told them, handing each of them a small purple candle from her cloth bag. "They will give you even more protection during the night."

But Marie did not go to bed at once after she reached the

room to which they escorted her. She closed her door and made herself a little altar upon the marble mantel in the huge and elegantly furnished room. She cleared the mantel of its ornaments, and set in its center a purple candle, a white one and a pink one—purple for protection in this case, white for purety, pink to bring love into the house, for love drove out evil. Then, at one side, she put small statues of a bear and a tiger, on the other side those of a lion and a wolf. The beasts would protect her. She untied her *tignon,* and loosened her hair. Then, stripped to her petticoat and baring her feet, she climbed into the immense bed, a four-poster with crimson canopy and side curtains, and went to sleep.

In the morning when she awakened, for the first moment she did not remember where she was; then, when realization came, she smiled. She had never slept in such a beautiful room. She arose and found that her candles were out, and she knelt and said her prayers, her forehead pressed against the side of the bed.

She had just finished dressing when she heard the woman shriek. She did not hurry, but moved slowly to the door and opened it. The morning sunlight was fiery on the furnishings in the hall, on the polished floor, on the stairway leading to the lower floor. The woman shrieked again.

In the lower hall a thin, almost emaciated old colored woman knelt at the feet of Madame Lefebrve. Madame was stroking the woman's *tignon* and saying, "Hush, Belle! Hush! You must not be afraid. You are all right."

Then she raised her head, her blue eyes wide and frightened. "A tureen on my sideboard flung itself at her," she told Marie, stammering a little. "Belle has been ill, but she came down this morning to fix breakfast for us because you were here. Go into the dining room and see. It is in a hundred pieces."

Marie walked quickly to the door of the dining room. Bits

of china lay all over the rug. She returned, put her hands under Belle's armpits and raised her. "Do not be frightened any longer, my child," she told her. "Go back to your kitchen and to your cooking."

Belle obeyed, but walked slowly, her face tearstained. "It is angry," Marie told Madame Lefebrve. "It knows it is being attacked by me. You must not be frightened, either. But we must find it as soon as we can after breakfast. Have no fear."

With trembling hands, Belle spread a sumptuous breakfast, carrying trays into the dining room from the kitchen across the yard. Marie ate heartily of chops and gravy, hominy grits, hot spoon bread, an assortment of preserves and jellies, and drank cup after cup of steaming coffee. She was the only one who ate well. Madame still seemed frightened, Monsieur depressed. "Do you think you can find this?" he asked her.

Marie raised her brows. "Do you doubt me?" she asked him. "If I cannot do this, I can do nothing! And, as you know, nothing can be done without faith. I beg you for your faith, Monsieur Lefebrve."

He said, "I did not mean that, Marie."

"The action of the tureen is a small thing," she told him. "It means little. It is just that the evil thing we must find is infuriated because I am here. It could not penetrate the *gris-gris* I set against it last night. It could only cause the tureen to be broken. It is strong and wicked, but not as strong as Marie Laveau, Monsieur." She wiped her mouth with her napkin. "I will go to work now," she said, rising. "I must be alone."

She went out into the kitchen first and talked to Belle, who knew nothing, and could say little, so shaken was she by fright and by the presence of Marie Laveau. There was nothing in the kitchen. Marie searched the huge open fireplace, in which hung the iron and copper pots Belle used in her cooking, the cabinets beneath the worn wooden table and

167

between the cracks in the brick floor. She left three purple candles burning in the kitchen and Belle seemed suddenly more comfortable.

"In the dining room," Marie kept telling herself, although it was almost like a voice speaking to her in her mind. That was where the tureen had attacked Belle. Perhaps the thing had betrayed itself.

The remnants of breakfast still remained upon the table, and the Lefebrves had vanished upstairs. Marie began her search of the dining room. Then she felt she must have help. She drew the draperies over the windows and closed the doors. She placed three purple candles upon the sideboard, then she lay down upon the floor with her head pointed toward the candles above her. She did not pray and she tried to clear her mind of every thought. She kept her eyes open, staring straight up at the ceiling. In a few moments the ceiling started to cloud and she began feeling strange. She was not frightened, but she knew something was pressing down from above her. It grew stronger and stronger. "You are here," she said aloud. "You are here, and I will find you!" She laughed. "I am talking to you as a person," she said, "and you are only a thing. But I will find you!"

She sprang to her feet and began her search. Crawling beneath the table, she saw it. It was a small bag, lightly nailed to the underside of the table. Snatching it free, she bore it to the sideboard and laid it before the purple candles. Then she ran out into the hall and cried up the stairs, "Monsieur! Madame!" She ran to the rear door and called, "Belle! Come here, my child! You must see it, too!"

When they were all assembled she opened the bag. "It is incredible!" she snorted. "Common filth! Yet it is evil, and could do much harm." She showed them the contents. The chamois bag held salt and gunpowder, saffron and dog manure, the dried testicles of a cat. "In time," she told Monsieur

Lefebrve, holding up the last, "this would have made you impotent!"

She burned it all in the fireplace in the kitchen. "You will have no more trouble," she promised. "It is over."

Both Madame and Belle were in tears, and Monsieur Lefebrve's face was ashen. "You did it so quickly," he said. "We are forever in your debt."

Marie smiled. "I came for payment, Monsieur."

Walking home, she could feel the gold coins they had given her rattling together within the handkerchief in which she had tied them and thrust them down into her bosom.

And as she neared her home she thought of her children again. Yes, she must do more for them. They were more her duty than all these other people. Today she would spend a time alone in her altar room. She would burn blue candles for Noemi and Felice, and feed the Vodu an extra portion of milk and poundcake for them, and then she would make a big *gris-gris* for husbands for them, and yet another to protect Jacques while he was at sea. The lives of her children must be good and happy.

By the end of two weeks Jacques had sailed for France. Marie did not cry, but she pinned a little bag to his shirt, and begged him to make only this one trip, to say his prayers, to be careful. She knew she would be unhappy until he returned.

Early in the spring Noemi married, and a month later Felice. Noemi's husband was a blacksmith and Felice's husband had a fine vegetable business in the market. Both young men were of good character and of respectable families.

The household seemed much smaller with only Christophe, Marguerite, Jean and little Marie there, but she was content that the twins had found husbands and that there was no bad news of Jacques. The *gris-gris* she had made for Noemi and Felice she began to use with her clients, and she found it good.

Many of her clients found husbands after she had used it for them.

To get husbands for the twins she had sketched crude pictures of each, and had set them up on her altar among the pictures of her saints. That the sketches did not resemble the girls did not matter; that they represented them was all that counted. The Vodu, the zombie, knew. At one hour before midnight, when all the children were asleep, Marie put the pictures on the altar. Then she mixed together in a bowl nine drops of vanilla, nine of wintergreen, nine of Jack honeysuckle, nine lumps of sugar, and nine rose leaves. She put this on the altar before the sketches, and before it she set up and lighted nine pink candles. Standing before all of it, she clapped her hands together lightly, and said, "Men have to come! Right men!" She repeated this again, "Men have to come! Right men!" In all she said it nine times:

"Men have to come! Right men!"

When she was through she cut seven notches in each of two blue candles, as she always did in furthering love affairs. Then she went out to make the sacrifice, carrying two plates of roasted chicken, cowpeas and rice. These she left at streets crossing behind Congo Square, near the prison, which was directly behind the square. When she returned home she lighted the blue candles, and let each burn down one notch. Each day for the next six days she burned another notch.

This, of course, only brought the young men. But within a week she had met both the young men who were to be husbands to Noemi and Felice, and when she met them she was certain at once that they were the ones the girls must marry.

She kept working. Every time the young men called she made the girls rub themselves with a verbena and sugar powder. Playfully they obtained locks of their sweethearts' hair, and these Marie placed in separate jars containing sugar water, sealed them tightly, and put the jars on the altar before the sketches of the girls. As the hairs sweetened so did the boys. Then came the proposals of marriage.

On the evening before St. John's Eve an old friend, Baptiste Dudevant, came to see her. He had long been her neighbor and he was a nephew of her friend Delia. He was a handsome mulatto, with tawny eyes and the mustaches of a pirate, which flared above a grin filled with brilliant white teeth. She welcomed him gladly, for he had been gone more than two years on a sailing ship that had encircled the world, and at sight of him she thought of Jacques.

He brought her gifts. One of these was a wooden god from Africa.

"Do you remember the god of Rosalie?" he asked. "I thought this was like it, but it is better and more powerful."

It was like the god of Rosalie. It had the same fierce face, the distended belly, the mocking, fearful eyes, but it was larger and handsomer. She took it in her hands with pleasure.

He brought her, too, a shawl. It was beautifully painted and embroidered with huge dragons and red and gold flowers, with pagodas and winding streams of blue water. Its silk gleamed with color.

"It belonged to the Emperor of China," he told her.

She put the statue down and draped the vivid shawl about her shoulders. "From the Emperor of China!" she cried. "I will wear it for him!"

"Tomorrow is the twenty-third of June," he said. "I thought you might want to show the god to the people then."

"I will show him to all my people," she promised. "They are my children and he is for them. I will wear the shawl. Sit down, Baptiste! You must have some wine and talk with me."

He remained a little while, and he answered all her questions about life at sea, assuring her that Jacques would be safe, and especially would the son of Marie Laveau be safe. She thought of the other Jacques; he had not been safe. But she had known little then; she had been young. "My power goes over the sea to him," she told Baptiste. "It goes out to protect my son. The evil sea shall not have him. He will come back." When Baptiste rose to go she said, "You must come tomorrow night, my child. You must come to St. John's Bayou and you shall sit at the feet of Marie Laveau. We will show them the god and the shawl, and they will know that you brought them to Marie Laveau from Africa and from the Emperor of China!"

All the next day she wore the shawl to give it extra luck, and she polished the wood of the god in the afternoon. She blessed it and showed it to the zombie in the alabaster box. She burned a candle for Jacques and one for Baptiste Dudevant, that he might have good fortune. Then she lighted a third one for the Emperor of China, and then a fourth, the last that the weather might continue to be rainless that night, for rain and thunder on St. John's Eve was an omen of terrible significance. Never had she known it to rain on St. John's Eve.

The women came to fetch her in the cart at dusk, three of those closest to her, who would help her prepare for the rites: Celia, Anastasie, and another named Marie Culotte; and she climbed into the back of the wagon, wearing her shawl and holding the African god against her bosom. As she climbed aboard and took her seat she blessed them by calling their names, "Celia! Anastasie! Marie Culotte!" Each touched her lips with a hand and then a place above her heart, then they loaded aboard the alabaster box that held the Vodu and placed it at Marie's feet. Marie Culotte took the reins of the horse, and in a moment they were off over the cobblestones. A breeze blew the trees in the distance, but the sky was a gentle pink and yellow. It would not rain tonight. The god was heavy in her arms.

Marie had made many changes during the year she had succeeded Saloppé as queen. The clearing that was the secret place on Bayou St. John had been enlarged and a shack had been built. This rough structure had three walls and a roof of tree branches and palmetto, with the whole front open to the area before it. Inside, there was at one end a brick enclosure for the building of a fire, a hole in the roof above carrying away the smoke. In the center against the back wall there was a raised platform upon which was a high-backed chair for the queen. Before the platform was a long, low wooden table. Into the dirt floor were stabbed receptacles like sconces in which pitch-dipped pine could be lighted.

The women left the cart at the side of the narrow winding road that had brought them close to the ritual place and went the rest of the way on foot, fighting their way through the brush and the tall grass and weeds; for now they came rarely except for this one night in the year, and no path remained for them but the faint track left by the men Marie had sent the day before to clear the space for the dancers, to beat down the earth within the shrine. The other women carried the heavy box with the snake in it and the rest of the things Marie had brought, but she still carried the statue. It became even heavier now; it seemed to grow. It was really only a bit more than three feet in height, but it seemed at moments to become nearly as tall as she was. And there were moments when it almost frightened her. Yet when she put it down on the platform it looked the same as it had before. She sighed and began to inspect the place. All seemed in order.

The women put the Vodu on the dirt floor directly in front of her throne, and unpacked the other things they had brought. There were two live cats, one black, one white; others dead and stuffed, but extraordinarily lifelike, which they placed each at an end of the long wooden table. They brought pine torches and filled the receptacles so that there would be light when light was needed. They went out into the brush and brought back wood and filled the brick fire-

173

place. They placed the pictures of saints upon the tables and set out the candles. Then they stripped off their outer dresses and their shoes and tied white handkerchiefs about their foreheads. Now they wore only white camisoles that reached to their knees and the white handkerchiefs about their brows. Marie took off her own shoes and stockings, but nothing else. She walked about on the earth in her bare feet, feeling the pleasure of it between her toes, her blue skirts whirling, her shawl and brilliant *tignon* and all her gold jewelry lighted into a blaze of color by the sunset. Then, as darkness came, she ordered the women to light the pitch-dipped pine, and she tied about her waist the blue cord that was the symbol of her office. When the musicians arrived, and the men with the rum and wine, and those with the roosters, and then the women with the already cooked gumbo, Marie was seated on her throne, ready to greet them.

From his place at Marie's feet, Baptiste looked up at her with a haze in his eyes. He put a hot hand on one of her bare legs. She slapped at him with her fan. "You have had too much rum, my child!" she scolded. "Go bring to me the offering to the goat." The meeting had been going on for four hours now.

He drooped his head in shame, and fetched her the money, and began adding it to the rest in the bag. He was returning the bag to its place beneath her chair, when he suddenly straightened. "Horses!" he said. "I hear horses coming!"

Marie heard them, too. "Go see, Baptiste," she told him, calmly, although she did not like the sound. "Go to the road and see." And, as he ran in the direction of the road, she rose and signaled the musicians to stop playing. Some of the dancers stopped, too. Manuel came to her, his body gleaming with sweat. "Quiet, children!" Marie cried. "Quiet!"

The noise abated, but did not stop. They were beyond stopping now. She did not like this. Only one vehicle had come to the meeting, the one that had brought her and her assistants. Her people walked here, many of them starting out early in the afternoon. They would walk home again at dawn, or as soon after as they were able. A few came by boats on the bayou.

Baptiste came running back across the clearing. "It is white people," he panted. "Two carriages filled with them."

Marie frowned. "The police?"

"Not police," Baptiste said. "They are people who look to be rich. There are even ladies. I counted four ladies. They have stopped the carriages now among the trees. They are watching. They laugh!"

Marie sat down, feeling anger grow in her. "What are they doing here?" she asked crossly. "How did they find it?" Whites had come to many of the meetings in her yard, in her home, but never here; this had always been secret. Of course she could guess how they had found it. Some servant had talked.

"What are we going to do?" asked Baptiste.

Marie was silent for a moment, then she rose again. "There is only one thing to do when one has callers, my child," she told him. "One invites them in. Go tell them to come here, Baptiste. Tell them they are welcome. They need not hide in the bushes like wood rats."

Baptiste stared at her for an instant, then he went to obey, and she sat there smoldering. Let them come if they dared! Let them watch! They would not laugh much after she had spoken to them.

Baptiste was back. "They are gone," he said. "They ran like rats. Listen!"

She heard the carriages departing. She laughed. "They only wanted a peepshow!" she told Baptiste. "They did not think we would catch them, and when we did they scurried away. They did not dare come before Marie Laveau."

She rose once more and clapped her hands for the drums to renew their beat, for the dancing to begin again.

It was the next afternoon before she had time to think much of this, and then it did not seem half so irritating as it had the night before. Slowly she began to feel differently about it, as she talked of it to Rose.

"They think we are queer, Rose," she said. "They found us amusing, too."

"I don't understand white people," Rose muttered. "They're not like us, Madame Glapion. The best thing you can do is not think about them much."

"They would like to see St. John's Eve at St. John's Bayou," Marie said. She smiled at Rose. "They would pay money to see our little celebration." She closed her eyes and opened them. "They would pay lots of money."

Long before the next St. John's Eve many prominent persons knew about the rites that would take place that night, and where they would be held. Their slaves and other servants whispered of it to them. The grapevine throbbed with it.

No great crowd of whites came that night, but there were enough carriages to line the roadside for some distance from the clearing where the celebration was taking place. The whites did not come into the light; none approached Marie. They remained hidden in the darkness. At first Marie heard a little laughter. But it did not last. Finally a few carriages departed, but the rest remained, and she sent Baptiste with a large bowl to collect an offering from them.

Chapter 9

AFTERWARDS it seemed strange to her that she had been thinking of the past the afternoon the man came. Jacques and Tinette had brought the baby to see her earlier. Jacques had been home more than two years now, and he and Tinette had married shortly after his return. Marie had enjoyed their visit and she was proud that she was a grandmother to 'Tite Tinette, as they called the infant.

When Rose showed the man into her parlor Marie was startled by the expression on the woman's face. Then she looked at the man, and she wondered if her own face was not much the same. He said, "I am Doctor John," and stood in the doorway, his hat in his hand.

She repeated after him like an echo, "Doctor John." She felt like adding foolishly, "Doctor John is dead." It was not that there was more than one resemblance to the other Doctor John, but that one was what amazed her. His coal black face was tattooed exactly as that other's had been— on the cheeks and forehead were symbols and snake-like patterns in bright reds and blues that twisted and writhed from his temples to the corners of his mouth. But above the bridge of his nose, between his eyebrows, was an additional marking that gave him the appearance of having a third eye; heavily outlined in black, it had a yellow and black pupil just as did his real eyes. He smiled now and the snakes moved on his cheeks, and the third eye seemed to wink.

Marie made a gesture with her hands. "Sit down, please." She could hear Rose rushing toward the rear of the house. "I once knew a Doctor John."

The man seated himself, sitting very upright and stiff, his hat held in his hands upon his lap. "I know," he said. "He taught me much when I lived here. But I have been in Charleston for some years. Now I have come home." He spoke good French, but in a stilted and self-conscious way. It was inconsistent with his appearance.

Marie scrutinized him. He was a huge man, tall, with broad shoulders and arms that bulged the sleeves of his coat, and with a barrel of a chest. He was hideous, and not only because of his tattooed face. He had a wide nose, so flat that he seemed to possess no nostrils, and when his heavy lips parted he showed jagged and yellowed teeth that seemed less than human. Marie noticed, too, that one of his ears was almost gone; only a ragged piece of flesh at the top remained. In the other ear he wore a small pearl.

She recovered herself and stopped staring. "Well, what can I do for you, Doctor?" she asked quietly, although she knew full well he had not come as a client. He would be a rival. Even so, it seemed a little strange to her that he should have called upon her, if that were the case.

"Your reputation has traveled far," he said. "Your name is known in Charleston. Since I have come back I thought perhaps we should meet. You work alone?"

"Always alone."

He gazed straight into her eyes. "It is best to work alone," he said. "But in the old days we always worked in pairs. The queen had a king. There was Papa as well as Mamma."

Marie moved her head slowly. "I work alone, Doctor."

His eyes were unchanged, as steady as her own. "You have made changes."

"I have made whatever changes I pleased."

"You have brought in Catholic saints," he said. "You were not the first, but you have given more power to them. You have invented new ceremonies and you have made new charms and *gris-gris*. But so have I. You are wise and you have a large following."

She was becoming angry. What right had this man to criticize her work or her methods? "I do what I please, Doctor," she told him again, "and let me repeat, I work alone. My people are pleased with my work—and with my working alone!"

He continued to stare at her for a moment. Then he said, "Have no fear. I did not come to ask to work with you."

She sighed. "That would have been quite useless."

"I came," he said, "because I thought we should meet since I am going to work in New Orleans. And perhaps I was curious."

"There are other workers here," she told him, shrugging. She wanted to add, "But they are small people—little people —who keep out of my way. You had better keep out of it, too!"

As if he had read her mind, he said, "There have been none like Marie Laveau."

His use of the past tense did not escape her. Her face was frigid. "There *will* be none, Doctor."

He rose. "I must go," he said, breaking suddenly into a wide but humorless grin. "We will meet again, and perhaps we can occasionally be of help to each other. I should like to attend one of your meetings."

"You will be welcome." She bowed her head politely, not meaning her words at all.

"Most of my work is quite different from yours," he said. "I hold no meetings of the type you do. I was born with a veil, and I see the future clearly. Sometimes I give protection to my clients, but I rarely do any other kind of work." He

179

strode to the door, seeming to crowd the room with his bulk. "Since I have been here I have accepted only one such case, but then I have been back only a few weeks."

Marie rose and followed him to the door. She said nothing.

"My client," he said, "is the woman Pauline."

"I wish you good fortune," Marie murmured. "I refused it."

They crossed the garden toward the front gate. "I will probably lose," he said. "It is a difficult one, and you were wise not to accept her. But her brother paid me well."

"She will hang," said Marie, with certainty.

He nodded. "She is a wicked woman, but the laws are too stern. Good day, Marie Laveau."

"Good day, Doctor John."

She shut the gate behind him, bolted it with a bang, and rushed back across the yard to the brick kitchen. Rose was stirring a pot of thick vegetable soup and the good aroma of it filled the small room.

"Why did not someone tell me that man was in town?" Marie cried passionately. "All such news is to come to me at once! That I demand!"

Rose blinked at her. "I've never heard anything about him," she said, cringing a little.

"Someone knew!" shouted Marie. "What good is my work if this can happen?" She took a white china cup and poured coffee from the pot on the fire. She was in such a rage that the cup trembled in her hand. "He is working for the woman Pauline. Much good that will do his reputation! Even *I* could not save Pauline. At least I would not be foolish enough to take the risk!"

Rose looked even more frightened. All New Orleans Negroes were greatly agitated about the case of Pauline, and many would not even discuss it.

"This must never happen again!" cried Marie. "I must

know when such men as this so-called Doctor John appear in New Orleans. I will punish those who know of it and do not tell me. Give them that message for me, Rose! Spread it in the market when you go!" She swallowed the coffee and hurried out, muttering, "I have an enemy! I have a bad enemy, Rose!"

For days she thought of nothing but Doctor John and the fact that her grapevine had failed to report to her his arrival in the city. Had he some power over her people? She did not fear him, but she did recognize in him a potentially dangerous rival. The very fact that he had dared to call upon her proved that, and the impertinence of his daring enraged her.

She found some consolation in remembering that he had been stupid enough to work in Pauline's behalf. That was bad judgment on his part, she felt, for although he might receive a little money for taking the case, he would lose prestige when he failed. And he would fail. He had almost admitted that he expected to fail.

All New Orleans knew about Pauline, and Marie knew even more than most of the citizens. Several years before, Pauline had come to her for a love philter. Pauline had not named the man she hoped to attract with it, and Marie had not asked; it was not her custom to do so. Pauline had used it upon her master, a white man named Peter Rabbeneck, a married man with three small children.

It had worked. Rabbeneck had taken the mulatto slave woman to be his mistress and gradually she had assumed command of his household, with Rabbeneck's own wife and children being forced to obey her orders. After several years of this state of affairs Rabbeneck had gone to St. Louis on business. He had been gone six weeks when Mayor Montegut had received an anonymous letter which informed him that Mrs. Rabbeneck and her children were being held prisoners in their home by the slave woman Pauline. When the police broke into the house they had found Mrs. Rabbeneck and the children locked in a tiny room without windows. They had been starved, deprived of decent human privileges, and beaten daily by Pauline. All four were covered with filth and ulcers and clotted blood; their eyes were blackened, and their bodies shrunken and emaciated.

Pauline's trial had been swift, but dramatic. A handsome woman of twenty-eight, she claimed that as a child she had belonged to President Monroe in Virginia. She testified that Mrs. Rabbeneck was insane and that her husband had ordered her, Pauline, to keep his wife prisoner and to beat her when she became violent. Pauline said she had been forced to beat the children because they were prompted to misbehavior and disobedience by their mother. The jury disregarded her testimony. Bitterness was extreme among the whites, and all New Orleans wanted an example made of Pauline. The Black Code was invoked for the first time since the city had been a part of the United States, and Pauline was sentenced to be hanged publicly in the courtyard of the parish prison. The execution had been delayed some months now because Pauline was pregnant. When she had been delivered of the child it would take place.

Marie knew that Pauline would be hanged. Doctor John would not be able to stop it, and he knew it, too. Yet he had taken money under the pretense that he could. He was not an honest worker, she thought with contempt.

Soon information about Doctor John was pouring in to Marie, and she ceased to worry about her grapevine. There had been a lapse, but that was all. Rose spread the word that Marie wanted any and all news of him, and Marie instructed others among her clientele to bring such information to her, too. She soon discovered that he had been trained well by that other Doctor John, and that he was imitating the older man in many ways. He was even using names the other had used, and the Negroes were calling him "Bayou John" and "John Bayou," as well as "Doctor John." There were even those who believed he *was* the older Doctor John; they believed the dead witch doctor had returned, and when they questioned him about this he did not make any effort to deny it.

"Charlatan! Faker!" Marie would cry when she was told of this. "He brings shame to us all!"

Doctor John, she learned, had taken a small house below the Esplanade, some half dozen blocks from where she lived, and there was a white woman living with him, who had come from Charleston shortly after his arrival and whom he claimed was his wife. To those who did not accept him as a reincarnation of old Doctor John, returned to earth a full-grown, middle-aged man, he told another fantastic story of his life. He said his father had been a king in Senegal, that he had been stolen as a child, sold into slavery in Cuba, had escaped as a young boy and come to New Orleans, where he had worked on the wharves. Then he had discovered his powers, studied with old Doctor John and other witch doctors, and at last departed for Charleston.

For the moment at least, Marie decided, and with increased contempt, he was behaving like nothing but a common for-tuneteller. He claimed to be able to read the stars and to find meaning in the casting of a handful of sticks upon the ground, in seeing his clients' futures in a glass jar filled with sand, and in other ways she considered sheer foolishness. He also practiced healing. Only now and then did she hear of his offering to sell *gris-gris* and charms, or to lift curses. But she continued to watch him and to query her contacts about his activities. Patiently, too, she awaited the execution of Pauline, hopeful that it would bring about his end, for she had taken care to circulate all over the city the fact that he had promised—and for a fee—to save Pauline from death.

Marie had no desire to witness Pauline's hanging. She had never attended an execution before. She went on thinking about this Doctor John, however, until she knew she must go and see the woman dead, and know that it was done, and that Doctor John had not saved her, had not demonstrated his power in that way. She must see it herself to have peace. Hearing of it from others would not do, would not be enough.

They hanged Pauline on a brilliant and sunny noon on a day near the end of March. A soft breeze blew, and the sky was cloudless and the air was sweet. To Marie it seemed terrible to die on such a day, but to most of those on the way to the parish prison there seemed to cling a holiday air. These were the whites and the free people of color, of course. They laughed and gossiped along the streets near the prison behind Congo Square, each group remaining apart from the other, but much alike in its attitude, for the free people of color were usually in agreement with the whites in such matters as this, especially the prosperous ones.

Marie did not arrive until after eleven o'clock, and the wide space between the two buildings that comprised the prison, as well as the streets surrounding it, were crowded with those who had come to view the hanging. But Marie had no trouble in passing through the crowd, for there were enough of her own people present to make room for her. The usual whispers went around: "It is she! It's Marie Laveau!" They made way, and she moved slowly and serenely to within a few feet of the scaffold, searching everywhere for Doctor John. He was not there, she discovered. He was so large and so unusual in appearance it would be impossible not to see him if he were.

The crowd continued to grow. "There're over five thousand people!" someone near Marie whispered. She glanced about again, but again she failed to see Doctor John. It seemed to her that everyone else in the city must be there. People talked and joked and laughed. Along the edges of the crowd vendors were selling gumbo, the rice cakes called *calas*, and hot coffee. It was like a circus, a carnival, except that beneath all the merriment there was nervous tension. A man would chatter and laugh, then become suddenly silent. A woman's laughter would be too high and shrill. There were serious, somber faces. Here and there stood a white master with several blacks before him. Marie knew these men had brought their slaves to witness the execution as a warning and a lesson. In the streets were several open carriages filled with gaudily dressed and heavily painted white women. The brothels had emptied for the occasion.

Pauline walked out of the prison with the Abbé Louis, the prison chaplain, at twelve-fifteen. There was a roar from the crowd, mostly whispers and gasps but deafening in its total effect, then almost complete silence. This was shattered when a baby began to cry, and Marie could hear its mother trying to hush it. Marie felt a shudder at the sight of Pauline, but she repressed it and kept her gaze upon the woman as she crossed the yard, walking steadily and firmly, held up her white robe with one hand, and climbed the steps leading up to the platform. There she sat down in the chair awaiting her. There was no expression at all upon her face. She stared down at the crowd before her—once, it seemed to Marie, straight into her own eyes—then down at the crucifix she held. She spoke to the Abbé Louis and he handed her a glass of water, from which she drank. There was no tremor in the hand that held the glass. Above her head the rope swung slightly in the breeze. She and the Abbé prayed, and the hangman came and stood behind her chair.

Marie wanted to close her eyes as the rope was fixed, but she could not do so. There were giggles in the crowd. A drunken man shouted an obscenity and other men shouted at him to shut up. Marie's eyes were open but suddenly her sight blurred, and she heard rather than saw the trap sprung.

When she could see again, the body of Pauline was swinging back and forth at the end of the rope. It swung with the steadiness and smoothness of the pendulum of a clock. It looked not like a human body at all, but like a ridiculous decoration hung in the prison yard.

Marie waited no longer but turned to leave. The crowd had become boisterous again. There was shouting and laughter. Some people gaped at what hung from the rope, but most of them were talking and gossiping among themselves. Marie thought of Doctor John. He had not come. As she reached the edge of the mob she talked aloud, so that those she passed might hear her. "That Doctor John didn't come!" she exclaimed. "That faker was going to save her, he bragged. He took money to save her! Doctor John is a faker and a cheat! He can do nothing!"

"That's Marie Laveau!" people exclaimed. "It's the famous Marie Laveau!"

Marie felt better about Doctor John after that, and during the weeks that followed thought of him seldom. But she often heard his name. Her clients sometimes mentioned it. "Is he good? Do you think he is good?" they would ask.

It never occurred to her to be delicate about expressing her opinion of the man with the tattooed face. She continued to tell them he was a fake, a cheat, a mere fortuneteller, who even imitated her, Marie Laveau. There could be but one leader, the queen, herself.

Those who mentioned him at this time were her colored clients. She heard nothing of him from the whites until one day when she accepted a summons to dress the hair of a Mrs. Bates, who lived in one of the mansions that lined Julia Street.

The block between Camp and St. Charles Streets, where Mrs. Bates lived, was one of the most fashionable in the city. Marie had visited it often, for Mrs. Bates had been her client a long time. Marie enjoyed working upon Mrs. Bates' stubborn hair with her pomades and bandoline and listening to her incessant chatter in the big front bedroom upstairs, the windows of which looked across the street to the row of splendid houses that most people called the "Thirteen Mansions," and which were the homes of some of the most elegant citizens of the American section.

Mrs. Bates, whom Marie thought privately to be somewhat less elegant than her neighbors, was consumed with curiosity about them and talked of them constantly, although never with envy or malice. She seemed to receive pleasure just by pronouncing their names.

"Mr. Lanfear's two girls are such beauties!" she would say. "Marie, you should have seen them leaving for a ball last evening. They both wore pink, and the sweetest little black slippers with narrow ribbons tied prettily about their ankles." Or, "They do say the Buckner girl is going to marry Mr. Eustis!"

She found it of absorbing interest that General and Mrs. Gaines frequently visited the Chinns, and once she had pointed out to Marie from a curtained window a tall, angular man wearing a claw-hammer coat, skin-tight trousers and a tall polished hat. "That is the great statesman, Henry Clay!" Mrs. Bates had exclaimed. "He always visits the Chinns when he is here from Washington."

The least kind thing Mrs. Bates might mention was that an elderly lady across the street wore false black curls pinned to the edges of the caps of Mechlin lace she always wore, a fact of which Marie was well aware. She made Mrs. Mathews' curls for all her beautiful little caps. But she had said nothing in reply to Mrs. Bates. She never discussed one client's hair secrets with another.

It was a question of Mrs. Bates', however, that brought about a discussion of Doctor John. "Did you know you had competition in your selling of lucky charms?" Mrs.

187

Bates asked Marie that day. Mrs. Bates was one of those people, and there were many white women like her, who had never taken Marie's other art seriously, but thought of it as merely the selling of "lucky charms." Mrs. Bates had bought them from time to time herself to send to friends in the North as fascinating novelties, but no more, and Marie had not discouraged her in this, for there was good money to be had from selling those concoctions of twisted wood or roots, scraps of cloth, and the gaudy pebbles with which she made them; and indeed they were not to be taken seriously, for Marie wasted no magic upon these.

Marie said nothing for a moment after Mrs. Bates asked the question. Then she replied in her halting English that there were many dispensers of lucky charms throughout the city.

"Oh, but I hear this one is different," Mrs. Bates said. "Mrs. Mathews told me all about him. You know she dotes on all that. Sometimes I really think the poor dear believes in it! She loves fortunetellers and all that kind of thing."

"Many believe, Madame," murmured Marie.

"This is a man," Mrs. Bates said. "A Negro. A very weird Negro in appearance, according to Mrs. Mathews. I thought you might have heard of him. He is called Doctor John."

"He is a charlatan," said Marie, without hesitation.

Mrs. Bates smiled. "Of course he is, my dear! They all are. *You* know that—of all people!" She winked at Marie, as if they shared a secret. "I've told you too many times how I really feel about all that, although I believe it is perfectly harmless if one wants to amuse one's self with it. I was even thinking of going to Doctor John and having him tell *my* fortune. I love to go to them, although of course I'm not like Mrs. Mathews."

If Marie had had a lock of Mrs. Bates' hair in her hand at the moment she would have pulled it. "Doctor John he is no good at all," she replied, willing herself to seem calm. "You save your money!"

Walking home through the streets Marie allowed herself to be engulfed with rage. She walked fast, her head up as always, but her eyes blazing so that people she passed stared at her. So Doctor John was after the whites now! He had even penetrated into the American part of the city—even Julia Street! Americans were such fools, too, that they might admire his trickery, they might not be able to distinguish between her power and his chicanery!

As she strode a few blocks down Canal Street, she had an impulse to stop strangers passing and tell them of Doctor John, and why they must have nothing to do with him. This upstart had deliberately returned to New Orleans to steal her place from her. This was one of the few times in her life she wanted to use evil—and upon him, to destroy him, to kill him.

Yet she knew she would not kill him. Rather, she must overcome him in some way, drive him out of the city if possible. She thought of the long-ago days of Saloppé, and how she had won victory over her. But Doctor John was stronger, and he was a man—a savage, she thought to herself, a black savage, but smart and ambitious.

The part of Canal Street on which she was walking was lined with residences, for some of the wealthiest people in the city lived here now. Farther toward the river there were places of business, mostly warehouses, but here were tall white homes with iron picket fences and gardens on the side, and upstairs balconies with iron lacework. The wide street was divided into two cobblestoned thoroughfares with a common, or neutral ground, in the middle, in which tall weeds grew, yet which gave off a warm fragrance at this time of year.

Many people were strolling along the *banquette* on this sunny afternoon—white men and colored men and women, and here and there a white woman with a fringed parasol raised above her bonnet and a green veil drawn over her face, her gloved hand tucked securely into the arm of her escort, for few white ladies liked to appear on Canal Street in the daylight, unescorted.

Marie continued walking until she came to where the houses ended. Beyond stretched a dank, swamplike region, spotted with grassy places. Here there was visible only some servants busy at beating carpets on the grass, which they had carried there for that purpose, a custom among those who lived in the vicinity. Marie stood watching them for a few minutes, her mind still occupied in attempting to plan the defeat of Doctor John, then she crossed the street and walked back in the direction of the river. A single carriage rolled past, its springs squeaking vilely. It was the first vehicle to have passed Marie in the street, but she was too profoundly absorbed with her thoughts to so much as glance at it. Absently she thought—some brazen Americans!

When she reached the Rue Condé (which was now called Chartres Street, although she never used the new name herself) she turned, and the narrow street seemed to embrace her as she re-entered the old part of the city that she loved. She would go to the Cathedral of St. Louis, she decided, and pray. It would clear her mind and help her. She went too seldom to church now; perhaps that was what was wrong.

She slowed her pace on Chartres Street. Even it was changing, she thought. It had become one of the principal business streets in the city, lined with specialty shops devoted to one type of merchandise. Each had show windows that displayed the commodity sold within, and Marie, the worst of her passion spent, paused now and then to glance at the samples on view in the windows. In the windows in Woodlief's there were beautiful soft marceline silks, organdies stamped in daring designs, and imported French calicos, all in the bold, bright colors that were in vogue. In Madame Frey's window there were mantillas, *visites* of thin muslin, magnificently embroidered, lined with blue silk and trimmed with blue cords and tassels. If her humor had been better she would have smiled. This fashion of the white women was almost like the symbols of her office as a voodoo queen! In other shop windows there were male garments—coats of blue and bottle green, bright vests designed in patterns of flowers and leaves, pantaloons of tan and green, and even bright yellow silk hats rubbed to a blinding brilliance. There were shops that specialized in mourning—at least two, Marie noticed, one for women, the other for men; both draped their windows funereally and filled them with black garments. There was a shop that sold veils, and two that sold gloves. There was Madame Olympe's, the window crowded with her imported Parisian *chapeaux*.

When she left the church, Marie wasted no more time but hurried home. As she entered her yard she saw little Marie Philome playing beside the house, wrapping pebbles and small shells and bits of dirt in small pieces of cloth. "Mamma, I'm making *gris-gris!*" Marie Philome announced proudly.

This forced a smile from Marie. She touched the child on the head lightly as she passed. "I hope it is good *gris-gris!*" she called back.

She went beyond the house to the kitchen. Rose was pounding a block of salt on a board and making a great noise. Rich smells came from the pots hanging over the low, glowing fire in the great brick fireplace.

"I will finish supper," Marie told her. "I have an errand for you." She told Rose what she wanted her to do. She wanted her to take a ball of black wax in which blood was mixed and roll it into the yard of Doctor John. It was a simple *gris-gris*, one she had often used to frighten people when it was necessary that they be frightened, and she did not really believe it would scare Doctor John. She knew only that she had to do something, and she imagined that it would make her feel better. Then she saw Rose's face. It withered. All the wrinkles deepened and she drew back her purple lips and showed her broken, yellowed teeth.

"You will not do it!" Marie cried in a temper. "Do you refuse me? I have never beaten you, Rose! I have never struck you!"

Rose said nothing, but she hung her head and sniffled.

"So you're afraid of him, too!" Marie shouted. "All right! All right!" She strode out of the kitchen and stood in the door, the last rays of the sun lighting her face. "I will take it myself! I will do everything myself!" She caught her breath, then she asked, "Do you think he's so powerful as that, Rose? Do you think he is more powerful than I am?"

Rose mumbled.

"Speak up!" Marie cried. "I cannot understand a word you are saying!"

"I said he wasn't as powerful as you," Rose muttered, her words seeming to come from deep inside her, "but people say he's bad. I don't want to take a chance." She began to whimper.

Marie walked away. "Fool!" she gasped to herself. "Fool!"

At the first moment of complete darkness Marie left her house and walked to Doctor John's and rolled the ball of wax she had prepared into his yard.

The next afternoon the bell on her gate clanged and Rose, appearing to be half-paralyzed with terror, brought Doctor John to her a moment later. He took the ball of wax from a paper wrapping and laid it on a table. Marie glanced down at it and then straight into his face. She could have sworn for a moment that the third eye, the tattooed eye on his forehead, gleamed.

Then Doctor John grinned. "You did not expect to frighten me with that, my dear?"

Calmer than she had been the day before, Marie felt a trifle ashamed, but she said only, "Do not call me 'my dear!' "

Still grinning, Doctor John returned to the door. "I have been wondering if a partnership would not be best for us both, Marie Laveau," he said.

Marie quivered. "Never! You are impertinent!"

Doctor John departed, and Marie sat down in a rocking chair and twisted her hands together in her lap.

Chapter 10

THE SUN was already hot and bright on the sloping roofs as Marie and Rose walked toward the market that morning. They were late, for even when Marie accompanied Rose they usually went at dawn, so they hurried. Most of the market stalls, the butchers and the fishmongers closed at ten o'clock.

They had been delayed because Christophe had not come home until well after dawn, and Rose had refused to leave Marie and go about the marketing until he appeared. Christophe was eighteen now, and lately Marie had been conscious of his growing restlessness, but it was the first time he had remained out all night, and from the moment she had awakened and discovered he was not home she had been besieged with fears. Many things could happen to a young man during a New Orleans night; there were the rough cafés, the evil waterfront, the thugs that haunted the town streets.

But Christophe's breath had been free of any smell of rum or wine, and he had looked sleepy but undissipated. He had been talking all night to a friend, he explained, a painter, an older man who lately had given him some instruction; and it had been in this man's home. Christophe had been painting for two years now. He painted and sketched in his room every evening he stayed home, and Marie would sometimes find him painting in the garden in the early, pale light of morning before he went to work, for he had a job now that occupied him three days a week, serving in a coffee-house near the Place d'Armes. Marie did not like him working there particularly, but he had insisted upon doing it. He contended that the finest gentlemen patronized the place, and he learned much there. The rest of the week he read and studied and painted.

"One must worry about each of one's children," Marie said, turning her head to Rose, who walked slightly behind her, the empty market basket on her arm. "If not in one way, in another."

"He is a good man," Rose replied loyally.

Rose was partial to Christophe, Marie knew, so this did not help her to stop worrying. Marie was not sure Christophe was making of his life what a young man should. He was strong and handsome and growing more like Glapion in appearance each year, but his disposition was too mild and gentle. She saw no use in his constant painting of canvases, except perhaps to amuse himself—and she believed there were better ways for a man to amuse himself—and she still held to her lifelong belief that too much education was not good for a man of their race. She would almost have preferred that he had spent the night in frivolity than in talking it through with another painter, although she did not mind his reading.

The market spread before them—all the open stalls, the stacks of green vegetables and red and golden fruit, the hanging sides of beef, the fowl, the game, the rabbits, the moss-filled baskets of writhing crabs, the fish. The market had changed not at all in her lifetime, she thought. There were the same flies, the same smells; it seemed to her the same Indians crouched outside, and that the same coffee women cried their invitations at the corners. No matter how often she came here, nostalgia rose within her at every visit. This morning she even thought of Jacques Paris and how she had once rushed through the market to meet him on the levee and tell him that Monsieur Charles was coming and that now they might be married. Dear God! she thought. That was more than a quarter of a century ago!

When they left the market, Rose walking behind with the filled basket, Marie was still thinking of Christophe. During the past months, worrying about his future had almost driven the rivalry of Doctor John from her thoughts. If only Christophe had a good trade—if only he had a girl! But he displayed little interest in girls.

Christophe lay languidly upon the couch in her small parlor when Marie reached home. He wore the long dressing gown she had given him the Christmas before. There were pillows piled beneath his head and an open book rested on his chest. "I couldn't sleep," he explained. "You know I can never sleep in the daytime."

"Rose can make you a hot rum toddy," Marie told him. "I will go tell her."

"Never mind, Mamma," he said, gaping. "I don't want to sleep. I want to talk."

Marie seated herself and watched Christophe as he rolled over on his side, facing her. The book tumbled to the floor, but neither of them reached to pick it up. "You need sleep, Christophe," she said.

"I will try again this afternoon," he promised. "I suppose I must if I am going to the theater tonight. I have a ticket and I want to go."

He was always going to the theater, the opera. That was nearly as much an obsession as his painting, his reading. "You must not be out too late this evening," she chided. "Tomorrow is one of your working days."

He scratched his head and made a wry face. "One of my working days!" he said. "But let us not talk of that. Did I tell you of the pair I saw at the theater last week, Mamma? No, I did not, and I meant to at once. It was the Mamzelles Laveau, Mamma—Mamzelle Eugenie and Mamzelle Emilie. I wish you could have seen them, Mamma! So ugly and fat, and both unmarried, I hear. They are my aunts, are they not?"

"In blood they are your half-aunts," Marie said, staring at him. "And how did you know them, Christophe?" Never in her life had she seen any of her father's other children.

He shrugged a shoulder. "Someone pointed them out to me, Mamma," he said. "I can't remember. Whoever it was knew who they were."

She rocked silently for a moment. She had no wish to pursue the subject. She heard Christophe laugh. "So fat and ugly!" he repeated. "Old maids!"

She made a clucking sound of mild reproval, but she smiled.

"They looked so prim and prudish," he told her. "And what would they have replied if I had introduced myself? 'Dearest Aunt Eugenie! Dearest Aunt Emilie! I am your nephew, Christophe Glapion.'" But he did not laugh now. "At work sometimes I hear the white gentlemen talking about their colored children. They do not realize I hear. When I bring them their wine I am entirely invisible."

She frowned. "That is of no importance, Christophe," she said. "Son, let us talk of your work."

"My work?" He shrugged a shoulder. "It is only temporary. I am like a servant. I wait upon them and clean their cuspidors, but I have learned much. I will not do it much longer."

"What *are* you going to do, Christophe?"

He swung his legs over the side of the couch and sat up, both hands gripping its edges. "I thought you must know," he replied. "I am going to be a painter, Mamma. Perhaps in time I will write a little, too. I am told that I have talent as a painter."

"And how will you make a living as a painter, Christophe?" she asked anxiously. "What will you do? Do you want to wander through the country painting portraits of rich planters, making a living of the barest sort? I have heard of men doing that, but they were white men. I have never heard of a colored man doing it."

"Mamma," he said without hesitation, "I want to go to Paris."

"I see, Christophe," she replied quietly.

His eyes became wide and bright and for a moment she saw herself in him as well as Glapion.

"It would not cost you much," he said, his voice excited. "I could work my way over as many do, and in a short time I am sure I could support myself."

"I am not worried about the money, Christophe."

"Then there is nothing to worry about," he said. "In Paris everything is different, Mamma. If my skin is a little dark no one will care. There are many men like me who have gone there from here. It is the only thing to do, Mamma. I do not want to be a blacksmith or a carpenter or to drive a dray. I am not made for such work. I want to use my mind and my talent—whatever it may be."

Marie's throat tightened. "I do not blame you for that, my son," she told him. "But how can I know what is best for you? How can I even know what talent you have? I have no knowledge of such things."

"No one can know even about himself, Mamma," he said, "unless he has a chance to try. But think of the men of my race who have become famous in Europe, in Paris! What would they have been here? At best they might have kept shops, or, if they were lucky, prospered on a plantation. I'll agree some have done that, but they are so few. And I have no taste for keeping a shop or for farming."

Marie stopped rocking. "We will think about it, Christophe." She waited a moment and then she asked, "You would be gone forever?"

"Perhaps," he said, dropping his head and not looking at her. "That is the dreadful part of it. That thought hurts me, too, Mamma. But what else is there to do? Perhaps I could come on a visit, but if I succeed I must live there. Most of those like me who have gone there from New Orleans have remained. But think how wonderful it is, Mamma. There are men like Armand Lanusse!"

Marie knew of him. He was a poet, a writer, and she had paid little attention to him, but she remembered that he had published a magazine, *Album Littéraire*, which accepted the writings only of quadroon and octoroon poets and authors, and that he had also brought out a book in which he had collected the poetry of colored authors.

"But Lanusse lives in Louisiana, Christophe," Marie told him. "He did not remain in Paris. He came home."

"There are those who did not," Christophe said. "There is Paul Dalcour. There are Camille Thierry and Victor Séjour. They know all the great of Paris, Mamma. Séjour has had plays produced on the stages of Paris, and they have been great successes. They are famous men, these men of color, Mamma! They are respected and admired!" He took a deep breath. "Of course, none of them are painters, but I want to show what a painter of my race can do. At least *I* must know. Then perhaps I will come home, Mamma!"

He ceased speaking, and although Marie did not look up at him she knew his eyes were upon her, anxious, pleading eyes, so she did not think long. What was there to think about? "All right, Christophe," she said quietly. "I will help you. I will give you money, my son."

Christophe smiled and his face brightened. "Thank you, Mamma. You are good."

Marie rose and passed him. She touched his hair lightly. "You must be happy," she said. "You must do what you please with your life. And now I must see to the others." As she left the room there was a cold feeling about her heart. When Christophe had gone she felt she would never see him again. Another one of her children would be lost to her forever.

She needed to make even more money now. When Christophe wrote to her of his arrival in Paris she began sending him a monthly allowance. Also, she liked to help Noemi and Felice and their children. Jacques made good wages, but the husbands of the twins did not earn so much, and Felice and her husband already had two children; Noemi had one and was pregnant again. With Jacques' two, Marie was now the grandmother of five. And her own children at home were getting older and bigger, and costing more each year. She began to plan ways to earn more money.

There was always Doctor John to fight, for there was no doubt but that he was taking more clients from her every day. She began leaving more and more *gris-gris* about in the houses to which she was summoned as a hairdresser. They were of a harmless variety—little packets and sacks containing pebbles and dirt—but when they were found by servants, many would come to her house in St. Ann Street to buy other *gris-gris* from her for protection. It was true they sometimes went to Doctor John instead, and thus she was inadvertently giving him business, but that could not be helped. Most of the servants and slaves, knowing she had been in the homes of their mistresses, came to her. Doctor John did the same kind of thing, planting his *gris-gris* with the aid of some of his followers. The war went on between them, although they rarely saw each other during the year after Christophe left home.

The greatest blow that came to Marie that year was when a woman named Tessa, long one of her followers, left her to go and live in the home of Doctor John. Even before her, another Negress had gone to live with him, and there was also the strange white woman, whom Marie had never seen. People told Marie that Doctor John now boasted that he had three wives.

Marie put great curses upon him when Tessa deserted her, but no harm came to him or to his business. She had not wanted to do him any physical injury, but she worked hard to fix him so that he would leave the city. He did not leave. "He is a fake and a cheat," she told Rose, "yet he must have some power. I cannot get rid of him."

A sly glance shot out at her from Rose's old eyes. "In the days of Dédé she would have fixed him," Rose said. "There were all kinds of ways nobody but the queens knew about."

"Poison?" Marie took a deep breath. "I'm not sure even Dédé used it, Rose. It was gossip. I will use no poison. You know that."

"Maybe Dédé did not use it," Rose told her. "But the old queens before her used it. That I know. My mother told me, and her mother told her. It was the truth."

"I will use no poison," Marie repeated.

Rose shrugged. "He grows in his power over the people," she said. "He grows rich. There are many who find his work suits them, and they say he does no harm, only good most of the time. Together you would be greater than either of you alone."

Marie's eyes flashed at her. "I will never join with him!" she cried.

"In the old days there were always two—man and woman," Rose said. "And the woman always ruled in the end. The man became as nothing compared to her."

Without another word Marie left the kitchen where they had been talking. She walked across her yard slowly, pausing to kick angrily at a tuft of grass. Was that the way, then? To join with Doctor John and conquer him? No, she would not do that. It was unthinkable.

She heard giggling beyond the gate, and she recognized it as Marguerite's. Probably some boy had walked home with her today. They waited now outside the convent where Marguerite attended school. As she entered the house Marie was thinking of Marguerite, her white one, her proud one.

She was sixteen now, and often it was the white boys and men who followed her in the streets. It was not good.

Marguerite's long hair still glistened with golden lights and every night she brushed it for a long time before the mirror in Marie's room. One night when the girl was nearly seventeen Marie sat and watched her, as she had often done, pretending to sew but with her eyes and her mind giving all their attention to this most different of her daughters. Marguerite had ceased going to school, and Marie felt that a good thing; she had gone too long as it was. It was time for her to marry now. She should marry soon, and safely, within her race.

Marie still felt she had cause to worry about this, too. Marguerite seemed to take none of the boys she knew seriously except perhaps one, and Marie was not too pleased with that one. "I want you to take a cake Rose has baked to Noemi in the morning," Marie told her suddenly.

"Send Jean, Mamma." Marguerite held back her bright hair and studied one of her pink ears.

She must look as she does because of Monsieur Charles, Marie told herself, as she had done many times before. Or perhaps it was some ancestor of Glapion's that relived in her. Marie knew of other cases like this, of course, but it had astonished her for seventeen years now that Marguerite was a member of her brood. It was true she had somewhat the same slight bone structure of Marie's mother and that her eyes were large like Marie's own, but her skin remained so fair, her features so delicate. Yet her jaw was strong and her brow stubborn when she frowned, as she was doing at the moment. She was not frail or delicate or weak at all, Marie knew. She was as strong as the rest of them, and her pride was determined and fierce. She was a vain one, too.

"It is you who will take the cake to Noemi," Marie insisted. "You have not been to see her for a long time, nor to see Felice, either."

"All right, Mamma," said Marguerite in an exasperated tone of voice. "I will take the cake to Noemi."

"And do not be cross!" said Marie. "You do not even see Jacques very often. It is not the way for a family to be."

"They all come here often."

"When are you home?" asked Marie. "First you were always at school, and now you are gone nearly as much of the day, and heaven knows where! I am going to make a *gris-gris* for a husband for you."

Marguerite had started again to brush her hair. She put the brush down and turned around, her face even whiter than usual. "Make no *gris-gris* for me, Mamma!" She rose. "I am going to bed."

Marie raised her gaze slowly, and laid the half-finished dress she was making for Marie Philome in her lap. "Oh, I know you do not like the idea of *gris-gris*," she said. "Are you becoming ashamed of your mamma, my child?"

"Of course not, Mamma." But Marguerite did not look at her.

"To be a queen and the daughter of a queen, as you are, are not matters for shame," Marie told her. "Is it Georges Legendre who puts such ideas into your head?"

"I am going to bed," said Marguerite again, and started for the door. "I am sleepy."

"Wait until I am through," Marie said. "You are my daughter and you will listen when I speak to you. I know it is Georges you like, and I hear many stories about him. People say he has left his family. He does not live at home any more, and he avoids old friends in the streets. They say he is trying to pass, that he pretends to be one of the white Legendres."

Marguerite sighed. "What is so terrible about that?"

"He is a laughingstock," Marie said. "Everyone knows who Georges is. He is light, but he fools no one."

"Mamma, I'm very, very sleepy," pleaded Marguerite.

"I do not care about *him*," Marie went on ruthlessly. "I care only about you. I know he is the one you prefer of all the young men you know. I know, too, what is in your own mind, and I need no voodoo to know that. Last Sunday you and Georges were promenading on the levees with the white ladies and gentlemen. You were imagining no one knew that you were not one of them. You were wearing a bonnet like a white lady, which I suppose you made for yourself. I found it this morning and destroyed it. If you must cover your head you will wear a *tignon* like your mother!"

"You did that to me?" Marguerite's eyes were bright with anger. "You did that to me?"

Marie felt her own eyes fill with tears. "My dear, I did not want to!" She shook her head grimly. "I want only to help you, my poor Marguerite!"

"I will have other bonnets," Marguerite was saying. "I will never wear a *tignon!* I would rather be dead!" She took a deep breath and began hurling words into her mother's face. "Listen to me!" she cried. "We did fool them on the levee! No one knew we were any different. I don't care that some nigger recognized us and told you. What does that matter? You and your nigger spies, Mamma! If it were not for them you could not live!"

Marie refrained from reminding her that she would not have lived so well herself without them.

"You do not care what Christophe is doing in Paris!" shouted Marguerite. "That is all right. He is a man. You let him do as he pleased."

"He is a man," said Marie. "But it isn't that, Marguerite. He is in Paris. You are in New Orleans and customs here are different. Nothing but unhappiness can come to people like Georges. That is why I don't want you to be like him, my dear. That is why I don't want you to behave as you did

Sunday. I don't want people making fun of you or laughing at you."

Marguerite collapsed on the bed and buried her face in a pillow.

"Child, I am only trying to spare you suffering!" Marie went over and sat on the edge of the bed and put a hand on Marguerite's shoulder. "It is all vanity, Marguerite," she said gently. "It is not good for young people to be so vain."

"Vanity!" Marguerite turned over and sat up, pushing Marie's hand away. Her voice was hoarse. "You talk to me of vanity! You're a queen, Mamma, remember? A voodoo queen! A witch! An African witch—from the jungles! And you think I'm vain! The way you walk through the street, with your head high, and the *tignon* you want me to wear tied just so, with its seven points just so! And you talk of people laughing at me! Do you know there are those who laugh at you? Georges laughs at you, Mamma! He says it is all ignorance and foolishness. It is the ignorance of savages, and I must not believe in it. Well, I've never believed in it, Mamma! Never! Not even when I was a little girl. I lied to you a few minutes ago. It shamed me! It shames me now. I won't live like a black, Mamma! I won't live like a savage! You may do what you like. Put your *gris-gris* on me, Mamma, and see if it works! I defy it!"

As the girl ran out of the room Marie whispered, more to herself than to Marguerite, "I will put no *gris-gris* on you, my poor child, my white one. I will pray for you."

Marguerite stopped speaking to her. She ate her breakfast with Rose out in the kitchen, and then vanished for the whole day, coming home at dark and having supper alone. Marie saw to it that food was saved, and although she grew sick with worry she said nothing to the girl. Marguerite, she thought, must be spending her days with Georges Legendre; so when Jean told her Marguerite was working as an assistant in a Chartres Street shop she felt some relief. At least she was not with Georges all day, although Marie knew she was still seeing him.

She was selling bonnets and hats to the ladies, Jean said. She was assistant to a French woman who had opened a small millinery shop. A big, strapping boy these days, only a year younger than Marguerite, Jean giggled when he told her about it. "She will love that, her," said Jean in English. "She will put them all on that yellow head of hers and strut up and down like a canary on a perch."

"Speak to me in French," said Marie automatically, as she did whenever any one of her children spoke to her in English. "And do not make fun of your poor sister."

"My poor sister!" said Jean. "Sometimes I can't believe she is my sister. And why is she poor? She and that Georges! He is all she cares about. She does not even speak to you these days. I would give her a good beating if I had my way."

"Hush, Jean," Marie said. "Go busy yourself. I have work to do."

She went into her altar room and closed the door. She seated herself in a rocking chair and stayed there a long time. But the quiet of the room gave her no peace. She should not have destroyed the girl's bonnet. It had been cruel, although she had not meant to be cruel. She had meant only to bring her to her senses. But children were not as they had been when she was young, and one could not use force with them.

The next evening Marguerite did not come home at all. In the morning Marie went straight to Georges Legendre's house and, when his mother came to the door, demanded to know Marguerite's whereabouts. Madame Legendre, a stout woman with sculptured, Indian-like features, nodded wordlessly and admitted her. When she had closed the door behind Marie, she said coldly, "They are married. If I were you I would let them alone."

"I will let them alone," said Marie, and, going out, opened and closed the door for herself.

It was more than two weeks before Marguerite came home for a visit. The first thing Marie noticed when she saw her was her bonnet. It was fashioned of pale blue silk, all fluted and ruffled about the edges, and within the halo of it Marguerite's face was prettier and blonder than ever. It was true, Marie thought; a stranger would never know.

She was in the altar room when Marguerite came, and the girl stood silently in the door for a moment, then walked over and kissed her cheek. They both found it difficult to talk, and oddly it seemed a long time since they had seen each other. Their conversation was trite. Yes, she was happy, Marguerite said, very happy. She had kept her employment in the shop. She would for a while. They had moved to the Faubourg Marigny, below the old city.

"I did not want to hurt you, Mamma," Marguerite said as she was leaving, only some thirty minutes later. "I did not mean all the things I said to you that night."

"If you are happy I am not hurt," Marie told her. "It was only you of whom I have been thinking." She gazed deep into her daughter's eyes. "You will come to see me? You will see your sisters? Your brothers?"

"Yes, Mamma," Marguerite said. "Of course I will see all of you."

But she did not invite any of them to call upon her and Georges.

None of the news that came to Marie in regard to Doctor John pleased her. Some of it became so fantastic that she had difficulty in believing it, yet most of it turned out to be true. He was prospering. There were more women in his home, a new home he had built out on Bayou Road, only a half mile or so from where Marie held her St. John's Eve meetings. Some people said there were at least eight women there these days, others stretched the number to fifteen. According to some accounts he had bought some of these women as slaves;

according to others the women were all there voluntarily. The house was filling with babies, it was said.

It was said, too, that his clients were increasing steadily, and that more and more rich whites were going to him. Whenever Marie lost a client she assumed immediately that she had gone to Doctor John. Yet it came, in a way, to bother her less, or at least she was beginning to accept the competition of Doctor John. She had all the business she could handle as it was. If a client did forsake her for Doctor John, there were always new ones coming.

She rarely saw him. She had heard of the fine carriage and pair of blooded horses he owned long before she ever saw them. Then one day she did see the carriage pass through the streets, with Doctor John gripping the reins. On this occasion she did not even feel much anger. Let him be a spendthrift and waste his money, she thought. She helped her children, but she saved most of her money. In the end she knew who would win. And she was the queen, the leader. No one could take that from her unless she chose to relinquish it, and she would not be ready to do that for a long time yet.

But Doctor John grew more and more conspicuous. Once Marie saw him gallop down Rampart Street on horseback, his horse a magnificent animal, his saddle a handsome one of silver-trimmed leather, and Doctor John himself a garish sight in a bright red coat and a top hat of yellow silk. People stared after him and some shouted, and suddenly Marie realized they were looking at Doctor John and not at her. This time she was furious and she walked home swiftly. Something must be done. If she could not overcome him, she must overshadow him. He must not get so much attention while she had received so little from the people along the street, as had happened on this occasion. This had never happened to her before.

It was days before she decided what to do, and then the plan came to her with a flash. Congo Square must be reopened for the Sunday afternoon dances. It had been closed for a long time now, and the dances had always attracted so much notice. If only the ban could be lifted! Slowly, a plan came to her.

She knew it would not be easy to accomplish, but it was worth trying. She sent out word through her grapevine that she wanted the square reopened. Within a few days scores of Negroes working in white households began complaining to masters and mistresses that they wanted their Sunday afternoon dances in Congo Square revived. Within weeks this had spread to a great rumble of discontent. Slaves and paid servants became shiftless; cooking deteriorated; there was pouting and sullen looks. Marie wondered why she had not tried this before.

Then one day Marie herself was called to the home of a Madame Cambre, whose husband was a member of the city council, and Madame talked with annoyance of the behavior of her slaves in recent days. All her friends were complaining, too, she said. What had happened to the colored people? Until a little while ago her own had seemed so contented. "I am so good to mine," Madame said. "I fear I spoil them terribly, but now they act as if they are angry with me."

"The poor Negroes have so little pleasure, Madame," said Marie. "It is diversion they need. I have heard they want their Sunday afternoon dances resumed."

Madame raised her hands. "If I hear anyone mention Congo Square again I shall scream!"

"The dances were harmless, Madame."

"Yes, Marie," said Madame, giving her a look. "I have heard that you led them once."

Marie smiled, and laid a soft stroke of the brush on her client's hair. "They *were* harmless," she insisted. "If Madame could prevail upon her husband to speak in favor of them to the mayor it would help to make everyone happier."

"I will prevail upon him!" said Madame Cambre with determination and a heavy sigh. "I would do anything to get the help back into humor again. We can't go on this way. It makes me too nervous!"

Even Marie was astonished when Monsieur Cambre and a policeman came to her house a few days later.

"We know you are a leader among the colored people," said Monsieur Cambre firmly, but politely, "and I want you to know that I for one do not entirely approve. However, it is true, also, that I see no harm in the Congo Square dancing. At least it is better to allow the dances than to have the blacks so discontented."

Marie suppressed her excitement. "Monsieur is wise."

"I can make no promises," continued Monsieur Cambre, with a scowl cast toward the ceiling. "I am neither the police nor the city government, but I have come to ask a promise of you. If the dances should be permitted to be resumed, would you cooperate in keeping order? Mind you, I do not say they will be."

Marie nodded solemnly. "I have always cooperated with the law, Monsieur."

Monsieur Cambre gave her a doubtful glance.

"I will attend all the dances, Monsieur," Marie told him, "and I will see to it that order is kept."

The ban was lifted in the fall, and again people poured into Congo Square on the first afternoon it was reopened to them. The only change was that a policeman was posted at the gate, but this did not matter to Marie. He was a man who had several times been her client, and she knew him well. At this very moment, she reflected as she entered the square, he probably carried *gris-gris* he had bought from her in his pocket.

Monsieur Cambre was at the gate, too, and she greeted him, expressing her pleasure that again there would be this recreation for the blacks. He wiped his brow. "It was mostly to please my wife that I prevailed upon the mayor to permit this," he confessed. "You know how women are! And now you must keep your word to me. If there is any trouble I will find myself in difficulty."

Two men carried in the cage containing Marie's snake, and she followed them, Monsieur Cambre staring after them and shaking his head slowly. "All my life I have had a horror of reptiles," Marie heard him remark to the policeman.

The musicians played and the dancers whirled. Marie did not dance this afternoon, but stood on the Vodu's box, sometimes calling out encouragingly. As the dancers passed her they often touched the box and sometimes her blue skirts. The crowd grew and grew, for word of the reopening of the square had spread swiftly through the grapevine of the slaves. Spectators filled the streets outside, too. They had come in carriages and on foot, and they lined the *banquettes*, vying with each other to peer through the pickets of the fence. Once Marie glimpsed Doctor John among those in the street. He sat high above everyone, on horseback. But he remained only a few moments before he rode away. Marie raised her head toward the sunny sky and shouted for another dance to begin:

> "*Danse Calinda, boudoum, boudoum!*
> *Danse Calinda, boudoum, boudoum!*"

Chapter 11

It was Marie's old friend, Baptiste Dudevant, who asked her to visit Numa Ballino in the parish prison. Baptiste still went to sea, but upon his return from each voyage he always visited with her. Upon this occasion he was in a state of great distress. He had returned to find Ballino, his cousin, sentenced to a term of five years for theft. Poor Numa, he explained, was really a good man with a heart of gold. Perhaps he was guilty of breaking into the sweetshop and robbing it of five dollars, and he must be, for he had been captured by a watchman as he had left the shop, but Numa had committed this crime only because he had been unemployed lately and his family was hungry.

Marie promised to go and to take him a bowl of gumbo, although, as she told Baptiste, she could do nothing more. The man was already sentenced. She would make *gris-gris* that might effect a shortening of the term he would serve, and she would take him a lucky *gris-gris*, too, but what else was there to do? Her heart always was with those locked within the horrible jail, but even she could not give them power to walk through its walls and bars. She confessed to Baptiste, also, that she had wished often to try to help these unfortunates. Real crime she detested, but the law could be more cruel than any criminal. Five years for five dollars! Was a man's life worth only a dollar a year? The law was not Christian! Neither were people. A man like Ballino should be able to go to the sweetshop and ask the proprietor for five dollars, and he should receive it without hesitation on the part of the proprietor. He did not do so because of the way life happened to be. Why had he not come to her, Marie Laveau? Poor Numa Ballino! Yes, she would take him gumbo.

Baptiste escorted her to the jail the next morning, carrying the bowl of gumbo in his hands, wrapped in heavy napkins. Ballino was a lean, gruff man. He grumbled at them, then grew silent, and let her gumbo get cold.

"Numa, eat!" Baptiste would beg.

At last Numa Ballino ate the gumbo, spooning it up noisily, spitting out bits of crab and shrimp shells upon the floor. When he had finished there was much belching. Then he leaned against the wall behind the cot on which he was sitting and closed his eyes and sucked on his teeth.

"Was my gumbo not good?" Marie asked him.

"What is good in a house of death?" Ballino replied, without opening his eyes.

"You are not to die here, my child."

His eyes sprang open, and there was terror in them. "You have not met my friends?" he asked. "They are to die."

"You have friends, Ballino," Marie said. "Only a good man has real friends."

"Did you bring me rum?" asked Ballino. "Rum is a friend."

"Numa, be quiet," Baptiste said.

Ballino touched the *gris-gris*, the pale blue bag Marie had pinned to his shirt.

"You must tell me about your friends," said Marie.

Ballino sprang from the cot. "Go!" he shouted. "Go! I must live worse than an animal for five years, and you will be free! I will be tortured and beaten! Go! Go!"

Marie and Baptiste left. In the corridor she touched his arm. "And who are these friends?"

"Let us go home," Baptiste said.

"Tell me!"

"They are white men," Baptiste told her. "Their names are Tony Deslisle and Jean Adam, Marie. Does it matter?" He put an arm around her waist.

Marie removed the arm with a firm hand. "I should like to see them now, Baptiste."

"Let us go home."

"No, Baptiste," she said. "And do not touch me like that again!"

The men sat listlessly in their cells.

Baptiste talked of the men behind the bars as if they were in a circus. "They are murderers," he said. "They are rapers. They raped and killed a young girl, a servant of Madame Chevillon's, who had hired them to paint her house. The law is just."

"Bless you, my children," murmured Marie. "I will come back. I will bring you gumbo."

The man named Deslisle laughed grimly. "Bring us gumbo and coffins, Marie Laveau," he said.

Baptiste was cross as they walked home together. "You must not visit such animals," he told her. "They are truly beasts. They are not like Numa, who is not really a criminal at all."

"We are judges of them, Baptiste?" she asked.

"In this case, yes!" he replied. "Let me tell you of their crime. They were house painters in the employ of Madame Chevillon when they discovered that she kept more than a thousand dollars in cash hidden in her home. One day when she was out they were taking it, and Madame Chevillon's young servant—a mulatto—saw them. When she tried to prevent them from taking the money, they raped her and cut her throat with a knife. They had been hiding in the swamps more than a month before the police caught them. Hanging is too good for those men!"

"I knew of the case, Baptiste," Marie said, "and I think

it as horrible as you do. Yet perhaps the wicked need our help and our mercy more than the good. I will take them gumbo."

Baptiste muttered to himself, and they did not speak again until they reached her gate. There Baptiste said, "You are good, Marie. Always you are too good."

She laughed. "Few people would say that of Marie Laveau!"

"Few people know you as I do."

He raised a hand as if to touch her and she saw an expression in his eyes she had seen often before. She stepped back a little, smiling warmly. "Good day, my friend," she said. "Come to see me again, my good friend."

When the gate was closed she walked slowly toward the house. She was fifty-five. It was nonsense to think of Baptiste as she was now. She had long known that he wanted her, but she had never given it serious thought. She had never thought that there could ever again be a man for her in that way. There had been Jacques and there had been Glapion. There would be no others. She had thought of Baptiste only as a friend. The men who had approached her she had always quickly repulsed. She prided herself always upon her respectability. There were the children and there was her work, and that was her life. It was enough. Don't spoil it, Baptiste, she prayed. Any woman can have a lover. Marie Laveau needs a friend.

She took gumbo to Adam and Deslisle the next day. They were still silent and sullen when she tried to talk with them on that occasion, but when she returned one morning a week later she saw gratitude in their faces for the food she brought to them, and even, perhaps, for her own presence. She returned within another week, and this time they welcomed her almost with joy. After that she went every morning with food, for she had seen the horrible prison fare. She and the two men, with the weeks diminishing between the present and the date of their executions, became friends.

They talked much, but it was curious conversation. They talked never of the immediate past, and of course never of the future. The crime for which they were convicted was never mentioned, and Marie asked the men no questions. Most of their talk was of the far past. Deslisle was a Frenchman, and he liked to recall his childhood in Marseille, from which he had come. He would ramble for a long time about his home there, his parents, his brothers and sisters and playmates, and it seemed that to him that had been his real life, and that it had all only been yesterday.

Jean Adam had been reared in the country, in a village on a Louisiana bayou. He had arrived in the city only a few weeks before "the trouble," as he on a single occasion referred to the reason for his present plight. He had a wife on the bayou and a young son, he told Marie, smiling boyishly, for he was only twenty-two. They were fine and healthy, and had had many good times together. He talked much of these times.

Marie often wondered after she had left them what had brought this about. Probably it was greed for money and nothing more, but why then had they not spared Madame Chevillon's young slave? When had the beasts been born within them? No one could ever know, probably not even the men themselves, she reflected. Now that they had become so friendly toward her, they seemed to her like any other young men. There were even moments when she felt almost as if they were her sons.

Nor in these conversations did she talk to them of voodoo. On the first few visits they had made feeble jokes about it, but when they discovered that she considered the subject no matter for joking they ceased this. She brought them no *grisgris*. She did bring them holy pictures, which they tacked on the walls of the cell they shared. And every day before she left she knelt and prayed with them, not for their release, but for their souls.

As she became a familiar figure in the prison corridors and in the yard outside, she came to know Father Casteau, the prison chaplain. The priest would often meet her as she left and walk across the yard to the gate with her. They would talk of the men within, of the weather, or only exchange pleasantries, but soon the priest met her so frequently that Marie began to suspect it was by design. He well knew her identity, but never did he, either, refer to voodoo.

Then one morning he said quite suddenly, "I want to thank you, Marie."

"Thank me, Father?" she replied.

"You have done much good for the worst of my poor charges." He was a small man who was compelled to look up to her, and now he looked up with sad, dark eyes.

"It is pity I have for them," she told him. "If I had not come, there would have been no one who would have done so."

He frowned slowly and kicked a pebble out of his path. "It has amazed me," he said. "I suppose that is a confession and it may even be a rude one. But you have brought them religion, too. I have wondered if you have not done more for them than have I. Yes, it has amazed me, I must confess."

"I am glad if I have brought them religious help, Father," Marie said, "although I doubt my powers to aid them much in that way."

"Your powers astonish me, Marie," he murmured. "I would not attempt to gauge them. But will you come to the prison often? I would be grateful if you would see others here, even after—after these poor men are gone."

Marie hesitated, but she could not stop her reply. "I will come to any who need me, Father," she heard herself saying.

Baptiste came to see her often during this period. He remained kind and gentle and he listened while she talked of her prison visits without noticeable disapproval, although she knew he did disapprove in his heart, and that it was only that he had decided not to openly oppose her in this again. He made love to her only with his eyes. He even consented to make the coffins. Adam and Deslisle wanted coffins badly, so that their bodies would not go naked into the lime pit, and they had no money.

Baptiste balked slightly when she told him she had bought the men a cheap grave and that she would claim the bodies. Father Casteau had won a consent from the authorities for her to do this. "It is going too far!" Baptiste said.

"The poor things!" Marie replied. "I must do this."

Neither did Baptiste want to accompany her to the execution. "You must not go, either," he told her.

"I must," said Marie. "I hate it, but I must!"

Baptiste stared at her with a peculiar expression. "Is there something in your head you have not told me?" he asked.

She tried to smile. "Probably many things," she said. "But in this instance, Baptiste, it is only that I must finish what I have begun. You must come with me to the execution. I cannot bear to go alone, for I have never been to one since the hanging of Pauline."

"Probably I shall become ill," said Baptiste with a sigh, "but I will go."

"On the morning of it I will take them much rum," Marie told him. "That I can do for them."

The rum had done them good. Adam had to be carried out of jail, across the yard and up the steps to the gallows platform. Deslisle appeared supported by two jailers. As he emerged into the pale morning sunlight he broke away from one of the men for an instant, although the other still gripped his arm. He flung back his head and shouted, "I'll fix you! I'll fix all of you!" As the jailer from whom he had released himself seized him again, he roared, "Have you noticed my fine coffin?" The coffins lay on the cobblestones beneath the gallows.

Marie grasped Baptiste's arm and looked up at him. His face was green, and she wondered if her own might not be the same. Her heart was pounding and her throat was constricted. "It's ghastly!" she whispered hoarsely.

They were almost in front, for they had come early. Father Casteau had persuaded the jailers to admit her to the men. She and Father Casteau had prayed with them, and she had given them the rum. Father Casteau had nodded in sympathy. Afterwards she had come out into the courtyard and joined Baptiste, who had awaited her there, leaving the condemned men with the priest. Looking at them now she knew that when Father Casteau's duties with them were completed they had consumed the rum rapidly.

When she had rejoined Baptiste the courtyard was already filling. They had waited for hours and all the time people had kept coming. Now the courtyard was filled with a crushing crowd that spread out to the street beyond. It seemed to her that all New Orleans must be here. It was a far larger crowd than had attended the hanging of Pauline, and there was the same atmosphere of a circus. Even at this moment, with the jailers dragging Deslisle up the steps to the gallows, the spectators laughed and shouted. There were children. Fathers held them on their shoulders so that they might see better. Men and women murmured that this was too easy a death for the monsters on the platform. Others munched on bits of bread and sausage or cheese that they had brought with them.

Above all the other chatter and din, Deslisle roared out, "I will have a fine funeral! I want a splendid procession!" He attempted to bow drunkenly. "You are all invited, my friends. All of you must·attend."

"Let us go," Baptiste muttered. "Why must you be here? There is nothing more you can do for them."

Marie glanced up at the sky; it was blue and serene; the sunlight was gently golden. "I must stay, Baptiste," she said. "It will not be long now." She forced herself to look toward the platform. Adam's arms were already bound. None too gently a deputy forced him into the chair that was his. His head fell forward, and he seemed entirely unconscious. Thank God, Marie thought. She looked again. There was still difficulty in forcing Deslisle up the steps. Twice he had fallen. He still shouted out at the spectators. "I am a citizen of France!" he roared. "I will not die to please barbarous Americans!"

"Marie, we must get away from here!" Baptiste had his hands over his face.

She turned to him. "Hush!" she chided. "It will be but a moment."

Then there was a piercing scream, violent, bleating, that drowned out all other sound.

Marie stared. Deslisle stood upon the platform now, his arms raised toward the sky, his head bowed. Beside him stood Father Casteau, his cross pressed to his chest, his gaze upon the sky. The sheriff, the jailers and the black-garbed executioner all were staring up at the heavens. Deslisle flung his head back and screamed again. Marie saw it too, now. In the blue and sunny sky hung a single black cloud. It moved swiftly toward them, and as it moved it spread and grew.

The crowd rustled and moved. People muttered and whispered. The light went suddenly and the whole sky was black. The courtyard had been bright. Now it was gray and shadowy. Baptiste squeezed Marie's arm. "My God! My God!" he muttered.

A woman cried, "It is just like the crucifixion!"

Marie shook off Baptiste's grip. Again there was movement on the platform. Deslisle was bound and forced into his chair.

Father Casteau stood before each of the men in turn, his crucifix held before him. Marie could see his lips moving. Deslisle made no further sound. His head wobbled on his neck, and Marie was certain he had fainted and was now as unconscious as Adam. The black hoods were fixed over both the men's heads, and the twin ropes were placed and tightened about their throats. Thunder roared and lightning split the sky, and suddenly rain came down in a deluge. The sheriff raised his hand in a signal, and the executioner sprang the trap. Behind her Marie heard people running from the scene. She knew they were running from the rain. Then she heard women who had remained, screaming.

Even through the blinding rain Marie could see the sheriff and the other men on the platform peering down into the opening of the trap. And beneath the open platform she saw Deslisle. He was crawling about on his belly, his face covered with blood, his mouth twisted in sobs she could not hear. People surged forward, carrying Marie and Baptiste with them. Policemen began forcing the crowd back, flailing away with clubs. Baptiste seized Marie about the waist and dragged her to one side, holding her tight against him. "I must go to them!" she cried. "They're alive!" She had seen Adam move, too. He lay upon his back, but one of his legs had moved convulsively. Lightning still rent the sky and the rain poured down.

"Hush!" Baptiste said, his mouth pressed against her ear. "Be still." She was still struggling to free herself from him. "We might be trampled to death by this mob!"

She realized vaguely that Baptiste was not as frightened now as he had been before, that somehow this hellish scene had strengthened him, and she ceased pulling away from him. The din went on. She could see almost nothing now. "What happened?" she gasped.

"The nooses slipped," Baptiste told her. "Poor fellows!"

Even Baptiste felt sorry for them now, she thought. Baptiste had released her since she had quietened, and she stared back toward the gallows. No one was on the platform. "They've carried them into the prison," Baptiste told her. "We must go, Marie."

She would not go. A man moved past them a moment later. "They're bringing them back out," he was telling everyone. "They're to be hanged again."

The mob was under control now. More people hurried away and vanished into the street, but many remained. They began talking again, and opinions were divided.

"Good! Good!" a man said. "The devils must be hanged if it takes all day."

"It was the will of God," a woman protested. "He sent the storm to save them."

The jailers carried Deslisle and Adam back up to the platform, and again Father Casteau stood before them, his garments drenched. The hoods again covered the now bloody heads, the trap was sprung. This time the ropes stretched taut. "We will go home," Marie told Baptiste. Wet to the skin like everyone else, she tried to arrange her *tignon*. She brushed raindrops from her face and raised her head.

As she and Baptiste left the prison courtyard, moving slowly with the crowd that had remained, she was conscious that many people were staring at her, recognizing her. The rain ceased suddenly, and before they were home the sun was coming out again. "A summer cloudburst," she remarked to Baptiste. "It is strange how they come and go so quickly."

Baptiste made a peculiar sound that might have been either a groan or a chuckle. "Don't you know what people are going to say?" he asked.

"Baptiste, my friend," she replied. "I am very tired."

It turned out that Baptiste had been right. She heard the gossip even before Baptiste brought her a newspaper a few days later. "Thousands among the citizens of this city," wrote a reporter, "give credit to Marie Laveau, the voodoo High

223

Priestess, for the storm that interrupted the execution of Deslisle and Adam. It did seem that the floodgates of the heavens were opened suddenly to deluge the world again. However, whether the dark sorceress had anything to do with the matter or not, our determined sheriff and his deputies overcame both witchcraft and weather and justice was done."

"The fools!" said Marie. She knew that her name was often in the newspapers now, but she seldom read them. Too many times had it been called to her attention that they made fun of her, and she had come to detest the sight of her name in print. She had often threatened within her own mind to put a curse upon anyone who wrote of her.

"Don't mind it," Baptiste told her.

She walked across the altar room, the newspaper in her hand. She stopped before the alabaster box wherein her Vodu slept and tore the paper to shreds and threw it on the floor. "I do mind!" she said. "Why should I not mind? They make a laughingstock of me. Doctor John will laugh at me, as I laughed at him when he tried to save Pauline." She stooped before the cage. "Vodu! Vodu!" she crooned. "We will show them, won't we? We will show them, my pretty one." Her Vodu was a new snake. When any one of them died, she had a new one brought to her in secret from the swamp, for many of her people believed the Vodu could not die.

Baptiste lifted her to her feet with his hands on her shoulders. "Marie," he said, "I wish you would retire."

She turned to him, her eyes blazing with anger, although she was not angry with Baptiste at all. "Retire!" she cried. "Do you think I'm so old?"

"I don't think you are old at all," he told her.

"Then why should I retire?" She raised her head. "When my time comes I will appoint another queen. That is the law, Baptiste, and you know it. I do not know who it will be yet, but I will. A queen can always tell. But I have a long time yet, Baptiste."

"Marry me, Marie," Baptiste said. "Marry me whether you retire or not. We are both free, and there is no reason why we cannot be married."

All the anger went out of her. It was the first time he had ever asked her to marry him. Baptiste was a bachelor, and she had never known him to want to marry anyone. He was more than ten years younger than she was, and the offer touched her and flattered her, as impossible as it was.

"We are both lonely," he was saying. "Yes, I know you are lonely, Marie. And soon you will be alone. Only Jean and Marie Philome are here with you, and you know it will not be long before they are gone like the others."

She said nothing, but she knew it was true. Her other children grew more distant every day. Christophe seldom wrote any more. Marguerite had not been to see her since Christmas. The others were busy, involved with their own families. She let Baptiste go on, tempting her almost, almost making her wish she were any woman but Marie Laveau.

"I have little to offer you," Baptiste said, "but my love and devotion. Yet I'll be a good husband to you, Marie. When your children are gone I will be here. That is something, is it not? Why don't you answer me, Marie?"

She left him and seated herself in her rocking chair and closed her eyes. "I thank you, my friend," she said quietly.

"You thank me?" he cried. "What does that mean?"

She looked at him. "It is best that Marie Laveau does not marry again, Baptiste," she said. "Besides, I've no mind for marriage now, nor taste for it. Let us be friends. As I've told you before, I need a friend, but not a husband, my dear. Or a lover."

"I will not force you, Marie," he muttered, staring into her face and moving his head from side to side slowly.

"You could not force me, my dear," she said. "But I thank you and I bless you."

She continued to go to the prison, to visit Numa Ballino and, eventually, other men locked in the bleak and dirty cells. As the weeks passed she decided that the gossip and rumors of her attempt to save Deslisle and Adam had actually been of great value to her. Her clientele grew to such volume that she had to select those for whom she would do her work and to force those who sought her out to make appointments in advance for visits with her at her cottage. The men in prison greeted her eagerly, even the gruff Ballino, and she saw to it that she went at least once a week, usually on Saturdays, a day when she received few clients at her home. At last she felt that if anyone had laughed it was only Doctor John, and she no longer cared if he did.

Father Casteau became even more her friend. They met frequently and chatted, but he never mentioned the storm that had occurred that day, and she had no idea what he thought about it. Neither did he ever say anything to her about voodoo. She knew the subject would be hateful to him, so she was glad he did not.

Toward the end of summer Baptiste returned to sea. She had continued to see much of him, but he had made no further proposals, no advances. She missed him after he had gone, but she thought his going might be best for them both. He might rid himself of the idea that there could be more to their relationship than there was now. Too, she had begun to depend upon his presence too much. Marie Laveau must not become too attached to anyone.

In August Rose died, and Marie was deeply grieved, although Rose was very old and had lately been of little use. Marie found her in the kitchen one morning, stretched on the brick floor, her eyes and mouth wide. Marie buried her in the tomb she had had built for Glapion and the children taken from her by yellow fever. She would have no more servants, she determined. Marie Philome, although somewhat loath to do so, could help with the household chores until she married. There were only the three of them now, and probably Jean would soon marry, too. Then she would really be alone, Marie thought. And she thought of Baptiste. Baptiste, my friend! My friend!

All her children, except, of course, Christophe, attended Rose's funeral, even Marguerite. Marguerite looked somehow furtive and frightened to be there, and Georges did not come with her. He had never come to see Marie, nor had she ever been to their home. Don't they know what they're doing, Marie often wondered. Why are they ashamed of our race? What is wrong with it? Even Monsieur Charles was proud of me, and he loved me. Didn't Marguerite and Georges, and all the others like them—for there were many such in the city—realize that by denying their race they were declaiming to the world that they considered themselves inferior to the whites they pretended to be? They must always wear masks; they must live secretive lives. It was so foolish, she thought; so pitiable.

All her other children, except perhaps Christophe, seemed to be so much happier—Jacques, with his brood; Noemi and Felice, with theirs; and even Jean, bringing his girls home to see her. Marie Philome was a little different, but it was nothing, Marie always told herself; at least she was not like Marguerite. About Christophe, Marie did not know. She had not heard from him in more than a year, although she still sent him money each month. But then the mails took such a long time, and he must be busy.

In the fall the yellow fever came, and it was not the usual, rather mild, epidemic. There had been nothing like it since 1832, people said, exactly twenty years before. They whispered, too, of the Asiatic cholera, and again the pitch was burned, the sky blackened; there were the flights to the country by those who could find refuge there; there was the rattling of death carts through the cobblestone streets, the cries of "Bring out yo' dead!" in the night, and the finality of lime.

Marie again became absorbed with the sick. She went no more to the prison, and all other problems became inconsequential; her clients sought from her only protection from the plague. She used all the old methods, the ones she had used in 1832 and in the smaller outbreaks since—the little bags of camphor, the burning of onion slices, the encirclements of salt. She lighted no fire in her yard and she instructed her neighbors not to do so.

When the epidemic subsided no one she knew intimately had died or even been ill, despite the fact that the newspapers reported thousands of deaths in the city, and she was shaken with amazement that her own people had been immune. It was true the newspapers said that old residents of the city, and colored people in particular, no longer contracted yellow fever, that it afflicted only Americans and other newcomers, but she did not believe this. It was more doctors' nonsense. Her people praised her and said that she had saved them.

Just after the first of the new year a letter arrived from Christophe. It was a happy letter. He was married to a pretty French girl, and he had secured a position in an art gallery that paid enough to support them. Mamma need send no more money. He adored Paris, and he wished he had the powers to describe it to her. The other evening he had actually met the great Corot at a party given by his employer, and once he had seen the great Rousseau, although he had not yet met him. Also, wrote Christophe, he had a young friend named Edouard Manet, who, though but twenty, painted like a genius. If only he could paint like Edouard! None of the names meant anything to Marie. Who was "the great Corot," who "the great Rousseau"? Only one thing she knew. Christophe was happy, and that pleased her. Yet mixed with the joy was pain, for she knew Christophe would never come home.

It was a week after she received Christophe's letter that she met Father Casteau on the street. He greeted her with a smile, but he demanded, "Why have you neglected us? We have missed you."

She promised to come and asked how his prison charges had fared in the epidemic.

Not one had been touched, he replied; then he asked, "Marie, are you glad of the new law, too? I have thought that you must be."

She frowned. "The new law, Father?"

"Child, do you not read the newspapers?"

She admitted that she did not, and added, "I do not read well, Father."

Public executions were now forbidden, he told her. They had been outlawed after the frightful ordeal suffered by Deslisle and Adam. "I thank our Lord for this favor," Father Casteau said. "They were barbarous exhibitions out of place in this modern age, that appealed only to the most cruel and evil emotions of men."

Marie gave a great sigh of relief. "Oh, Father, I am so glad!" she cried. "You cannot know!"

"So we must thank our Lord for the storm," said the priest, "and for the sufferings of those poor men." He stared coolly into her face for a moment; then he smiled. "Come to visit us, Marie."

"I will, Father," she promised again.

So she went back to the prison a few days later, a basket on her arm. She walked through the corridors, stopping at each cell to give each man some of the food she had brought in her basket.

It was Numa Ballino who said it. She had just entered his cell one day and seated herself on his cot. He was standing, leaning against a wall, drinking the hot coffee she had brought him and munching a rice cake. He smiled in a way she knew meant he was glad to see her; then he said, "They are thanking you for the law against public hangings in murderers' row." He smiled again. "I thank you, too. Some day I may want to commit a murder, and then I may choose to be hanged in private."

She smiled back at him. "Ballino, you are a fool."

He shrugged. "Perhaps."

"Once," she said, "men were sawed in half in the Place d'Armes. That, too, is no longer the law. Times change."

Ballino shoved another rice cake into his mouth and washed it down with coffee. "Perhaps," he said.

When Madame Chevillon sent for her, Marie thought at first it must be pure coincidence. The note was delivered by a slave. Would the Widow Paris come on Tuesday afternoon to arrange the madame's coiffure? Marie even wondered for a moment if it were the same Madame Chevillon. It was so much a coincidence.

Madame's mansion was on Royal Street, however, the note said. Marie knew the house well. She gave balls of which all New Orleans talked. She was said to be beautiful and eccentric, even a little mad. On Tuesday evening she was giving another ball. Marie sent a note of assent by the slave. At least she would gain admission to the house of the Chevillons, and who knew what might be gained by an acquaintance with Madame?

The house on Royal Street was of gray stone, three stories in height, its entrance set flush on the *banquette*, with an impressive gate of iron lacework leading to steps that, in turn, led to the immense doors of bronze, each with thick panes of cut glass. On both the front of the house and its sides were arabesque figures and scrollwork in classic designs, and above the windows at the upper stories were stone figures of angels and cherubs. Hesitating to enter at the front, Marie went down the side street at the corner of which the house stood, searching for another entrance; but there was only a carriageway far to the rear, with barred iron gates shut and bolted, so she returned to the front. The gates were open and on the door was an immense knocker in the form of a cherub. She lifted his legs and rapped several times, as she supposed she was to do.

It was only a few moments before a butler, an elderly black man in a peagreen coat, cut in an old style, and maroon trousers, answered. He led her up curving mahogany stairs, across a wide hall floored with marble tiles of white and black, and into huge drawing rooms. "Madame'll be here in a minute," he said in English, and left her.

Marie stalked about for what seemed hours, yet she knew it was actually only a quarter of one. Yet she was not entirely sorry for the wait. It gave her an opportunity to inspect the rooms, for, although she had been in many fine houses, until now she had never seen such a residence as this.

The rooms were huge and divided by folding doors, pushed back now into the wall, and the division of the rooms was unbroken by portieres, as was the fashion. There were pale golden draperies at the windows, but these increased rather than diminished the bright light pouring in from the sunny day outside. The walls and the ceiling were pure white, and from the ceiling of each room hung a crystal chandelier of enormous proportions, each prism glittering and gleaming as if it had been polished only a moment ago. The divans and chairs were all done in white and gold, the carved mantels were of impeccable white marble, and each held only a clock of the French fashion, also in white and gold. There were no pictures, no portraits, no mirrors. The total effect was bare and stark, and yet somehow of incomparable elegance. Marie kept wondering why she had been received here, in these rooms. In most houses she was directed straight to her client's boudoir.

The butler came to the door. He had a stony, roughhewn face, but he smiled faintly when Marie started at his appearance. "You come on with me," he said, and Marie followed down the hall toward the rear of the house. "Widow Paris?" called a woman's voice from an open door, and Marie entered.

Madame Chevillon walked toward her. She was a small, pretty woman in her middle thirties with golden hair done in the Grecian style, bright curls adorning her smooth forehead and her cheeks before each ear, and the great knot at the back of her head caught in a net embroidered with pearls. She wore a loose white tunic of a filmy material that fell to her ankles, and golden sandals. With one swift glance Marie saw that Madame's boudoir was all white and gold, as were her drawing rooms.

"Did you feel her in there?" Madame asked. She smiled faintly, widening her blue eyes and lifting her perfect eyebrows. "I put you there in hope that you would, although it is the wrong time of day."

Marie raised her own brows, not knowing what the woman was talking about. "Madame," she said, "I am afraid you have the advantage of me."

Madame Chevillon laughed, and it was musical laughter, as pretty as her person. "You are the great Marie Laveau," she said, "and you felt nothing? It is too much." She turned her back, walked gracefully to her dressing table and sat down. "Come in," she added. "Marie, I did not invite you here to arrange my coiffure. I arrange my own."

"Then why was I asked here?" Marie remained in the doorway, hating the woman. She was not used to being taunted.

"Come in! Come in!" Madame Chevillon repeated. She was looking at Marie in the mirror above her dressing table. "You are the great voodooienne. I have a ghost. She is the ghost of the girl who was murdered by the painters I hired, in whom I am told you took so much interest. The girl's ghost

232

does not bother me, nor frighten me, but I prefer my house without her." She turned and looked Marie in the eyes. "Can you get rid of her for me? She was killed in my beautiful drawing rooms, and at times she returns to them, usually at dusk. It is annoying and embarrassing, at least at times. You will please remove her for me. I will pay you well, Marie."

Marie entered the room and stood over Madame Chevillon. "I know little of ghosts, Madame," she said. "It has little to do with my work. But I will see what I can do."

Madame smiled again, this time more pleasantly. "Good," she said. "Come tomorrow at five-thirty. We will be alone. My husband is in Charleston, and there will be no servants here but Herbert, my butler, who, strangely, is not afraid of poor Melanie. Goodbye, Marie!"

As Marie left the house, her only feeling was that the house was too quiet. Where were the other servants? A couple like the Chevillons should have many, yet it seemed no one was there but Madame and the stony-faced Herbert. Madame *was* a little mad, she decided, just as people said.

But she returned the next afternoon, and when Herbert led her into the drawing rooms Madame was awaiting her there, seated on a golden divan and wearing a white riding habit with immense and flaring skirts, slit at one side. "It is good to see you," she said at Marie's entrance. "She will come today. I am sure of that. Did you bring what you need? Poor Melanie! I do not want to hurt her! She has been through so much! I want only that she stay where she belongs now."

Marie put the bag she had brought upon a table. "I understand, Madame."

"You will not harm her?"

"Of course not, Madame," Marie reassured her. But she felt compelled to repeat, "I know little of ghosts. My spirits serve me, Madame, my saints answer my prayers. I am not even sure I believe that the ghosts of ordinary people ever return to us. Your note did say that I was invited here to dress your hair for a ball you were giving."

Madame Chevillon laughed so coarsely that the sound did not seem to come from the pretty woman on the divan. "I did fool you, didn't I?" she said. "Sit down, Marie Laveau, the great voodoo queen! You should indeed be able to help my poor murdered Melanie!" She picked up a short, thick riding crop from on the divan beside her, which Marie had not noticed before, and began tapping the side of one of the boots she was wearing. "We listen, Marie." She spoke in a whisper. "We listen!"

Marie seated herself. Madame Chevillon was really insane, then, she was thinking. There could be no doubt. After a few moments of silence she said, "I can purify the rooms for you. I have brought salt and brick dust, and they will give you powerful protection. I have brought candles and *gris-gris* that will help you."

"Hush!" whispered Madame. "That will do no good in the case of Melanie."

Marie frowned. She wanted to rise and walk about the room. Madame's monotonous beats with the riding crop upon her boot were getting on her nerves. The minutes passed, and she heard nothing. She asked suddenly, "Why did you ask me here? Perhaps I cannot help you."

The woman gave her boot an especially hard blow. "You must be quiet, Marie Laveau." Her face was suddenly twisted, her eyes wide and venomous. "If you will not be quiet," she cried, "I will give you this whip in your face!"

Marie sat upright in her chair, too startled to rise.

"I hate you!" Madame raved at her, and slashed the whip through the space between them. "Did you not know that? You loved those men who murdered my Melanie! The gossip travels, Marie. Your house is filled with the skeletons of babies, I have been told, and you attend criminals and murderers in the parish jail." She dropped her arm, and the

234

riding crop fell from her hand upon the rug. She bent her head and began to cry. "Yet I thought you would help me! But even Melanie's ghost will not come when you are here."

Marie rose. "Good day, Madame," she said quietly, picking up her bag.

Then a woman shrieked. It was a piercing scream that came from somewhere above them and to the rear.

Madame Chevillon's face was buried in both her hands. "That is not Melanie," she whimpered, almost like a child.

Marie felt her body growing cold from head to foot, and her legs trembled beneath her as she walked out of the room and down the stairs.

She was almost home when she noticed people coming out of their gates and their houses and moving toward her. And then she heard their excited conversation. There was a fire. They were rushing to a fire. She turned around and forced herself out of the shocked state she had been enduring. Gray and black smoke was rising in huge rolling clouds against the sky. Then she smelled it and wondered why she had not done so before. She stopped a man, a neighbor she knew well. "It is a fire," he told her. "They say it is the mansion of the Chevillons on Royal Street."

She thanked him and went through her gate. Marie Philome was coming toward her across the garden. "Mamma, a fire!"

"Yes," Marie said. "Yes! Let us go together."

They stood together in the crowd on the *banquette* across from the house. Smoke belched from the roof, and firemen were setting up ladders and clambering in windows, although the front door was sprawled open. "They say she tortured her slaves," Marie Philome said, "and that one of them set the place afire."

"Where do you hear such things?" Marie asked. "And why do you pay attention to such gossip?"

"It is true," said a woman standing near them. "I have heard it for years."

"Mamma, you never pay attention to anything," Marie Philome said. "If I were like you, if I could do what you can do, I would know everything."

"Be quiet," Marie scolded. "No one knows everything, child." The crowd grew, pressing upon them. "I was in there only a few moments ago. Madame is sick. It is her brain. But I do not believe all the evil I hear."

"Perhaps it was the ghost of Melanie," Marie Philome said. "Perhaps the ghost of Melanie set the place on fire."

Marie gave her a stare. She had not heard of the ghost of Melanie until she had heard of it directly from Madame, yet this child of hers had known. But then young people got about more and so heard more talk than their elders.

"Screams come from that house every night," said a man. "I have heard them. All the neighbors have."

Marie thought of the shriek she had heard, that of a creature in torment, and a creature alive, not dead. Madame herself had said it had not been the ghost of Melanie.

There was a sudden movement in the crowd then, and Marie Philome gripped her sleeve, pulling her toward the corner. Marie went with her, with the crowd. Everyone seemed to be shouting at once, as the mob moved in that one direction. Marie's head throbbed with the noise and she wished for a moment she had remained home, but she was helpless now. There was nothing to do but move. Marie Philome was yelling in her ear, "Mamma! Mamma!"

Then Marie saw it. They were at the side street, and she saw Madame Chevillon's carriage gates swing open, and a white carriage rush into the street. On the box was Herbert, the butler, still clad in his antique uniform, and behind him was Madame, standing up in the carriage, fierce and erect in her riding habit, slashing her crop down on Herbert's shoulders, just as he flailed the two horses with his whip. The crowd sprang back, people screamed, dust blinded them, and the carriage was soon a faint speck in the distance. The crowd made a deep breathing sound in unison that was like a giant's sigh.

White men began rushing into the house—policemen, firemen, neighbors.

"We will go home," Marie told Marie Philome, and took her firmly by an arm, for she knew the girl would not want to go. "It may be there are things you should not see, my child."

She heard the rest of it the next day, and it was Marie Philome who told it to her. Marie Philome had been out all morning, and she came rushing in at noon with the news. The police, the firemen, and the other men who had entered the house had conducted a thorough search. In the attic they had found nine Negroes, slaves of the Chevillons, chained to the walls, and obviously victims of torture. Taken to the hospital, they had mumbled stories about Madame. They had been beaten with whips, burned with fire, starved, and kept bound in terribly painful positions. The instruments used to torment them had been found, too—the whips and spikes and rusty nails. An old cook had set the house on fire, deciding that the excitement might bring an end to this cruelty in one way or another, for even had the tortured slaves died they would have been better off than living such lives as were theirs.

"The poor things said," related Marie Philome, "that Madame would sometimes excuse herself in the middle of a ball she was giving, and go up to the attic to amuse herself for a while with the whip."

"There was no ghost of Melanie," Marie said. "That was only Madame's conscience and her insane mind."

"She and her butler got aboard a ship," said Marie Philome. "She must have paid well, but then she is very rich. People say she has gone to Charleston to join her husband." Marie Philome's cheeks were flushed with excitement. "The crowd was so angry they tried to destroy the house. They tore down the big chandeliers and sent them crashing to the floor, they stripped wallpaper from the walls, and tore carved banisters from the great staircase. Only the police stopped them from razing the house to the ground with their bare hands, Mamma!"

Marie was not pleased with the girl's excitement. "Let us talk no more of this," she said. "Madame Chevillon will never return to New Orleans."

"Mamma," Marie Philome asked, "did you not feel anything was wrong when you were in that house?"

"Only that there was no ghost of Melanie," Marie replied, "and that Madame was mad. I was not there very long."

"I think I should have felt it," said Marie Philome.

Marie looked up and saw something not far from scorn in her daughter's face. "Go busy yourself in the kitchen," she said quickly. "There is much work to do. And do not boast to me again. The chick must never boast to the hen!"

Alone, she sat frowning and rocking. She had not liked what she had seen in Marie Philome's face.

Chapter 12

Marie resumed the Friday meetings in her yard in the spring. She had suspended them during the epidemic, and had not resumed them in the winter, for it had been a cold and rainy one. She planned an especially elaborate St. John's Eve celebration that year, at which her people would give thanks to the great powers that protected them for escaping the plague, and so she gave much time that spring to preparing for the bayou meeting.

But it was not to be. Early in June the fever returned, and this time with far more intensity than the previous year. Once again any attempt at normal living became futile, and once more all Marie's work was concerned with the protection of her people. All summer it raged, until there came what was to be forever known as "Black Day," which was the last day of August. Later the newspapers reported that 230 persons died of the fever on that one day. After that it began to abate. As it faded away Marie made inquiries through her grapevine about her followers. None had died, and only a few had been ill. Jean brought home newspapers, and in them it was stated that among those residents born in the city there had been comparatively little illness, relatively few deaths. It was true that more than seven thousand persons had died from yellow fever during that frightful summer, yet of these only eighty-seven had been native New Orleanians.

In October, after a time when not a single case of the disease had been reported, Marie resumed her Friday night meetings, the Sunday afternoon dances in Congo Square, and her Saturday visits with the prisoners. Again her clients came to her with problems concerning love and money and luck. Also, that month, Baptiste came home, and to supper.

She was delighted to have him back again, although she tried to conceal from him the magnitude of her elation. She had missed him and she had been lonely for him; and this afternoon she was particularly lonely. Jean was out as usual, and her young Marie Philome was in one of her bad moods; there were frequent such bad moods lately, when Marie Philome was cross and sullen. Even with Baptiste there she scarcely spoke through supper, and afterwards went to her room, saying she had sewing to do.

Baptiste had been quiet during the meal, too. He had not looked at Marie often, and it seemed almost that he was somehow embarrassed, which Marie supposed might be natural enough at this first meeting since his return. But with Marie Philome gone and his wine glass filled he brightened and talked of his trip, and asked for news of her and what had gone on in New Orleans during his absence. They talked of such subjects for more than an hour, and he became more as he had been before. He did not try to make love to her. He understood how things between them must be, she thought. She had been right in her belief that his going away would be good for them both. Poor Baptiste! She felt that her affection for him had increased, although not in the way he had once wanted.

At last he asked about the children, and she confessed that she worried about all of them at times, but that now—she supposed it was natural—she was concerned mostly with the two who were home. "As I once told poor Rose," she said, "one worries about each of one's children. If not in one way, in another."

Jean was a good boy, she explained, but he was never home. She had bought him a fruit stall at the market, which was not what she had wanted for him. But even that did not matter. The truth was that he was not diligent. He would stay out late at night and then not be able to wake early enough in the morning to open his business. He chased all the girls, but did not settle upon one. It was true he was but twenty, but she was distressed about him and had been for some time. Only the epidemic and all her work had delayed her having to do something about it.

"And Marie Philome?" asked Baptiste. "She is so like you."

"Do you think so?" she asked. "Many people do. She looks like me, I suppose, or as I did at her age. Yet sometimes I think she is not like me at all, Baptiste. You saw how she was at supper. She is quite angry with me."

Baptiste smiled. "She is young. Many young people are like that. It is a phase that passes."

"Nonsense," Marie replied. "She is eighteen. She should be married. I like to see my daughters married. I was so old when I married first. Twenty-five! Baptiste, do you know she pays no attention to young men? She ignores them. Until now not one has called upon her. It worries me."

"A beauty like that!" Baptiste's face was filled with amazement. "Like you, Marie. So much like you, as I said a moment ago!"

"It is not that they don't seek her out," Marie told him. "They do. Baptiste, I wish she were different! There were reasons for my late marriage. My mother was ill, and I had to care for her. There is not that in the case of Marie Philome."

Baptiste shook his head. "Give her time. Some girls are slow to be women."

"She is stubborn," Marie sighed. "She grumbles about everything. I must force her to do the simplest household

241

chore, and I hate forcing my children. Do you know what she wants to do, Baptiste?"

He replied with an expressive movement of his eyebrows.

"She wants to help me with my work," Marie confessed, and saying it made her tremble slightly. She had told no one before, and she wondered why she was telling this to Baptiste.

He shrugged. "And so?"

"None of my other children have been interested in it at all," she said. "Noemi and Felice married young, and before that they cared nothing about it. They would sometimes watch the meetings from the side gallery or from a window, but only out of curiosity. That was all. As for Marguerite, she despised it and hid from it. The boys were not interested. The first of my children to be so is my youngest, my Marie Philome. When she was a child she played at making *gris-gris*. Then I thought it was only a game. Later she asked me to teach her things. I did teach her a little. It was still a game. Do you know why she is angry with me at this moment, Baptiste? It is because I will not consent to let her assist me. I have women to do that, Baptiste. Not my child!"

Baptiste's eyebrows were very high now, but his eyes were narrowed. "Why, Marie?"

She frowned and took a long time to answer. Then she said, "I don't know, Baptiste."

"She is like you," he said once more. "Don't you see? She is you again."

"No!" she said vigorously. "No! No! No!"

"I do not understand, Marie."

"Perhaps I don't, either," she admitted. She made a futile gesture with her hands. "No, I suppose I don't really know. Or perhaps it is only that I want her to have a better life than mine."

242

"And what is wrong with your life?" he asked. "You have power and money. You have had love and children."

Marie nodded. "Yes. Yes. I know."

"You are respected."

"And feared?"

"Perhaps that, too. There are those who delight in being feared."

She nodded again. "There may have been times when I have, too," she said. "Baptiste, it has been a good life for me, yet it isn't one to pass on to my child. You know all about my life, my friend; I believe I have told you everything. If Jacques Paris had not gone away, and we had had children, and I had not entered the work . . . but what is the use of going into that? I did begin the work, and Jacques went away and died. Baptiste, do you think we make of our lives what we want? Not what we think we want, but what we really want?"

"Who knows?" asked Baptiste. "And who knows that Marie Philome is not right in what she wants? You must have a successor. You have often explained the law to me, and I have heard you say that once it was not unusual for daughter to succeed mother."

Marie felt the blood rushing to her face. "I will not have it, Baptiste," she said. "I will never allow it!" She sighed heavily. "I do not mean to sound angry." Then she asked, "Why am I such a child with you, Baptiste?"

It was late one Saturday afternoon when she caught Marie Philome. She had come home from visiting the prisoners, and as she opened her gate a woman was coming down the walk from the house. The woman was heavily veiled, and Marie could tell nothing about her appearance except that she was white. In her hands she held a small parcel. Marie saw her eyes give her a piercing look through the veil; then the woman bowed curtly and went out. Marie slammed the gate, and the bell hanging above it jangled loudly. She grasped her skirts and ran toward the house.

Her intuition told her where to go. Marie Philome was seated in the rocker in the altar room. On her head was one of Marie's *tignons*, tied in seven knots. Marie stood in the door for a moment, staring at her, and thinking for the most part: My God, she is like me! Baptiste is right. She is almost exactly like me! The girl glared back, her eyes as wide and as large as her mother's, the clear whites showing beneath the pupils. Her red lips were slightly parted; her nostrils quivered noticeably.

Marie crossed the room, and with a gentle movement took the *tignon* from her daughter's head. Marie Philome rose, her head raised, her chin proud, and her long black hair tumbled down her back. They faced each other in silence for a long moment; then Marie Philome lowered first her lashes, and at last her head. Marie was the taller of the two, and she looked down upon the creamy center part in the girl's hair. "Did you tell her you were Marie Laveau?" she asked suddenly.

Marie Philome raised her head. "No, Mamma."

"What did you tell her, then?" Marie twisted the *tignon* she had removed from her daughter's head in her hands.

"I told her nothing, Mamma. She did not ask. A friend had sent her here."

"But she accepted you as Marie Laveau. A child like you!" She appraised Marie Philome with her eyes. Did she look so much a child? She was not so large as herself; she was shorter, slighter, but she was not small, and with a *tignon* on, and in this darkened room, she might not look a child to a stranger.

"She wanted only a love philter and some candles," Marie Philome was saying. "I knew enough to instruct her in their usage. I was only trying to help, Mamma." She drew some crumpled bills from her bosom. "Here is your money."

"Keep the money," Marie said coolly. "Buy yourself material for a dress or something for your trousseau—something appropriate for a girl your age." She waved the *tignon* in her hand at her. "Go start supper. I'll come help you in a few minutes."

Marie Philome turned her back, went to the altar and laid the money upon it; then she went out and closed the door.

As she prepared for bed that night Marie studied herself in her mirror. Her face had not changed much, she told herself. She did not look her age; she looked no age. The lines running from her nose to her mouth had deepened, it was true, and there was a crease between her brows, but there were no wrinkles in her face. There was no flabbiness. The skin still stretched tightly over her high cheekbones and her chinline was clear-cut and hard. She unwound her *tignon* and began brushing her hair. There was white in her hair; streaks of it ran from her part to the very tips. She removed her gold earrings, laid them down and rubbed the lobes of her ears.

"Mamma."

In the mirror Marie saw Marie Philome standing in the door in her nightdress, her hair hanging in two plaits over her shoulders. "Yes, Marie Philome?" Marie was more out of patience with her than ever. They had had another of those sullen, silent suppers. Of course Jean had not come home to help matters. Now he was sometimes gone for several days at a time.

Marie Philome came in and sat on Marie's bed. She had been through this so many times before, Marie thought. There had been the scene with Marguerite in this very room. That had been very different, but she wanted no sort of scene. There must not be one now. "I'm very tired, Marie Philome," she said.

"Mamma, why won't you teach me?" Marie Philome turned her head a little to one side and fingered one of her plaits. She smiled, almost wistfully. She had never looked like that before.

What to answer her? Marie did not know. She said, "Don't be coy with me, Marie Philome. You are not like that."

Marie Philome let go her plait and raised her chin. "I am never coy," she said. "I am like you. So why won't you teach me?"

"For one thing, you are too young," Marie said hastily. "Go to bed, child."

"I am nineteen," Marie Philome said.

"I was nearly ten years older than you before I started learning," Marie told her, "and I was thirty-five before I really knew anything." She turned from her mirror and faced the girl. She knew the question was foolish, yet she asked it. "Why do you want the knowledge? Why do you want the power?"

Marie Philome met her gaze evenly. "Why did you?"

"I want you to have another kind of life, my dear," Marie told her. "I want you to have a husband and children and a home. I do not want you to have the problems I've had. I want a better life for you."

"You had a husband," the girl replied. "You had children." She kept looking into Marie's face. "I care nothing for a husband or for children. Mamma, I want to rule after you. I want to be queen. I can go on learning until I'm thirty-five —until any age. Then I will be ready."

Marie was suddenly so chilled that she wondered if her face had changed and if Marie Philome noticed. She thought even her heartbeat must be loud enough to be heard. She wondered why she was thinking now of Dédé and Marie Saloppé. Then she heard her own voice saying, as if she had been speaking to a stranger instead of to her own child, "Marie Laveau will choose her successor when the time comes."

There must have been something awful in her face then,

she was to reflect later, for Marie Philome rose suddenly from the bed and the color drained from her face.

Marie took a deep breath and somehow composed herself. "Oh, go to bed, Marie Philome. This is all nonsense. It is a phase you're going through, that's all."

"All right, Mamma." Marie Philome's voice was hoarse, and she started toward the door. At that moment she looked like a little girl. Her white nightgown fell straight from her shoulders to her bare feet; her plaits dangled; her expression was one of injury.

"Come here, my child." Marie closed her eyes and stretched out her arms. "Come kiss your mamma goodnight."

Marie Philome turned and went back to her. She kissed Marie, and then crouched on the floor at her feet, her cheek on Marie's knee. Marie stroked the smooth head fondly, affection welling within her, and shame for the things she had felt and said. "My youngest," she whispered. "My baby!" She kissed the girl's forehead.

Marie Philome looked up at her. "Mamma, may I come to the bayou on St. John's Eve?" she asked. "Just this one time? I've always wanted to see the celebration. I will be very quiet. I will sit close to you and take no part in it."

"No," Marie said. She shook her head firmly. "Perhaps some day, but not this year. Do not ask me again, Marie Philome."

The girl was already on her feet. "All right, Mamma," she said. "I will not ask again this year. I will go to bed now."

Marie sat watching the door through which Marie Philome had passed for a long time after the girl had gone. Why must she have this trouble with Marie Philome? And why did she mind that her youngest wanted to be a voodooienne? Perhaps another queen would be proud that her daughter wanted to succeed her, but Marie knew she was not. Perhaps later she would learn to be so if Marie Philome persisted in wanting to do the work. When she is much older, Marie thought, when I am much older. In any case she would not have Marie Philome coming to the St. John's Eve rites at this time. The girl did not know what went on during them, and although Marie knew she could protect the girl she did not even want Marie Philome to know, let alone to see.

It was during that spring that Marie began teaching young Marie Philome her hairdressing art, however. Marie Philome had long shown talent for this, and Marie thought she should develop her skill. It would be a way for her to make a living whether she married or not. Too, Marie was accepting fewer and fewer clients, and she planned eventually to hand over all of them to Marie Philome.

She was soon taking Marie Philome with her on all her calls at the great houses along the Esplanade and to the mansions of the rich Americans uptown. Her customers were all amazed and charmed with Marie Philome. The first time a client saw them enter together, so startlingly alike, and dressed in similar fashion—for Marie saw to it that Marie Philome wore a *tignon* too during these visits—the reaction was always the same. The lady would cry out in surprise. She would never have expected to see such a resemblance in her life, she would gasp. It was unbelievable! Everyone in the house must come and see the two Maries. How remarkable! Marie was proud of this. One afternoon she went shopping and she found a pair of gold hoop earrings that duplicated the ones she always wore, and she fastened them to Marie Philome's ears with her own hands. After that some people declared that, at least at a quick glance, they could not tell one from the other. People stared after them in the street and as they rode uptown in the horsecars, and whispered. One a little older than the other, one a little taller than the other, Marie would sometimes overhear them saying, but as much alike as twins otherwise.

The whole matter seemed to disturb Baptiste, however.

248

He was, insofar as Marie knew, the only person who disapproved of it. "I do not like it, Marie," he told her bluntly one evening. "You discouraged her learning to be a great voodooienne such as you are, yet in every other way you encourage her to imitate you."

Marie smiled. "It amuses us both and it attracts attention," she told him. "Surely it is no harm. Why do you object, my friend?"

"Perhaps I do not know the answer to that," he replied. "Except that there can be but one Marie Laveau, and I think it's unwise to allow Marie Philome to be a second one. Do you know some people who have never seen you point her out on the street as 'Marie Laveau'? It is not good."

"And why not?" asked Marie. "It can do no harm. I am not jealous of my child, Baptiste. I hate mothers who envy their daughters. It is not for that reason that I forbid her to do voodoo work."

"Then perhaps I am jealous for you," Baptiste said.

Baptiste aided her more than ever in the preparation for this St. John's Eve. And when the fires were lighted and the people had gathered, he sat on the platform with her. He was not truly a "king"; he did not wear the blue cord, nor any of the insignia; but he was as close to that rank as any man in her cult had ever been. As the dances began she was wondering whether she had been wrong in always refusing to have a king reign with her, but she felt she was right. Marie Laveau must always reign alone.

The ceremonies were almost over when Marie saw the girl standing at the very edge of the clearing. She was half-concealed by some brush, and she must have thought she could not be seen, but Marie saw her plainly. The figure was unmistakable, the way she held her head, the tumbling black hair, for she had left home her *tignon*.

"Baptiste!" Marie gasped. "Look at her, Baptiste!"

Instead Baptiste looked at Marie herself, as if he thought her ill, for she was groaning to herself.

"Baptiste," she moaned again, but as an order now, "get her and bring her to me! How did she get here? I cannot understand it!" She had heard no sounds of horses' hoofs, but there was so much noise.

Baptiste had seen the figure now, and in a moment he was pushing his way through the dancers. Marie Philome ran, but he caught her, and brought her back to the platform. She did not struggle when she stood before her mother with Baptiste still grasping one of her arms. Instead she raised her head defiantly and pulled away from him.

"You deliberately disobeyed me," Marie said slowly, still finding this hard to believe. "You came, anyway. You broke your promise."

"Mamma," Marie Philome said, "I did not promise not to come! I promised not to ask you again if I might come this year. That is all I promised you."

Marie shook her head, gazing about her. No one seemed to be noticing this scene, except the two women assistants who sat on the steps leading up to the platform. Marie rose slowly. "We will go home," she said. She turned to one of the women. "Malvina, you will take my place for the rest of the night. Baptiste, you will take us home, please. Bring the collection of money, and we will go."

No one spoke again until they were in the little cart in which Baptiste had driven her to the bayou. Then Marie asked Marie Philome quietly, "How did you get here? Did you walk?"

Marie Philome tossed her head. "I did not walk."

"Then how? I must know."

Marie Philome was silent for a few seconds; then she said, "Perhaps I had better not tell you."

"And why not tell me? I will know in time. I will find out."

Marie Philome squirmed in her seat. "All right," she said. "I suppose you will. Doctor John drove me to the bayou in his carriage."

"Doctor John!"

"He came to the house just after you left," Marie Philome said. "He wanted your permission to come to the bayou tonight. Then he offered to take me."

Marie could scarcely speak through her rage. "He has not been to the house for years!" she cried. "He did this on purpose." She turned violently toward Marie Philome. "Have you ever seen that man before?" she demanded. "Have you ever talked with him before?"

"I have never talked with him before," said Marie Philome, sighing. "I have seen him, yes. And what harm is it to talk to him? He was very nice, at least at first. But then he left me here. We were supposed only to take a look at what was going on and then he was to drive me home in his carriage. Then I lost him, and when I searched for him he was gone."

"You little fool!" Marie snapped at her. "Don't you know he did it to hurt me? He did it on purpose. You asked him to take you to the meeting. I am positive of that!"

"All right," admitted Marie Philome. "I asked him. It was an opportunity to go, so I took advantage of it."

"My child, what am I going to do with you?" Marie cried. "What *can* I do?"

"Teach me the work," Marie Philome replied blandly. "Give me the power, Mamma."

"I must think," Marie muttered, more to herself than to Marie Philome. "I must think." They both sat in silence all the rest of the way home.

Marie Philome was silent for a week. Then when Marie came home one afternoon from a walk during which she had tried to clear her thoughts and to decide how to handle Marie

Philome, the girl was gone. Her bureau and *armoire* were empty of clothing, but although Marie searched her room there was no note.

For a while Marie stalked aimlessly about the house, her mind numbed by a sense of panic. She sighed heavily when she heard footsteps and she knew that for once Jean had come home when she needed him.

"Go out and make inquiries," she directed him. "But be discreet about it. We want as little gossip as possible. We must protect her reputation."

Looking frightened himself, Jean departed without protest, but he had been gone only a few minutes when she realized she must do something herself, and she knew exactly what it was she must do. She must go to Doctor John. That devil would do anything.

To her, the yard surrounding his house seemed filled with children. They tumbled past her, playing some game or other as she approached his front stoop, and she glimpsed two women washing clothes in the side yard. A small yellow woman she had never seen before answered the door after she had rapped noisily upon it. She demanded to see Doctor John, and the woman replied that he was not at home, shrinking back a little in a way that showed she knew Marie Laveau. "Let me talk to Tessa," Marie said. At least she knew Tessa.

Tessa appeared, hugely pregnant, her eyes filled with shame at the sight of Marie.

Marie glared at her fiercely. "Doctor John is really not here?" she asked.

"He is out," Tessa said meekly. "Louise told you the truth."

Marie hesitated, peering into the darkened house over the women's shoulders. She hated to tell them of the disappearance of Marie Philome. Now she was growing sorry she had come. She tried to reason that Marie Philome would not be here, that she had been a fool to come. If Doctor John had been here, or if she confessed her worry to these women, she would humiliate herself in the end. "Good day," she said suddenly, and turned and left them standing in the door, walking through the yard with her head held as high as possible, her wide skirts swinging past the romping children, her heart pounding.

Yet she was quieter when Baptiste came that evening. He grew angry for her as she told him about Marie Philome. "You can make her come back," he said. "She is still under age. You can get the police to help you!"

"Not yet," she said. "I will wait a while."

Baptiste stayed with her until Jean came home late in the night. By then Marie had become impatient with him. But she felt as soon as she saw him that he had really spent all this time searching for his sister.

"I've had no luck so far," he said at once. "But I have friends who will help."

"Get the police at once!" cried Baptiste to Marie. "Jean and I can go for them."

"No," Marie said firmly. "I will still wait. She was not kidnaped. She must have had plans. I won't make a fool of myself running to the police."

It was three days before news came to her, through the grapevine, of the sign in the window of a house in Bourbon Street that read: MARIE GLAPION, *Hairdresser.*

"I will go fetch her," raged Jean. "I will drag her home by her hair! She should be put into a convent!"

Marie smiled faintly, for her first reaction was one of relief that at least she knew the whereabouts of Marie Philome. "No, Jean," she told him. "You will not go after her and neither will I. She must come to me." She rose as the bell on her gate rang; she had an appointment. "After all, she is doing nothing wrong," she added. "I taught her to be a hairdresser. She must come back to me. I am her mother."

Doctor John came. She was alone in the house at that moment, so she answered the bell herself. She did not greet him politely. Still holding the gate with one hand, blocking his path, she demanded, "What do you want?"

He swung the hat he had removed a little in front of him. "You called upon me and I am returning your visit," he told her, grinning broadly.

"My purpose for coming to your house no longer exists," she said.

He leaned on the gate lightly. "Marie, don't you think we should cease to be enemies?" he asked. "We take nothing from each other."

"I disagree." She widened her eyes and stared straight into his. But then she released the gate. "Come in, if you like," she said coldly.

She led the way through the yard and into the house. She seated herself, and without invitation he took a chair opposite her. "What do you want?" she asked for the second time.

He shrugged his immense shoulders. "To be friends. We grow old, Marie."

"I can be a friend to one who is a friend," she said. "But you've never been that. Why did you bring my daughter to the meeting, John?" It startled her that she had called him by his name, and she saw in his face that it had not escaped his notice.

He still held his hat and shuffled it on his lap, yet his gaze was on her face. "The girl would have gone anyway," he replied, "if not this year, next. You know that as well as I do. That is one reason I came here today. I know the girl has left home. She sent me a message. She wants to become my pupil. My reply advised her to return home."

Marie willed herself into remaining outwardly calm, to let nothing show in her face. "This is your gesture of friendship toward me?" she asked gravely.

"I think it is that."

"Then I thank you," said Marie.

Still shuffling the hat, he rose. "Good day, Marie," he said.
She bowed quietly. "Good day, John."

Marie Philome came home the following morning, but she
brought none of her possessions with her. At first she seemed
somewhat subdued, but by no means contrite. As Marie let
her in, she said, "Mamma, I hope you do not hate me. I
want to come to see you whenever you'll let me." Suddenly
her stubborn expression changed. Her eyes filled.

"I don't hate my children," Marie said. She took her in
her arms, and with their cheeks pressed together, she whispered, "Marie Philome! My little Marie!"

They both wept openly when they were inside the house.

"Why did you go to *him?*" Marie cried. "To Doctor John
—of all people!"

Marie Philome buried her face in her hands. "I'm so
ashamed, Mamma! I was angry with you. You know what
an evil temper I have! Mamma, I'm so ashamed!"

Marie wiped away her own tears. "Do you want to come
home?"

"Do you want me to?"

"You must do what is best for you." It was difficult to
say that, but Marie knew it was what she must answer.

"How do I know what is best for me, Mamma?" Marie
Philome asked. She hesitated; then she said, "Mamma, perhaps I should live alone for a while. Already I think I can
make a living. Madame Desforges was passing in the street,
and when she saw my sign she came in to see me. I went to
her house to arrange her hair that very evening."

Madame Desforges was one of Marie's oldest clients. Marie
smiled, and waited.

"Mamma, you do not mind me taking her for a client?"

'Of course not," said Marie. "Marie Philome, when Doctor

John came to see me he said we grow old. It is true. For some time I've been considering abandoning hairdressing. If you like I will give you all my clients."

"Mamma, I did not mean for you to do that!"

"Of course not," said Marie. "But why shouldn't I? I am tired."

Marie Philome laughed. "That is nonsense! You're as young as I am, I sometimes think."

"That is something you do only think," Marie said lightly. "But never mind. I will direct them all to you. I will only do the work." She waited. There was something she wanted Marie Philome to say.

"I am not going to think about that any more," Marie Philome said at last. "I will be only a hairdresser."

Marie studied the girl, searching the young face—she hated to admit to herself—for any trace of a lie, for any deception. She saw nothing of the sort. "Make no hasty decisions," she said. "None of us know what we may want to do tomorrow or next month or next year. But, for the present, I will teach you only the trade of hairdressing. You must learn it well."

"I will work hard," Marie Philome promised. "I will be good. I will be as good as you, Mamma."

Marie winced slightly. It was always like that with Marie Philome. I will be as good as you. I will be better than you. Marie wondered what it was that she felt toward her daughter when she said those things. I am not jealous, she told herself. I am not jealous of my own child! It is like I told Baptiste. I could not be!

Chapter 13

EARLY on a Saturday afternoon Marie and Baptiste walked slowly through the Place d'Armes. It was a dark and chilly winter day, yet many people were out, and they stared at Marie as they always did. "Does it annoy you?" Baptiste asked. "No, I suppose you are used to it."

Marie smiled faintly, and kept moving on, her head held as high as ever, her gaze straight ahead. She was always perfectly conscious of the staring, and she knew what Baptiste meant. "If it annoyed me I should have lived my life in a rage," she said. "Does it make you nervous, Baptiste? My poor Baptiste! If it upsets you, you must discontinue our little walks."

"Never!" he said. "I was thinking only of you."

She paused and looked about her. "I have been walking here for so many years." She sighed. "It almost hurts me to come here now."

The changes. The old square was not even called the Place d'Armes any more, except by people like herself who would not change such ways of theirs as calling places and streets by their old names. It was now called Jackson Square, after General Jackson, who had saved the city from the British in 1815. Once it had been a parade ground for soldiers. Now it was a park, with curving paths and flower beds, stretches of grass and tall trees. In the center was a statue of General Jackson on his horse.

Marie looked at the statue. "I saw him many times," she told Baptiste. "Did you know that? I helped nurse some of his wounded, and I watched his parade of victory as it passed through the Rue Bourbon. It seems like yesterday." She sighed once more. "I am talking like an old woman."

"You will never be an old woman."

"Lately I feel very old," she said. "How do I look, Baptiste?"

He grinned. "You're still a vain woman. You look the same, Marie."

"Fool!" she said affectionately. "I'm in my sixties, and you know it. And you are no young colt yourself."

"I will wither of old age and blow away," he declared, "and you will still be the same."

But she had stopped listening to him for a moment. She was studying the changes about her. There were steeples on the St. Louis Cathedral now, three of them, one on each side and a third, and taller one, rising in the center. To her the Cabildo and the Presbytère seemed unaltered. Perhaps it was the buildings on each side of the square, on the north and the south, that made the whole setting look so different from the way it had once, for on these sides rose identical buildings of red brick, four stories high and each a whole block in length, with galleries adorned with black iron lacework and green shutters. On the ground floor were shops and above, for living quarters, were fine apartments still much talked about in the city.

Marie remembered the old shops and coffee houses and Monsieur Tremoulet's hotel that had once stood at those sides of the square. "But she loves the past, too," she said idly.

"Are you talking to yourself, Marie?"

Baptiste's voice brought him back to her attention. "I was thinking of the Baroness," she told him. "The Baroness Almonester Pontalba." She knew that the Baroness had built these fine buildings with the hope of coaxing businessmen and other people back to the old quarter of the city and away from Canal Street and the uptown section toward which business had long been drifting. "Do you know I knew her, Baptiste?" she asked. "She came to see me ten years ago. I think it was for curiosity, but she came. She has red hair and a long face like a horse, but she is charming, and very kind. She promised to write me from Paris if she ever heard anything of my Christophe."

"I did not know you knew the Baroness." Baptiste sounded impressed.

"She was returning to Paris that year," Marie told him, "and she came to buy *gris-gris* for her friends—I suppose to make them laugh, but I am not unused to that. What I sold her was harmless. Foolishness, perhaps. But she stayed and talked to me a long time. She talked about her father, Don Almonester, who built all that." Marie gestured toward the cathedral and the Cabildo. "Now she has built these new buildings. Father and daughter! All this is of their doing. She remembered so much. She is a bridge across time. All people who grow old are bridges. I am a bridge."

"Do you hate the changes?" he asked. "Everything must change—cities, people."

"No," she replied. "I do not hate them."

Marie began to walk again, Baptiste following. "You are in a nostalgic mood," he said.

"I told you I was old," she said. "But let me forget that. Perhaps the new things are better. Jackson Square is handsomer than the Place d'Armes."

"And you are handsomer than when I first saw you," he replied gallantly.

She glanced up at him. "You are incorrigible," she said. "Come walk home with me. I must go to the prison. It is my day to visit my birds." Lately she had taken to calling the

259

convicts this. "If I am late, they grieve. If you will stop at home for a moment I will make you a *gris-gris* that will compel you to tell the truth to old women."

Marie's nostalgia remained with her all day and into the night. She was much afflicted with it these days. Because she knew she would have trouble sleeping, she puttered about the house until after midnight, until after she heard Jean come in, walking unsteadily, yet, she knew, trying to be quiet. That one! she thought. He no longer even made a pretense of working, or of doing anything but drinking and chasing after women. When there was no sound from his room for a long time she went in and saw that he was sprawled across his bed in his clothing, sound asleep, having removed only his shoes. She covered him with a blanket, extinguished his flickering lamp and left him. What would become of Jean? she wondered. Perhaps he would just stay here with her. Well, at least he was here, and even when he was like this there was comfort in his presence.

When she went to bed sleep did not come for a long time, and as usual her thoughts were of her children. It had been five years since Marie Philome had left home, but she saw her often, and she did not worry too much about her, except for the fact that Marie Philome was still unmarried. She is almost the age when I married Jacques Paris, Marie thought. Would she and Jean ever marry? She determined she would make a *gris-gris* for a husband for Marie Philome the next day. Why had she not done so before? She could not decide, except that she had always known Marie Philome did not care whether she was married or not. With Noemi and Felice it had been a different matter. But, anyway, she would do it for Marie Philome, whether she would want it or not. It would be best for her to marry. Marie Philome was famed as a hairdresser these days, and she seemed to have forgotten the ambition she had once had to follow Marie into voodoo work. Marie wondered if she had really forgotten it. Did she practice a little, perhaps with some of her hairdressing clients? Of course not, Marie told-herself. Surely she would have heard of it. But Marie Philome must have a husband. It did not occur to Marie to make a *gris-gris* for a wife for Jean.

She often saw Jacques, of course, and Noemi and Felice, and their large families. Jacques had ten children, and he could not have supported them without Marie's help. But she did help him with money, and so he and his family were all right. Noemi and Felice each had many children, also—a half dozen or so each, Marie was always losing count of them— and she helped them, too, although they did not require as much financial aid as did Jacques. Those three, Jacques and Noemi and Felice, had always been good and affectionate, she reflected. Were they her best after all? They had been no problems except in regard to money, and that was nothing. Money was so easy to give.

Marguerite had never asked her for money. Indeed, she had refused it on the several occasions Marie had offered it to her. Marguerite came to see her perhaps three times a year now, bringing her three little girls with her, but always seeming nervous and ill at ease when she was there. She had given the three little girls American names, Agatha and Harriet and Margaret—in the latter case, Marie had noted, she even used the English and not the French form of the name. Marie suspected that Marguerite and Georges spoke much English, too, and she had come to feel this pretension was rather pathetic; they would never speak it without an accent; it would always be an attempt. Their whole lives were an attempt to be what they were not.

It had been years since she had heard from Christophe, and it was he over whom she perhaps worried most. At least the others were here; she saw them or heard of them. If only Madame Pontalba, the great Baroness, would write and say she had seen Christophe. She had promised to make inquiries. But Marie knew it was improbable. Paris was a large city.

Madame the Baroness was a busy woman. Perhaps Christophe would write again some day, perhaps not. It would be wonderful to know what he had become, what his life was like. Or perhaps it would not be so wonderful? At times Marie imagined dreadful things might have happened to Christophe, but she always shut out these visions as quickly and as completely as she could. If he had trouble he would write to me, she told herself. When there is no news he needs nothing. He is a man, and he can take care of himself. Perhaps he had become a famous painter in Paris? If that were so Marie knew she would be unlikely to hear of it, unless he were to write and tell her. She knew nothing of such matters.

At times like this night when she could not sleep, Marie would see all her children before her. She would stand them in a line and look at them closely, the seven of them that were left to her of all those she had borne. In that way she drew them close to her, and all at the same time. It had been years since all of them had been together. All, in one way or another, were gone from her now, except Jean—her poor Jean, who lay sleeping amidst the fumes of sour wine and cheap rum in his room at the rear of the house. She turned over in the bed restlessly and found a softer place on her pillow. Yes, she must sleep herself. There were clients to see before noon in the morning, for some insisted on coming on Sundays these days, and in the afternoon she must go to Congo Square. Perhaps she could coax Jean to go to Mass in the morning if his headache was not too severe.

It was Monday before she had the time to make the *gris-gris* for a husband for Marie Philome. Then she made it, and it was exactly the same as she used for her clients—women who wanted husbands for themselves or for their daughters. She sketched a picture of a man, a rough drawing, but of as handsome a man as she could manage. At midnight she put it on the altar; she mixed the bowl, putting into it drops of wintergreen, vanilla and Jack honeysuckle, lumps of sugar, rose leaves. She placed this on the altar before the sketch. She lighted nine pink candles and one blue one, cutting seven notches into the blue candle before she lighted it. She recited the simple ritual asking for a husband for Marie Philome. Then she took the sacrifice, a plate containing roast chicken, cowpeas and rice, and left it at a place behind Congo Square where the streets crossed. All through it she remembered how this had worked for Noemi and Felice, as well as for many of her clients. She prayed it would work for Marie Philome, too.

She waited weeks for it to do so, and she watched Marie Philome each time she saw her. She asked no questions of the girl, for Marie knew Marie Philome would object to being questioned, but she waited hopefully for some indication in Marie Philome's manner that she had a suitor.

Marie Philome seemed happy these days, but she had seemed so almost from the time it was first agreed between them that she should live away from home. This fact Marie had respected, even though it had depressed her at first. When Marie Philome came to see her she was almost always gay and animated, most of her talk being filled with gossip of the clients she attended as a hairdresser. She seemed to have no other life, and to be contented that way. On the rare occasions when Marie had visited her, it was the same. As far as Marie could tell, no friends came to her rooms; apparently there were no friends. This worried Marie. No one should be so alone.

As usual she gave her confidence to Baptiste. "She should bathe herself with verbena and sugar water," she told him. "But if I tell her to do that she will laugh and reply as usual that she does not want a husband."

Baptiste smiled at her, although kindly. "You are becoming obsessed with this," he said. "Why don't you let her alone, Marie? If she is contented, let matters remain as they are."

"I'm growing old," she said.

"You're becoming obsessed with your age, too," he replied. "You talk about it constantly."

She sighed. "It is true I am growing old, no matter how much I talk about it. What will become of her when I die?"

"You will not die for a long time yet," Baptiste said.

Marie almost laughed aloud. "Do you know that is true?" she said. "I will live a long time yet, Baptiste. Still I worry about Marie Philome."

Sometimes Marie Philome brought her gossip from the houses of her white clients that was useful to Marie. The grapevine of the servants still operated well, it was true, but, being more intelligent, Marie Philome often gave her information that was more useful than most of that that came to her from slaves. Then, a few weeks after she had made the *gris-gris* for a husband for Marie Philome, Marie one day became suddenly conscious of the fact that it had been a long time since Marie Philome had told her anything of this sort. She thought about this for days, trying to convince herself that it meant nothing. Yet it was strange, or it seemed so to her.

She was sure, after careful thought, that it had been several months since Marie Philome had mentioned Monsieur Pelletier to her. This was just an example, but Marie Philome had been very much interested in the strange arrangement in the Pelletier household, where Monsieur lived openly with a slave who belonged to his wife, and apparently with the full knowledge of Madame Pelletier. Marie had always thought Madame would in time come to her, and Marie Philome had said she would hint to Madame that she do so. Why had Marie Philome stopped talking about it so abruptly? There were other cases, too, but this one struck Marie as being the oddest. Marie Philome had said Madame was so miserable, so anxious for help. . . .

One afternoon Marie walked over to Marie Philome's rooms

in Bourbon Street. She would ask her no outright questions, she determined as she started out; she would simply hint a bit.

Luckily Marie Philome was home. She greeted Marie with a kiss, and Marie studied her with admiration. Marie Philome was not wearing a *tignon*, and her hair was done up in a great thick knot. She had on the earrings Marie had given her, and there were gold bracelets on her arms like Marie's own. Her dress was the same blue that Marie always wore.

They talked idly of the family, of trivial matters for a while. Marie kept thinking that Marie Philome was growing more beautiful, more as she herself had been. We are no longer quite as much alike, she thought, although without bitterness. Her beauty ripens, and mine fades. In a few years no one will say we are alike, as they used to do only a few years ago.

"And your business?" Marie asked finally. "It is good, my child?"

Marie Philome replied that it was very good indeed. She now had the patronage of the wife of a wealthy banker, a great beauty. Never had any woman had more beautiful clothes and jewels! She would have attended her for nothing, she vowed, just for the privilege of seeing that magnificent wardrobe.

"You never mention Madame Pelletier," Marie said lightly. "The poor thing never came to me. I had hoped she would. Perhaps I could have helped her."

Marie Philome said that Madame Pelletier had not called for her services for a long time. She shrugged. Perhaps Madame was one of those who did not believe she could be helped by such means.

"Perhaps," said Marie, "she went to Doctor John or some other worker."

She went on to other matters. They chatted on, and then Marie became conscious of the fact that Marie Philome seemed nervous. She began wandering about the room, straightening things here and there, moving objects from one place to another. At last it seemed to Marie that Marie Philome's hands were shaking a little. Finally she took a *tignon* from a bureau drawer and bound the red and yellow silk about her head. Marie asked, "You are going out? Do you have an appointment, my dear?"

"I must, Mamma," said Marie Philome, nodding. "I am sorry. I hate to make you go."

"Nonsense," said Marie. "Will you come to dinner next Sunday?"

"Yes, Mamma," Marie Philome said, but vaguely.

"I will stew a chicken with brown gravy, the way you always liked it," Marie promised. "Perhaps I will ask Jacques and his family, but it is such a crowd when they all come at once. Well, we will see."

"Yes, Mamma."

Then someone rapped on the street door.

Marie Philome did not answer it at once. She did not move. Marie started to speak to her; then she saw her face. The blood drained from beneath her rich coloring, slowly, completely. Marie did not need her voodoo to know instantly that the girl was afraid, or ashamed; it could be either.

"Shall I answer it?" Marie asked.

"No," said Marie Philome. "No. I will." She was almost stuttering. She opened the door. A middle-aged white man entered, smiling, his hat in his hand. When he saw Marie his smile faded, and he looked confused.

Marie bowed and went out into the blinding afternoon sunlight. She could feel the small muscles in her face twitching. She knew the identity of the prominent people in the city too well not to have recognized Monsieur Pelletier.

She did not invite Jacques and his family for Sunday dinner, but Sunday morning she cooked the chicken and the other dishes for the meal. She was calm now. All week she had brooded, and she had not yet decided what she would say to Marie Philome if she came, or whether it would be wise to say anything at all to her. Perhaps she would not come.

Jean rose late, and came out into the kitchen to pour himself hot coffee. The kitchen was fragrant with the good smells of Marie's cooking, and he sniffed appreciatively and asked, "Company for dinner?"

"Marie Philome," she said. "At least, I asked her. I'm not sure she is coming." She glanced at him and decided he did not look so bad this morning. "Going to Mass?"

"Guess so."

Perhaps I should go to Mass, Marie thought. It has been so many years since I have been. Perhaps it would improve my luck. She would pray for Marie Philome, she knew. She always prayed for all her children in her heart.

"You worry too much about Marie Philome," Jean said. "It is all right to have her for dinner, but she can take care of herself, that one."

"What does that mean?" asked Marie.

He shrugged and rose to pour more coffee. "Nothing, Mamma," he said in a cross tone.

She gave her stewing chicken one last stir, replaced the pot cover and turned from the fireplace. "Jean," she said, wiping her hands on her apron, "if you hear any gossip of your sister you must tell me, do you hear? It is your duty as her brother. She may need our protection."

"Oh, my God!" bellowed Jean. "That one!"

"It is always 'that one,' 'that one'!" Marie cried impatiently. "It is no way to speak of your sister." She took a gentler tone. "What have you heard about her, Jean? You are out so much and you must hear gossip. No one would tell me anything because I am her mother."

"Mamma, I've heard no gossip about Marie Philome," he said. "I don't know what you're talking about."

"Nothing about men?"

Jean laughed and put his coffee cup down on the table. "Men? Men and Marie Philome? No, Mamma. I don't believe she has ever looked at a man!" He rose. "I am going to church."

"Come home soon," Marie said. "Do not stop at your friends' to drink wine and ruin my dinner."

She walked out into the yard behind him, wiping her forehead, for the kitchen was so hot. She gathered some small roses from a vine that climbed over a fence and carried them into the house, but she hardly knew what she was doing. When she found them in her hand she placed them in a vase and put it on her altar before the holy pictures. She fed the snake and went back to look at her chicken.

Marie Philome came, and before Jean returned from church, for which Marie was glad. She said, "I want to talk to you before your brother comes back." She led the way into the house, holding her head high, her back very straight.

"Mamma," said Marie Philome, "I intended to come to see you before this, but I was afraid, I suppose. I want to explain, as best I can explain. I know you will be angry, anyway."

Marie kept pacing the floor. "I am no moralist, Marie Philome," she said. "But Monsieur Pelletier? Of all the men in the world to choose! It is disgusting, Marie Philome. I cannot understand it." She frowned sternly. "I made a *gris-gris* for a husband for you. You may as well know that now."

"A husband for me?" asked Marie Philome. Then she laughed. "Oh, Mamma!"

"Do you think it is funny?" Marie cried. "I don't think it is funny at all, I assure you. A husband would be much better for you than Monsieur Pelletier. I have always been proud that all my daughters married. None but you ever formed such an alliance! None but you! You were never taken to the Quadroon Balls!"

"Oh, Mamma!" Marie Philome was gaping now. "It is not that at all. It is not what you are thinking!"

Marie looked at her; then she went to her rocking chair and sat down. "What do you mean it is not that?" she asked. "I saw the man there! A man like Monsieur Pelletier has interest in a woman like you for only one reason. Marie Philome, somehow I must have failed you as a mother, but I am not a fool."

"Mamma," begged Marie Philome, "please listen to me. I have been helping Monsieur Pelletier. His problem is difficult. He has reformed, Mamma, and now he wants his wife's love back, and she has refused to forgive him. Mamma, you may hate me for this, but you must know the truth."

Marie stared. "That never occurred to me." She could see in Marie Philome's face that she was speaking the truth.

"I wanted to tell you before this," Marie Philome said, "but I knew how you felt about my doing the work."

"I have suspected that you were doing some work," said Marie coolly. "I have long suspected it. When I came to see you the other day I had been thinking about that. But when I saw Monsieur Pelletier it did not occur to me he was there for that reason."

Marie Philome blushed. "I did not want you to see him. I would have given anything if you had not met him there."

The bell over the gate jangled, and Marie knew it was Jean returning from Mass. "Say nothing of this to your brother," Marie told her. "It is best if you don't. He will go out again after dinner, and you must remain a while. I won't go to Congo Square this afternoon."

When Jean had gone, Marie Philome helped Marie clean the kitchen, and after this was done they sat on the side gallery, and for a while they sat in silence. Then Marie asked, "Have you had luck in helping Monsieur Pelletier?"

"It is difficult," the girl said. "No, I have had no luck yet."

"Send him to me," Marie told her.

"No," said Marie Philome. "At least not now. I want to do this myself if I can."

Marie spread her hands in a hopeless gesture. "Then what can I do to help you? Shall I tell you what Monsieur Pelletier must do to win back his wife? All right. I will tell you this one thing, since it is important to you."

She told her. It was very simple, if one just knew. It was necessary that Monsieur Pelletier secure some strands of his wife's hair and sleep with them under his pillow. That would not be difficult; probably he could obtain the hair from his wife's brush or a comb. If he could not, Marie Philome could do it for him next time she went to dress Madame's hair. Then he must write his wife's name and his own on a piece of paper, cut the names apart and pin them together in the form of a cross, with his own name on top. He must bring this to Marie Philome, and she must put the paper cross into a jar containing sugar and orange water and burn a red candle before the jar for nine days. This should work, but no sudden miracle must be expected. After all, from all reports Madame Pelletier had good reason to be angry with her husband. It would take time.

Marie Philome's eyes were huge with excitement. She told Marie she had been using ordinary love charms; she had not known of this way to bring the Pelletiers together again. Monsieur had promised to pay her well. Marie must accept the fee. But this Marie declined. "I have told you even this against my better judgment," she said. "Keep the money. You will have earned it. But I wish you would not do the work, Marie Philome. I wish you would not."

"I must, Mamma!" Marie Philome cried. "Don't you see that I must? You must teach me more. I am older now, and it is what I want."

Marie would not answer that. Instead, she said, "I'll go and make a fresh pot of coffee. Then we'll talk about a husband for you. I will try other *gris-gris*, if you'll help me. There is still much I can do." She started to rise, but Marie Philome was on her feet first.

"You won't teach me, will you?" she demanded. "You never will! Mamma, you're jealous of me, do you realize that? That is the truth. You're afraid I'll take your place. Well, I will, Mamma! You will see."

"Jealous of you!" Marie cried, and could say no more; for an instant it was impossible to speak.

Then Marie Philome was gone. She strode swiftly across the yard, her skirts whirling, her head high, and the gate slammed behind her, the bell jangling wildly. Marie sat down again, her heart throbbing with anger, rage blinding her. The garden before her seemed filled with the blackness of night. She wanted to scream, to run screaming after Marie Philome, to catch her and pull her hair and slap her face. But instead, she sat immobile, like a statue, as if she were dead.

She told Baptiste of how she had felt at that moment. "I hated her," she said. "I hated my own child! It lasted only a few minutes, but I hated her. It was a dreadful feeling."

"It was natural enough," said Baptiste gently. "It was only temper."

"Once I told you I despised women who were jealous of their daughters," she said. "But I'm not sure I wasn't jealous of Marie Philome then, that I'm not still jealous. Perhaps I *do* fear her taking my place."

"It is just that you both have tempers," Baptiste again insisted. "It is because you are alike. She will come back, or you must go see her."

"I do not want to see her," Marie said. "At least not for a while."

"You will feel differently in a few days," he told her. "You will make it up with her."

"I am not ready to be displaced yet," she said. "I am Marie Laveau."

When Marie heard that Marie Philome had attended one of

271

Doctor John's meetings it was no shock. She felt only a strong sense of disappointment.

"Perhaps I always knew she would go to him in time," Marie told Baptiste. "Let her. Once I would have interfered, but I will not make a fool of myself as I almost did then. Let the man teach her his foolishness. He has little true wisdom, little knowledge but for that which he has copied from me. What can she learn from that charlatan?"

She watched Baptiste reply with a frown, and she knew that he thought she was bitter and that he hated to see her that way. Well, perhaps she was, but had she not reason? It has been months now since she had seen Marie Philome. Once she had made Jean go to his sister and demand that she visit them, and he had done it as if it were his own idea. Marie Philome had half-promised to come and then had not done so. Perhaps, Marie thought often, she could go to Marie Philome, but was it not the place of the child to come to the parent? Marie grew more and more unhappy, but she held to her decision. Marie Philome must give way first. Then, Marie told herself at last, perhaps she would teach her some of her knowledge. At least that would prove to everyone, including herself, that she was not jealous of her own daughter.

To make the matter even more unpleasant, Marguerite came to her one day in a rage. Marguerite was getting stout now, and she looked far from angelic as she sank heavily onto Marie's sofa, and tugged at her corsets impatiently. She had heard, she told Marie, of Marie Philome's voodoo practices. Was the family to be disgraced by her?

Then Marie heard herself defending Marie Philome. "Do you think I am a disgrace to the family?" Marie asked at once.

Marguerite pushed fading strands of her hair back into place under her bonnet and gazed at the toes of her shoes. "You belong to a different generation, Mamma," she said.

"Times are changing. Anyway, I never approved of voodoo, as you know."

"Yes, I know," said Marie. "But whether you approve or not, I can do nothing about Marie Philome. You know I refused long ago to teach her the work."

"I've tried so hard," Marguerite said, shaking her head wearily. "I've wanted my children to have a respectable background, to *be* respectable. But they are growing up now, and already they know too much. Marie Philome danced at a meeting at that terrible Doctor John's home one night, I am told."

Marie studied Marguerite. She looked shabby. Her shoes were worn and her dress was an old one. She had had a hard time. Poor Marguerite! But she would accept no help. "I suppose Marie Philome was imitating me," Marie said. "I've decided to let her alone, Marguerite."

The bell clanged above the gate, and Marguerite rose quickly and pulled down her veil. "I suppose you have a client," she said. "I will come another time."

When she was through with the client, Marie thought about Marie Philome a long time, but it did her no good. There was nothing to do. She would not go to Marie Philome with either threat or supplication. She would not go to Doctor John. She rarely saw him, and they had never become real friends. Once he had promised not to help Marie Philome in the way he was doing now, but he was not a man to keep a promise, especially after this long a time. Besides, Marie knew, he owed her nothing. She had not given him her friendship.

Perhaps the time had come when she must fight to retain her position. It had come to Dédé. It had come to Marie Saloppé. It had come to others before them and it must always be so. But in the cases of Dédé and Saloppé it had not been their own daughters who had tried to displace them as leaders.

Marie's thoughts filled her with horror. It was not true!

Was she losing her mind? Marie Philome would not do that. The ideas passing through her mind were preposterous. Marie Philome was foolishly ambitious, but she loved her mother, of that Marie was certain. Perhaps she would at last teach the girl, but that would be at some time in the future. At least one thing was certain. Marie Philome could not learn all she must know from anyone else. Even if Marie Philome did want to be the leader, and Marie kept telling herself that was absurd, she could never be, without her mother's knowledge. Only Marie Laveau could pass on the power that was her own.

She would make a good *gris-gris* for Marie Philome, Marie decided, one that would make her better and kinder, that would "sweeten her up," as the Negroes would have expressed it. She would pray for her, too. Jean must burn a candle in the cathedral. She might even go there herself.

Marie decided, too, that on this year's St. John's Eve the celebration must be greater than ever. She would send word of it through her grapevine to remind white people that they were invited, for many forgot from year to year unless that was done. Her friends among the police must come and those among the politicians. It was a good year, this 1860, and people had plenty of money. She must make much money. Perhaps she could even find a way to help her poor Marguerite. This St. John's Eve must show the whole city how great was Marie Laveau.

Chapter 14

MARIE was indignant when she learned that the police and the city officials would oppose her St. John's Eve celebration that year. Word came to her from these sources that there must be no gathering at Bayou St. John. It was true that it came in the form of a request, but there could be no doubt that it was really an order.

She went to the City Hall at once and demanded an interview with a councilman she knew, taking him as a present a lucky charm for gambling. It was useless. Of course Marie had heard, he said, of the trouble brewing between the North and the South. The southern states, he explained, were being persecuted; their rights were threatened. He prayed there would be no war. This was why at the moment it was so important that there be complete quiet and peace in New Orleans. Even here there were individuals and groups spreading nonsensical yet dangerous talk among the slaves. It was best that the blacks did not gather in such large numbers as they did on St. John's Eve.

Marie replied that she could control her people. The city councilman said he did not doubt that, but he was only one man; the others were afraid. Perhaps this would pass in a few months; the situation might be different next year. She would be permitted to hold a gathering in her home, if she chose, providing it was properly policed, which he could arrange for her. Above all, she must remember that this was not the fault of the local authorities, but of the corrupt government in the north.

The councilman was a Creole, so Marie agreed. She told him she had never liked Americans. "Monsieur, I can remember when New Orleans did not belong to them."

"The tragedy is that it ever came to!" he said, sighing.

She had heard much talk, but she had paid little attention to it until now. Politics did not interest her. But people chattered so incessantly about it all that the subject could not be ignored. The black slaves even talked of being freed, which Marie considered sheer foolishness. What good would freedom do them? Jean talked of it, and Baptiste. Once when Jacques had visited them, he and Jean had spent the whole time in conversation on that one subject. It had bored her; all of it bored her. She felt its only real importance, insofar as she was concerned, was that it had ruined her St. John's Eve.

But that evening she asked Jean what he had heard lately about it; what were the newspapers saying; what was the latest gossip in the streets?

Jean became excited about it. He said the slaves would soon be freed; white and black would be equal. "That," Marie said, "is the babble of fools and clowns!" She was profoundly shocked. She widened her eyes at Jean and added, "No black slave will ever be my equal!"

"It will come, Mamma," said Jean. "It is the new way."

"And what do you imagine the white people will do?"

"They will fight against it, but they will lose."

She laughed. "And so you can foretell the future!" she said. "I did not know you had that talent!"

On Saturday she went to the parish prison and saw to it that she had an opportunity to speak to Father Casteau. "Will there be a war, Father?" she asked. "Will there be actual fighting?"

"Let us pray not, Marie," he replied. "No one knows yet."

The meeting in her yard on St. John's Eve was small, with many of the ceremonies omitted through necessity. No white people came, and a policeman in uniform stood at her gate. The collection was small, too.

Baptiste remained until dawn and drank coffee with her. "Next year will be different," he said. "It may all be rumor."

"Whatever it is," Marie answered angrily, "it has done me harm already. My people asked me why I allowed the law to interfere with me. I should have had my meeting at the bayou in spite of it! They would not have dared to stop it!"

"It is best to avoid trouble," he told her. "You do not want that."

She sighed. "I suppose you are right. I have never had trouble." She felt better, resigned; Baptiste always comforted her. She said, "It is strange, but all day I had a feeling that Marie Philome would come tonight, and I am seldom wrong when I feel that way. Yet she didn't come."

"She must have been considering it," Baptiste said, "and then changed her mind at the last moment, probably because she was afraid to come."

Marie nodded. "That is it. I know that is right, now that you've said it."

She thought of Marie Philome constantly, wanting to see her, and yet unwilling to do anything about it. But the summer passed slowly and still the only word of her came from other people. One afternoon she deliberately walked up Toulouse Street, crossing Bourbon, and she caught a glimpse of Marie Philome entering her house. Marie quickened her pace, but her eyes filled with tears. Marie Philome had not seen her. If only she had looked that way! They might have come together then.

News of Marie Philome came from every source. She was well; she was the same. She still practiced her trade of hairdressing, and in her rooms she sold *gris-gris*. She also occasionally appeared at the meetings held by Doctor John. Jean brought gossip about her too, and, infrequently, Jacques, Noemi and Felice had also heard talk of her. They were grieved that none of the family was in close contact with her, and both offered to go to her, which Marie forbade. Marguerite fumed about it all and threatened to tell Marie Philome what she thought of her at their first accidental meeting. "Of course I cannot be seen going there!" Marguerite cried. "But if ever I meet her, and no one else is around, she will hear how I feel about the disgrace she is bringing to our family!"

In September Baptiste went to sea. It was to be a short trip, only to the West Indies, and he would be gone only two months, but as usual Marie missed him. He was getting on in years, too, now, and his hard life had aged him beyond their number, so he tried to avoid long voyages. Soon he would retire, he promised. He had saved money. He might open a little café in a year or two, he had decided. The times were so prosperous that there was always room for more business. If only all this talk of quarreling between the southern states and the Federal Government would stop! Marie would smile when he spoke of this, for during the summer she had ceased to believe the talk meant anything. "I have been through so much in my life," she told him once, "that I refuse to let this bother me. I have money, Baptiste. It is the one thing I do have. If ever you need any, it is yours, my friend."

She had become more thankful for her money as she grew older. It was true she had given much of it away, and she still gave it freely—to her children, to neighbors and to her followers when they needed it—but there was much left. For years now she had been buying property, too. Jacques, Noemi and Felice all lived in houses that belonged to her, for which she charged them no rent, and she owned other houses, too. Lately she had begun buying empty lots "downtown," in the Faubourg Marigny, for she had been advised they would increase in value as the city grew. She had large deposits in three banks. Her clients paid her well, and her fees had increased with the passing years. The collections at her Friday night meetings were large, and those on St. John's Eve, except for this past one, much larger.

She was a rich woman, yet until she stopped to remember that she was, she was rarely conscious of it. Her personal expenditures remained the same from month to month, from year to year. She lived as she had lived most of her life, and she wanted nothing more for herself. A newspaper reporter had once asked her if it were true that she was the richest free woman of color in New Orleans, and she had replied that she did not know nor care. Her wealth gave her a sense of power and of gratitude, increasing gratitude, but that was all. "Mamma, you could retire," Marguerite had said more than once, and that always angered Marie far more than she had been angered by the behavior of Marie Philome, although she understood Marguerite's motive, and forgave it far more easily than she could altogether forgive Marie Philome.

There were even moments when she thought she would never retire, when she could come close to believing she was immortal. She was a ruler, a queen, almost a goddess. The powers she understood spoke through her. When she stood upon the alabaster box in which the Vodu twisted and writhed, her body twisting and writhing, too, and vibrating with mingled ecstasy and pain, words she did not believe she really spoke pouring from her lips, and the people before her fading away, nothing about her but mist and strange lights, she forgot altogether that she was Marie Laveau, the Widow Paris, the Widow Glapion. She was someone else then, or *something* else. Then she was only a medium, an expression, of the powers she served.

Of course most of the time she knew she was not immortal. There were the times when she felt old. There were the times when she looked into her mirror. It was true she did not look her age, and she found it hard to believe she was sixty-seven, but she was changing. There were even the times when she was obsessed with growing old, with wondering, "How long? How long?" It was then she was most grateful for her money, and mostly this for her children's sake. It was good to know they need never want for money.

The tension caused by the brewing trouble increased in the fall. Marie tried to ignore it, but gradually it began to seem that no one could talk of anything else. The greatest event of that autumn, as far as she was concerned, was a letter from Christophe. Yet even that had to do with the political situation. Was everyone well, he wanted to know. And, then, what was the effect upon them of all this gossip one heard in Paris? He hoped it was exaggerated, but he was frightened for them. They must take care of themselves, he said. Would it be possible for any of them to come to Paris? He could offer a home to any who could. He ran an art gallery of his own now, although he still painted. He had four children, two boys and two girls. He begged forgiveness for not writing, but the writing of letters was torture for him. Still, he would start to write regularly, anyway. Mamma must please send him news of everyone.

Marie wrote him, telling him everyone was well. She told him nothing troublesome, omitting any mention of Marie Philome's estrangement from the family or of Marguerite's unhappiness. She also wrote that she believed the Paris gossip must be a bit exaggerated. She was worried about nothing. Could he come for a visit one day soon? She did not indicate it in the letter, but there was a little bitterness in her. He worried about them now, but he did not know, actually, if they were alive or dead; it had been so long since he had bothered to inquire!

The authorities closed Congo Square. Marie found notices posted on the fence one day. She did not protest, as she might have at any other time. She told Baptiste she would be content with the meetings at her own home for the time being. Baptiste, who had arrived home in early November, agreed. She must bide her time. It would be useless to complain. Some of the Negroes were talking a great deal, boasting and bragging about their future. The whites to whom Marie talked seemed both boastful and filled with fear.

One of her clients, an Anglo-Saxon, expressed most clearly to her the sentiments of the white people. Mr. Dodson was a gambler who came to her often for charms and lucky *gris-gris*. He credited her with all the good fortune he had enjoyed for several years now, and he paid her handsomely, especially when his winnings were large, and usually they were.

"We could take Washington in two weeks," he said. In the North, he told Marie, there were fanatics who would destroy the South, if they could, by depriving them of their Constitutional rights, one of which was the holding of slaves. He said that northern industrialists and others were envious of slave labor in the South, as well they might be, and, of course, of the prosperity of the South and its Eden-like way of life, which provided, as he expressed it, "the most noble mode of existence ever known to the Caucasian race, as well as an Elysium for our African bondsmen!"

The new president, Mr. Abraham Lincoln, was described by Mr. Dodson as "a man holding to what he probably considered high principles, but weak and sentimental, and enslaved by the fanatical Abolitionists, unfit for such high office, elected by a purely sectional vote in a deliberate design to pervert the powers of Government to the immediate injury and eventual destruction of the South." But, Mr. Dodson concluded, the South would, if it must, fight for its honored institutions and there was no chance that it would not succeed.

Marie did not listen too carefully, but afterwards enough of all Mr. Dodson had said remained upon her mind to worry her, and she began to question other white men who sought her out as clients. All expressed much the same opinion as Mr. Dodson.

In December the governor of the state made a speech to the State Legislature, and Jean read it to her from the newspaper. Governor Moore sounded not unlike Mr. Dodson and the others. In fact he was a little stronger in stating his sentiments. "I do not think," said the governor, "that it comports with the honor and self-respect of Louisiana, as a slave-holding state, to live under the government of a Black Republican President!"

It was in January that news spread through New Orleans that Governor Moore had ordered all military barracks, arsenals, forts, as well as all Federal property in the state, seized by the state militia. Forts Jackson and St. Philip on the Mississippi River were taken over, as was Fort Pike at the Rigolets near New Orleans. The customhouse and the United States Mint were seized. Excitement roared like a consuming fire through every section of the city, and Marie's followers descended upon her in great numbers, some afraid, some simply ignited with the passion of the moment. Marie did her best to quiet all of them. She recalled another war, the one of forty-five years before. We—or our parents—endured that, she would say. So can we this, if war comes. Perhaps it won't. Then the newspapers and public gossip reported that on January 23 the State of Louisiana had seceded from the Union, and that even before that, other southern states had done so.

There was a great clamor and universal joy when news came that Fort Sumter in Charleston Harbor had been bombarded on April 12. General P. G. T. Beauregard, a New Orleans Creole in charge of the South Carolina defenses, had ordered the first shot fired. As if this were a signal intended especially for them, New Orleans men rushed to join the Confederate forces. A Monsieur Brisson, an old customer of

Marie's, came to buy her protection for his son, who had already gone, and explained, "All the men of New Orleans are willing to follow the great General Beauregard to victory! It will not be long. If only I were a younger man!"

Marguerite came to see Marie, and as soon as the gate was closed burst into loud and uncontrolled weeping. Marie put an arm around her quivering shoulders, led her into the house, and made her sit down. She removed Marguerite's bonnet with her own hands and smoothed her pale hair. It was minutes before Marguerite was able to speak, then words poured from her, wildly and hysterically. Georges had left her to join the Confederate forces. He had enlisted in the Washington Artillery, and he had already left the city. He had left only a note.

Marie was stunned. "How could he be such a fool?" she cried. "He would not have had to go!"

"They will not question him," sobbed Marguerite. "They will not question his color. You know how Georges is about that. What am I going to do, Mamma?"

"He will come back safely," said Marie. But she was really thinking that Georges had not done this because of patriotism toward the Confederacy. He had wanted to get away. She knew that he and Marguerite had not been getting along well for some time now. "How much money have you, Marguerite?" she asked. "You must tell me."

Marguerite's white face was twisted with misery. "I have less than ten dollars in the world, Mamma!" she blurted out. "What am I going to do about my poor children?"

"You know I will give you money," said Marie. She crossed the room and poured Marguerite a glass of wine from a decanter. "Drink this and try to quiet yourself."

Marguerite took the wine with a trembling hand, tasted it and put the glass down on a table.

"As you know, the banks have shut down," Marie told her, "but everyone says it is temporary, and fortunately I have kept enough money in the house to last us for a long time." She sat down beside Marguerite and asked quietly, "Would you and the children come here to live?" Thank God she had hoarded gold pieces!

Marguerite wiped her eyes and her blanched cheeks that were streaked with tears. "Would you want us, Mamma?"

"Of course I want you," Marie said. "How can you ask me?"

"I think I would go crazy at home without Georges," said Marguerite. "It is so lonely even with the children, and no one knows what will happen if this war continues." She began crying again, her nose buried in her handkerchief. "I've been wicked, Mamma. My pride has been too great. Forgive me, Mamma."

"You must come here," Marie said firmly. "There is lots of room for all of you, and it will be easier for everyone. I will get Jean and Baptiste to move your things. We will close your house until Georges comes back." Already she was making plans in her mind. Marguerite and the youngest girl could share one room, the two older girls another. She could not feel shame for the fact that she would be glad to have Marguerite and her children there. There would be nothing to embarrass Marguerite. Marie knew she would not even be able to hold the meetings in her yard while the war lasted. She hoped she would continue to have as many private clients as ever, but the children were not likely to pay too much attention to that.

The next months were oddly uneventful. There was much talk; young men disappeared, and some older ones, too; soon it was being said that one never saw a white man on the streets of New Orleans who did not have gray hair. Confederate flags flew from poles, from public buildings and balconies. The banks reopened, but they issued Confederate money that was confusing to everyone. All prices rose and as time went on it became apparent that deciding upon the value of the money one possessed was nearly hopeless. The State issued oné sort, the city another. Finally some banks began to issue bills of their own invention and manufacture.

Marie and her family were as careful as possible. The banks held much money belonging to her, but the amounts seemed to decrease rapidly. Her tenants could not pay their rents in many instances, and she would not press them. She and Marguerite bought only the barest necessities. Jacques and Noemi and Felice reported that their households were being run the same way. Marie worried about Marie Philome. There was no word from her and little gossip about her. Even Marie's best informers were too occupied with other matters to bring her much news of Marie Philome.

Clients still came to her, but fewer and fewer. Nearly all were white people, for, with the exceptions of her closest followers and her neighbors, most of the colored ones seemed afraid to come, or were prevented from doing so. Slaves were kept at home. Even the white people who came could often pay her little and then it was in one or another of the types of script that was now money.

During this first period of the war Marie took more interest in the newspapers and in the verbal reports that spread through New Orleans than she ever had in her life. News came slowly, and all of it was not to be trusted, but in a short time all New Orleans knew that Fort Sumter had fallen, that the flag of the Confederacy flew over Mount Vernon, home of George Washington, that it was expected that the city of Washington would be taken in a very short time. Pictures of Jefferson Davis were everywhere, people began talking about General Robert E. Lee, and bands marched through the Vieux Carré playing *Dixie* and *La Marseillaise*, urging the few young men who had not already done so to follow them to recruiting stations.

But with all this there was little action reported. It was a period of preparation. Crates of arms appeared on the wharves to be shipped up the Mississippi, and the railroads carried more. The talk in the streets grew impatient. Why was it not already over? The Northerners should not be permitted to carry on this long. Creoles expressed the view that the appointment of Lee was a mistake. General Beauregard should have had the appointment as commander of the Confederate forces.

It all gripped Marie's attention, but most of her feeling about it was personal, concerned with herself, her family, her fortune. To be sure she felt the South must win, and she was faintly patriotic in this regard, but she did not feel this was of great importance to her, to her race. They were already free, and she could imagine no other way of living for herself. But neither could she imagine living in a world in which slavery did not exist.

She and Jean often argued over this, for he disagreed with her. Jean changed during these months. He drank less, went out less, and he became in many ways a more agreeable person. But he wanted a northern victory, and this frightened Marie. She was afraid he would express his views in public. The bitterness was growing and the hate. If a white man heard him, it could mean Jean's life. He promised to say nothing outside of the house, but still she worried.

Marguerite and Jean argued, then fought, and, finally, almost ceased speaking to each other. Her first shock over, Marguerite had turned out to be not too greatly changed. The pride and the vanity for which she had apologized to Marie were still there. She and Marie had no quarrels during the first months she lived in Marie's house, but she often showed she was the same as she had always been. Now she had taken on the airs of a Confederate lady whose husband was a hero, or on his way to becoming one. She had never heard from Georges, but this did not prevent her from singing his praises constantly. Her views regarding the war were fiercely southern and Confederate. Once she even threatened to report Jean to the authorities, and she had shrieked at him in English, perhaps in some hope that Marie would not understand, "You talk like a nigger!" Marie had quieted them, but it was then that they ceased speaking.

Marguerite did not protest in these days about Marie's practice of voodoo, but she could not conceal her dislike for it. There were no meetings now, no Congo Square dances, but on rare occasions Marie would assemble a small group within the house. Then Marguerite would take her children to their rooms until Marie's followers had left. When clients came it was much the same; Marguerite would see to it that her daughters remained in another part of the house. On Sundays she took them to Mass, and every Sunday she made an issue of this, always remarking in Marie's presence that at least her branch of the family were good Catholics. Too, she never allowed her children to enter the room where Marie kept her altar. Once when Marguerite was out Marie took them there. It fascinated them, especially her snake, but she made them promise never to tell their mother.

The rumors concerning the war continued all fall and winter; then late in the winter came a report that was no rumor. A large Federal fleet and an army had arrived at Ship Island and was preparing for an attack upon New Orleans. The city began to seethe with preparations. People talked of the eighteen warships sent down the river to guard its lower passage, of the batteries below the city, of the strength of Fort Jackson and Fort St. Philip, of the most powerful warship in the world, the *Mississippi*, that was as yet unfinished.

Months went by, and Marie endured a small, private war in her own home. Marguerite and Jean engaged in no civil conversation, but they yelled invectives and accusations at each other in quarrels usually begun by Marguerite. She had still not heard from Georges and she vented her grief and rage upon her brother. If he were a man he would be doing something to defend his city, his mother, his sisters! "I am a nigger," he would reply. "Don't you remember? This is not my war. Let them come and set us free!" This would make Marguerite almost ill, but she would bring it upon herself over and over again. Marie would try to quiet them. She wanted only for the war to end, and for life to be as it had been before. There were no clients now, and the money she could scrape together bought less and less. In the spring, she determined, she would plant vegetables in the garden; she must get some chickens, for she had kept none for years.

The bombardment of the forts began in April. On the twenty-third of that month word swept through the city that the United States fleet was approaching the city. Marguerite, who had been out, came into the house, screaming the terrifying news. "I'm going to the levee!" she cried. "I'm going to the levee! Everyone is going!"

She ran out again, and Marie behind her, crying, "Marguerite! Marguerite!"

She caught up with her in the street and went with her. The streets were crowded with people, all moving in one direction, walking swiftly, resolutely, as if all drawn in that direction by a force too powerful to resist. When they reached the wharves the crowd was vast and jostling. Men shouted that Farragut's men would never enter New Orleans if they had to fight them with their bare hands. Women yelled and shouted with them, some of them ladies in fine silk dresses, now torn in their struggle to get to the river's edge, their hair undone and blowing wildly in the river breeze. "Marguerite! Marguerite!" Marie pleaded. "Let us go home! You cannot stay here!" It took her more than an hour to coax Marguerite away from the wharf.

Marie and her household stayed home for the next few days, but friends came to tell them of the approaching northern fleet. Beyond the high fence there was always noise in the streets. All night there was noise, people passing and talking to each other, shouting at each other. Horses' hoofs clattered over the old cobblestones constantly. Sometimes martial music could be heard in the distance, as if some men in some band were playing to keep up their courage.

At night the sky was lighted by fires. A crowd had set fire to twelve thousand bales of cotton on the levee. Ships were set afire, too—among them the unfinished *Mississippi* —cut from their moorings and sent floating down the river in flames. Warehouses were broken into and molasses and sugar were added to the burning cotton; more molasses was dumped, and the gutters of the city streamed with it. Great clouds of black smoke shut out the warm spring sunlight, and Marie could think only of the yellow fever epidemics.

Before the week was over they knew that Farragut had taken the city. There had been no resistance; there could be none. The United States flag flew over the City Hall.

Then Marie answered her bell one afternoon and Marie Philome crumpled into her arms, crying, "Mamma! Mamma!"

Marie Philome was almost starving. For months she had not earned a cent. Jean fetched her belongings from her rooms and brought them to Marie's cottage. She had come home. Marie asked her no questions—what was there to ask?—and despite the conditions that existed in the city was happier than she had been for a long time. They shared what they had with Marie Philome and she seemed grateful and glad to be there. Even she and Marguerite had no quarrels, at least for the time being. Marguerite spent most her time going about with a look of misery on her face and saying that they were all lost, that they would all be better off dead.

She did protest when Baptiste came to live with them. One day he told Marie frankly that he was hungry. He had no money, could earn none; he had no one to whom he could go but to her. She made up a bed for him out in the

289

kitchen and told him he must remain there. "How many can we feed, Mamma?" cried Marguerite. "There are enough mouths now. I must consider my children!"

They would all eat, Marie promised. They would survive this just as people had survived the yellow fever epidemics. It would end one day.

So they lived as on an island apart from the city. Jean sometimes went out into the streets, and Marie would occasionally walk to the market to see what could be had that she could afford, but the others spent nearly all their time behind her high fences.

But they all knew, of course, everything that was going on in the city. General Benjamin F. Butler arrived on the first of May, and almost at once the apparently peaceful atmosphere seemed dissipated. The rumbling grew louder and louder. At first New Orleanians said he was a crude, ill-mannered man, not a gentleman, which meant much to them, but that was all. Soon they were saying he was a tyrant.

For almost from the beginning of his "rule" the citizens were subjected to grave indignities. A New Orleans woman was sentenced to two years on Ship Island under Negro guards because she laughed at the passing funeral of a Federal officer. An aged bookseller received the same sentence for displaying a skeleton in his shop window, which he told passers-by was that of a "damned Yankee." A famed city judge, also aged and much beloved, was sent to Ship Island for displaying a bit of bone attached to his watch chain and boasting it was from the thigh bone of a Federal officer. A young man tore down the United States flag from the roof of the Mint and was hanged for doing so.

All New Orleans retaliated, and the women were the most violent in this regard. They emptied bedroom vessels upon the heads of passing Federal soldiers, including one upon Admiral Farragut. They left the mule cars when Federal soldiers boarded them, or feigned illness at the sight of them.

They swept aside their skirts when any passed them in the streets. They sang insulting songs about Butler. Finally, Butler delivered an order that any woman insulting or reviling a soldier of the United States should be treated as "a woman of the town plying her vocation," as the order was phrased.

Through all of it Marie and her household remained as much as possible on the little island that was their home. The almost useless money had now become entirely useless. The gold pieces Marie had hoarded dwindled. Few clients came; at times weeks would pass when there would be none. Then, and they all considered it a miracle, Jean accepted work as a porter in a warehouse on the wharves, and brought home his pay. Marie smiled and thought that poverty might be the making of him. At last a few messages reached Marie Philome that certain ladies, who were, as Marguerite said, probably northern sympathizers, sought her services as a hairdresser. No one else cared about the women's sentiments about the war, and Marie Philome accepted. So they lived, and they remained always quiet and discreet. When an edict came from Butler that all citizens must take an oath of allegiance to the Government of the United States, all of them took it, even Marguerite.

In December Butler was removed from office and he left the city hastily. His place was taken by General N. P. Banks, who, the Creoles said, was a gentleman even though he was a Yankee. Reports of a season of balls and theater and dinner parties began to reach Marie, but it was confined, it was said, to the Yankees and their sympathizers. Yet the reports cheered Marie. Soon the worst, as far as they were concerned, might be over.

Then one day the bell above her gate clanged, and she answered it herself. Outside there were three fashionably dressed women. One asked in English, "Is it true you tell fortunes? Would you tell us ours?"

At another time Marie would have slammed the gate in

their faces, but, instead, she nodded politely and invited them in, speaking English, too, for she knew they must be northerners. She took them into her parlor, and, keeping her expression serious and intense, pretended to read their palms, telling them all kinds of foolishness, and only half listening when each of them told her over and over how right she was in everything she said.

As she escorted them back to the gate, the good, real money she had exacted from them clutched in one fist, the one of them who had talked the most during the hour they had spent with her giggled and asked, "Is it true you practice hoodoo?"

"Claire!" gasped another of them in embarrassment.

Marie did not smile. She looked the one who had asked full in the face and said, "Yes." Then she bolted the gate behind them with satisfaction, and ran as fast as she could toward the kitchen where Baptiste was lying down on his cot. "Baptiste! Baptiste!" she cried, waving the money at him. "I think I can begin to work again!"

Chapter 15

FOLLOWING Marie's instructions, Baptiste hired a cart and horse one warm afternoon in late February, and the two of them set out for St. John's Bayou. They told no one they were going, for as yet the plans in Marie's mind were only half formed, and she had decided to say nothing to the others until she again saw the place where she had for such a long time held her annual rites.

As the horse pulled the jogging cart over the bumpy road that followed the winding bayou into the swamp, she turned her head and studied Baptiste. There were moments now when she thought him the best man she had ever known; and there were even moments when she regretted she had not married him years ago. But then she would tell herself she had been right, and they had this friendship; perhaps it was better than marriage. Theirs was a complete and mutual devotion. At their ages no marriage could offer more.

"You are staring at me," Baptiste said, without turning.

She nodded. "I was thinking what you mean to me," she told him. "It is a great deal, Baptiste."

He smiled, and all the wrinkles in his face crinkled with pleasure. "And you to me, my dear." Baptiste's hair was turning white now, as was her own beneath her *tignon*, and there were many lines in his face, but they were kindly lines and not aging ones. He was thinner than he had been once and

293

a bit stooped; yet somehow this did not make him look old, either. "We are almost there," he said.

She was surprised that the clearing and the shed were not in worse condition. Grass and weeds had grown high, and the roof of the shed needed repairs, but otherwise it all looked much the same. Yet she was not satisfied. "I would like a much better place," she told Baptiste. "Let us drive a little farther down the road."

There had been time to think since the war had almost suspended her work, and as yet she had not told even Baptiste of what was in her mind. He drove on down the road for a mile, until the road itself ended at a place where it almost met the bayou. "Here!" she cried. "Help me out, Baptiste."

They walked about in knee-high grass, over the uneven ground. At last she stopped, clutching Baptiste's arm. "We'll build a house here," she told him. "You and Jean, and any other men who will help. Just a one-room house, but a big room! I'll hold the meetings here. We'll destroy the other place."

"But can you, Marie?" he asked. "Will the authorities allow it?"

"Of course I can build here!" She almost snapped at him, although it was not intended for him at all, but for all the circumstances that had nearly ruined her. "This is my land. I bought it years ago. We'll paint the house white, Baptiste, and it'll have doors that I can shut and lock and keep out prying eyes." She walked down the sloping land to the bayou. "I'll arrive by boat for the meetings!" she added, deciding that at this very moment.

He nodded, and then he smiled faintly, and Marie wanted to smile, too, for she knew she never ceased to startle him.

"Baptiste," she said, climbing back to him and taking his arm again, "you will take charge of this for me, won't you? The house must be built by St. John's Eve. Then I will put on a show for them that they will never forget, my dear!"

Yet from the beginning there were difficulties. Baptiste had a hard time finding the men he wanted, experienced carpenters and a painter. Jean, who still worked at the warehouse, could devote only spare time to the project. A man would work a day and not appear again. The trouble was that the colored people were living under great tension. In January the Federal Government, through a proclamation by President Lincoln, had ordered the freeing of all slaves in those parts of the nation still under Confederate control, but this did not apply to slaves in former Confederate territory now occupied by Union forces. However, General Banks, acting upon his own initiative, ordered all slaves freed in New Orleans, and an almost audible outcry swept the city at once.

During the following months Marie saw more and more the chaotic results of this order. Everyone, whites, slaves and freedmen, was confused. Most slaves walked out of the homes of the white families where they had spent all their lives, although many others remained. Those who left suffered terribly; some were reduced to begging in the streets. Many whom she had known for years came to her in panic, but she could do nothing for them. Her entire grapevine fell to pieces, and she often wondered if she could ever put it back together again, knowing in her heart she would never be able to do so.

Yet she was making a living again. Clients came to her, most of them white, many of them newcomers to the city, Yankees. She did not care; they paid her well, even though many of them treated her as if she were merely a fortune teller.

The white house on the bayou was built before St. John's Eve, but then she decided against holding a meeting. "Not this year," she told Baptiste. "Next year will be different." How did she know next year would be different? she wondered; yet she said it to Baptiste.

Getting the house built had been a terrible job, but he agreed with her.

Then two white men came to her house and rang the bell, and Marguerite answered at the gate. Marie was on the gallery, and she saw Marguerite slam the gate in their faces and come running back toward her. "Do you know what they asked me?" Marguerite cried, her face livid with rage. "They asked me if I was the hoodoo woman! The hoodoo woman! When I opened the gate they expected to see a witch!" Marguerite burst into tears.

There was never any way to comfort Marguerite these days, so Marie said only, "Let me answer the gate from now on. Don't you do so. I know how to handle such people." All Marguerite did these days was to indulge in self-pity and in frequent outbursts of tears. There had never been a word from Georges, and Marie had always felt there never would be. Marguerite was miserable. Marie reflected that she had always been a person who collected misery.

All winter Marie's business grew, although it was of a kind somewhat different from that which it had been once. Yet did it matter? They must live. Jean still worked, and Marie Philome continued to receive hairdressing appointments, but there were so many of them in the house, with Marguerite and her three children. And there were the others to help, too. Jacques and the husbands of Noemi and Felice earned less than ever, and prices were so high they were sometimes hard to believe. Baptiste occasionally got a day's work, but most of the time there was nothing to be found.

On an afternoon in March Marie and Baptiste walked to Congo Square and joined the crowd there. Every black citizen seemed to be present, some dressed in high fashion, others in rags. There was a parade of colored regiments, and then carriages filled with white Republican officials followed in procession. Banners bore statements that white supremacy was over, that slaves were the equals of their masters, that the old ways had gone forever. Governor Hahn, General Banks and Mayor Hoyt made speeches, then Negro leaders began brief talks.

After a few of these had spoken, Marie squeezed Baptiste's arm, and they left. She felt confused and a little stunned, and for a few minutes she said nothing; then she said, "I do not think I can ever call Congo Square mine again, Baptiste. It is lost to me."

"They've all gone crazy for the moment," he said. "It will change."

"We are always saying that," she told him, "and yet we know it isn't really true. Things change, but they never go back to what they were before. I do not believe I will like this new world, Baptiste. Perhaps it will do for others, but it is not for me."

All the way during the short walk home they could hear the shouting behind them. Then a band played. Even after that, when they were sitting in Marie's yard drinking coffee, they heard more shouting and noise. "I will not hold any meeting at St. John's Bayou this year, either," Marie said. "I will wait."

Neither did she use the house on the bayou during the year that followed, but when the war ended in the summer of 1865 she began to feel better. There seemed to be as much disorder and chaos as ever, but she hoped it might fade before the June to come, and she called a meeting in her home, gathering a few of her women together to make plans for the next St. John's Eve. She chose a young woman, Malvina Latour, to be her principal assistant, for Marie felt tired these days, and she could not perform all the rites alone any longer. She had been watching Malvina for some time, and she thought the girl possessed great talent for the work. But just after she had done so she saw Marie Philome's face, and she said hastily, "You may assist, too, Marie Philome."

297

After they had all gone, Marie Philóme asked bitterly, "Why did you pick Malvina, Mamma?"

"But I told you that you might assist, too, my child," Marie said. "I let you attend the meeting tonight, and you may come this St. John's Eve."

"I am not a child!" cried Marie Philome. "You must not tell me what I may or may not do!" Then she stalked out of the room.

Marie sat down heavily, for she had been walking about, putting the room in order after the meeting. Was that going to start again? Marie Philome had said little about wanting to do voodoo work since she had returned home. Marie had taught her how to make some *gris-gris* during the past several years, but she did not know if Marie Philome had been doing any work as she went about her duties as a hairdresser during this period. She realized now she had not wanted to know. She wondered why she still felt this way. Marie Philome was right, of course; she was not a child, but thirty-one years old. Well, let her come to the meetings, Marie decided. It did not matter any longer.

She was still sitting there when Marguerite came into the room. Marie prayed Marguerite would not start ranting, or weep, or even remain; she felt she could not bear it at this moment.

Marguerite sat down, and she looked quiet enough; there was only a steady gaze, but with that weary expression of hers. Georges had not come back, of course, and though Marguerite pretended to believe he was a prisoner, Marie knew she really believed nothing of the sort. "Are you actually going to begin holding those awful meetings again?" Marguerite asked finally.

"Yes," Marie told her, "I am going to begin holding the meetings again."

Marguerite twisted a handkerchief and stared at the floor.

"I am so defenseless," she sighed. "If only my children and I had somewhere to go. But you know we are dependent upon you."

"You are welcome here," Marie said. "But you know, also, we need money. Now go to bed, Marguerite. I don't wish to discuss this tonight."

"Mamma, you must retire," said Marguerite, pleading this time. "You are past seventy."

"Am I?" Marie asked vaguely. "Sometimes I forget."

"If only my poor Georges could come home," said Marguerite, rising.

"Stop whining and go to bed," said Marie crossly, and then remembered that Marguerite was no child, either.

She went to her bedroom and undressed, and when she had removed her *tignon* she glared at herself in her mirror, almost angrily. How did she appear to others? Did anyone ever really know? To herself she did not look young, yet nowhere near her age. There were lines in her face, but no more than she saw in the faces of women much younger than herself; her eyes were still black and clear. Did she look in any way like the witch some people who came to her expected to find? It was true times were changing and some of her visitors seemed different from those in the years past. Often they seemed so furtive and scared, they might believe the ridiculous stories they had probably heard—that she kept the skeletons of babies in her cottage, that she had been guilty of poisoning people. Long ago Marie had become used to such stories. They amused her and in a way they increased her prestige. In her work it was good that some fear her.

Then she thought of the first man who had called her a witch. She thought of Jacques Paris, and of the young woman racing over the levee a half century ago to meet her lover. That seemed a long time ago, yet it seemed yesterday. Probably no one in the world remembered Jacques Paris, even that he had ever lived. Time was horrible, she thought. Then she thought again of the Baroness. The old were bridges across it. But of course the bridges did not last. In the end all were broken. Go to bed, you fool, she told herself.

She was reaching to turn out her kerosene lamp when Marie Philome came to the door. She had a worn straw valise in one hand and a bundle in the other. Marie almost cried out impulsively: "Oh, no! We have done this before!"

Marie Philome spoke quietly, and she seemed perfectly composed. "Mamma," she said, "I am leaving. I have found a room that will do for a time, and I believe I can support myself now. The rest of you will be better off for my not being here."

"Do as you wish," Marie said. "You are welcome here, but leave if you prefer."

"I want to be fair," said Marie Philome. "I am going to do the work. I will never conceal that from you again."

Marie nodded her head, as if she were talking to a stranger. "I know you are going to do it," she said. "I know also that you are leaving because I chose Malvina Latour over you for the meeting. As I told you, for years I have tried to keep you out of the work only for your own good, for your happiness."

"That is not true." Marie Philome opened her eyes wide, until they were huge and almost hypnotic in their intensity as she glared at Marie, but she displayed no other signs of anger. Her voice was still low. "You chose Malvina because of your same reason for trying to keep me from practicing. You are jealous of me, Mamma. You have known that for years, as have I. Now that you are old it is worse."

Marie could say nothing for the moment. Marie Philome had never been this cruel before.

"I do not mean to hurt you, Mamma," Marie Philome continued. "I am grateful for all you have done for me. I know what I owe you. I know that but for you I might have starved only a short time ago."

Marie rose from the edge of the bed. "You had better go, Marie Philome," she said. She tried to control her voice, but it came out with a tremble in it and a little cracked—cracked, she thought to herself in a flash, like an old woman's! "Do what you please, but go!"

"Yes, Mamma," Marie Philome said, and picked up her valise and cloth-wrapped bundle, and left the room.

Marie sat down heavily on the bed, pushed back her long white plaits and put her hands over her face. But she could not cry. Only a single thought rang through her mind, and over and over again. "I am Marie Laveau! I am Marie Laveau! I am Marie Laveau!"

Baptiste rowed Marie and Malvina Latour down the bayou toward the meeting place. In the distance they could see the flares Jean and Baptiste had set up along the bayou's edge near Marie's new meeting place a little while ago, and as they came closer they could see the white house itself; Baptiste had given it a fresh coat of paint only a week before.

Although she had been depressed since Marie Philome had left, Marie now began to feel the depression drain away and excitement take its place. Why had she not thought of this years ago? Her arrival by water would impress the people, her white house looked splendid, and there had never been so many flares, so much light. She did have some apprehension about the attendance, for it had been long since she had held her last St. John's Eve meeting. But her closer followers had promised to spread word of the meeting, and if it were not large this year, it would be bigger next, and the next.

As they approached the shore, Marie narrowed her eyes, trying to see if she could detect a crowd waiting for her. But the lights blinded her and she could see nothing. Neither could she hear anything. By now there should be shouts of greeting. "It is so quiet, Baptiste!" she remarked.

"It is early," he said.

He helped her and Malvina from the skiff and tied it to an old stump near the water's edge. Marie walked along the shore, with the others trailing her. "But there is no one here!" she cried. "No one at all, Baptiste!"

He touched her arm. "It is early."

"We will go look inside the house," she said. "Still, I do not like this. Could there be some mistake? This is St. John's Eve."

Baptiste nodded. "Perhaps there are some at the house."

She led the way to the stoop before the house, and as she reached it two men stepped out. They were white men and policemen. She knew neither of them.

"Are you the woman Laveau?" one asked.

She stared for a moment. There had been a time when not even a policeman would have dared address her that way.

"That's the old hoodoo queen," the other policeman said.

She raised her head. "I am Marie Laveau," she said. "What are you doing here? Have you driven away my people?" That was it, she thought hastily. These young fools had come and frightened her people away! "You had no right to do this! I still have many friends with influence. You will be punished for this!"

"You had better come inside," the policeman who had last spoken told her.

Filled with rage, Marie followed him inside, then stopped just within the door. Once she opened her mouth and thought she was about to scream, but no sound came. From behind her she could hear Malvina Latour releasing shriek after shriek. It went on and on, as if she could never stop.

For on the altar in the center of the room lay Doctor

John. He was dressed in all his finery, but all of it now was drenched in blood. Blood covered the altar, and still dripped, drop by slow drop, on the floor. It seemed to Marie that his head was still attached to his body by only a few pieces of scarlet flesh.

Chapter 16

THE EARLIEST of her followers to arrive at the meeting place had found Doctor John. They had run away, as must have all those who came later. However, one of them, braver than the rest, had sent an anonymous message to the police. All of this Marie had learned since her arrest.

She sat with Malvina Latour in their cell, trying to think clearly, to plan. This was all absurd, she had been telling herself. The police must know that. The body had been there long before she had arrived. She had told them that over and over again during the long night through which they had questioned her. She could have been there, gone away, and then returned, perhaps intending to dispose of the body, they replied.

All night they had hurled monstrous charges at her, often repeating the lies that had been told of her in New Orleans for years. Had it not been said that she committed murder in secret, that she used human bones and babies' skeletons in her rites?

"Is it not true that you have practiced blood sacrifices?" one of the police had asked. "My father told me once that it was rumored you had performed human sacrifice."

"Rumors! Rumors!" she cried, sitting very straight in her chair, her head high, her eyes bright with indignation. "Lies! If your father believed such things he was a worse fool than you are!"

"Hold your tongue, woman!" the policeman shouted in her face. "You are forgetting yourself and your place. I can make you talk."

Marie realized that he was now referring to the difference in their races. She still forgot how the racial situation had changed since the war.

"Everyone knows you hated Doctor John," he continued, after composing himself for a moment, "and that you were rivals in your savage practices. You were enemies. Perhaps it would have been a triumph to have sacrificed him upon your altar?"

"If it were not for my own danger I would laugh." Marie spoke quietly, but she did not intend to shrink from this man. "Why don't you spend your time trying to find the murderer instead of tormenting me with this nonsense? Turn me loose and I will help you."

"With your *gris-gris?*" the policeman sneered.

"Perhaps with my *gris-gris!*"

After hours they had returned her to her cell, and taken Malvina Latour with them.

Although it was now late morning Malvina still trembled. "You know how they are with colored people now," she said once. "They don't care whether they hang the guilty one or not, just so they hang a colored person. I wish they were Yankees, but they're from here, and they have hate in their hearts."

"These police," Marie said, "have no power to hang anyone. They are not high officials. Rest yourself, my child. Try to get some sleep. They can hold us only on suspicion. They have no proof against us." Marie lay down on her cot. She wondered how Baptiste was, knowing he was somewhere within the jail. Then she began thinking of the days when she had visited prisoners here. Never had she imagined herself confined in a cell. She thought a little of Doctor John, and not without pity. Who could have done this? She won-

306

dered if it were not true that in time old, old enemies can become to one almost as friends. Somewhere dislike and affection met.

In the afternoon Marguerite came, bringing a basket of food. Marie was surprised she had come at all, and she noticed that Marguerite's face reddened as the guard admitted her to the cell. "Oh, Mamma!" Marguerite whispered hoarsely and began to weep. "Mamma! Mamma!"

"Hush!" Marie said. "No tears! I have shed none."

"A charge of murder is a disgrace to a family," Marguerite said.

Marie kissed her, smiling faintly. "My Marguerite is always the same!" she exclaimed. "But thank you for coming, my dear."

"Jean was coming, but he got drunk in his grief."

"That Jean!" sighed Marie.

"I have not told my girls," Marguerite went on, "although I suppose they will have to know. I will get a good lawyer— the very best. I do not know how we will ever pay him, but we must get you free."

"Wait a bit," Marie told her. "I have committed no crime, Marguerite!"

Marguerite blew her nose. "Oh, I know that, Mamma!" she said. "But I should not have allowed you to go to the bayou last night. Now perhaps you know what savages your followers are. And at your age, carrying on with them!"

"My age!" sighed Marie. She sat back upon her cot. "First Marie Philome reminds me of it, then you. I think it is my children who are making me old!" She looked up at Marguerite. "And none of my savages, as you call them, killed Doctor John; I am sure of that!"

"It must have been one of them," Marguerite said.

"No," said Marie. "I think he was brought there."

"Mamma! Mamma! Always excuses!" said Marguerite. "I will find the best lawyer."

307

"But I do not want a lawyer!" cried Marie. "I have done nothing!"

Malvina Latour had been sleeping. She began to moan, and then awakened, crying, "What are they doing to us?"

"I will return, Mamma," Marguerite promised. She kissed Marie's cheek again and departed.

Marie sat in silence. As she watched, Malvina Latour went back to sleep.

It had been as she had thought only a moment ago, Marie decided. Doctor John had been brought to her white house, and against his will. Probably he had been under the influence of some narcotic—there were many of his followers who would know what to use—and there his throat had been cut.

Marie Philome came the next morning.

"I just heard, Mamma!"

It was difficult for Marie to look into her face. She was so much as she had been. Yet it seemed strange to her that she should be thinking of this now. Marie Philome had always been like her. Marie Philome had walked in with her head held proudly and defiantly, her blue skirts swishing, her gold hoop earrings swaying, her eyes unafraid.

Marie had not spoken, and Marie Philome said, "Mamma, I want to help you!"

Then Marie had her in her arms. She kissed her cheek, and then she told her, "You must keep out of this. You do not know what it is like! What they say of me they may say of you."

"I want to help, Mamma!"

They sat down together on Marie's cot.

"It will take much *gris-gris* to help us," muttered Malvina Latour, who stared at them from the other side of the narrow, tiny cell. "It will take more *gris-gris* than I have ever known."

Marie watched Marie Philome as she smiled at Malvina

308

with unveiled contempt. "Perhaps it is not *gris-gris* I will use," Marie Philome said.

"You will use?" Marie patted her daughter's knee gently.

"Yes, Mamma. I will use what I must."

"Perhaps you can help," said Marie. "But first I must have more time to think. Then I will tell you what you can do."

"Mamma, I know what to do!"

Then Marie found herself staring at Marie Philome, and she realized she had been talking to her as she always had, as an elder, as one of superior wisdom. Certainly she was both, but now there must not be contention between them. There should never have been that. "And what will you do?" she asked.

"Mamma, I am sure Doctor John was not killed at the white house."

"So am I," said Marie, only faintly surprised that Marie Philome had arrived at the same conclusion as herself.

"There are those that hated him," Marie Philome said, "and hated him more than you. Some of his women did. There is one called Hattie. Once I heard her threaten his life after she had been beaten by him. He beat them whenever it pleased him. You must remember, Mamma, that I knew him better than you, that I have been often in his home."

"Yes, yes," said Marie, "I know. But, Marie Philome, there must be no trouble for you! You must be calm. I am not too worried for myself. I worry for Malvina and Baptiste, but not for myself."

"And I not for myself," Marie Philome told her, rising. "I will be back soon, Mamma."

"Be careful!" Marie cried after her. "Be careful! Do nothing to hurt yourself, Marie Philome."

Malvina Latour rocked from side to side on her cot, her dark face contorted with worry. "What will become of us?"

she kept asking Marie. "What will become of us? They will hang us!"

"My Marie Philome knows what to do," Marie replied. Then she thought it odd that she had said that, and that she was filled with faith in Marie Philome, with faith such as until now she had felt only in herself.

There was noise in the street below, and it awakened Marie. She noticed it was late. Sun streamed through the barred windows of the cell and it was hot. She was drenched with perspiration. Malvina sat up suddenly, swinging her legs over the side of her cot, and began searching for her shoes on the floor, her face dripping, the chemise in which she slept sticking to her stout body. "What is it?" she asked Marie. "Have they come to hang us?"

"Hush!" Marie said. "You are foolish! I will take a look."

The noise grew louder.

Malvina began to tremble. She muttered, "It is like a riot!"

"You would be a voodoo queen?" Marie chided her. "With such fears?"

She pushed over their one stool and stood upon it, grasping the bars on the window, and peered down into the street below them. Beneath was a great crowd, and in front of it was Marie Philome and two black women. Marie Philome had a stick in one hand, a thick cudgel Glapion had once cut in the swamp and then dried and polished, a formidable weapon he had always kept for protection. As the women cringed before her, weeping, their hands over their faces, their bodies bent, Marie Philome struck one of them across the shoulders, and then the other. The blows were not hard, but were sufficient to keep the women moving on and on toward the entrance to the jail. Behind the three trailed an immense crowd, who shouted and roared with laughter. Marie Philome's voice sometimes rose above all the others.

"Murderesses!" she cried. "You will hang until you are dead! You will hang, sluts!"

Marie laughed as heartily as the people in the crowd below, and swung away from the window. Malvina was staring up at her as if she thought her mad. "It is my Marie Philome!" Marie told her. "She struts and swings her skirts. She lets all others see her power. She is magnificent!"

Malvina only nodded her head.

"We will soon be out of here!" Marie shouted, not caring that her voice must be reaching to every part of the jail. "Do you not understand? Marie Philome has brought the murderesses of Doctor John to justice, and they will not be able to hold us any longer!"

She waited outside for Baptiste after Malvina had hurried away, still nervous and shaky, as if she scarcely realized she was actually free. Poor Malvina, Marie kept thinking. Poor Malvina!

When Baptiste joined her they walked home together. The police had told Marie what had happened. Marie Philome had gone to the home of Doctor John and, armed with her cudgel, had forced her way into the house and confronted the woman named Hattie. With threats of beating and even death she had made Hattie talk. Hattie had at last admitted that she and another of Doctor John's women, one called Lurine, had put a drug in Doctor John's wine, and then had carried his unconscious body in a cart to Marie's house on Bayou St. John. There they had severed his throat with a sharp razor and left him, hoping the blame would be placed upon Marie and her followers.

But Marie Philome had used methods other than the cudgel, too. She had remembered what her mother had taught her. She had made known to Hattie and Lurine that she had a cassava stick and an egg to place on Doctor John's grave, that, furthermore, she would burn black chicken feathers in a black pot before it. This had frightened the women much more than her threats of physical violence.

Later, deep in the afternoon, Marie and Baptiste sat in her small parlor, no longer talking of the murder, but of other subjects. As yet Marie Philome had not come, and Marie wanted most to see her. Yet she talked not of her, but of the other children. "I never hear from Christophe," she told Baptiste. "I wish very much to hear from him."

Baptiste reminded her that the mails had been erratic and unreliable since the war, and promised her that she would hear in time.

"I wish Marie Philome would come," she said suddenly.

"She will," he promised, too. "She will."

"Isn't it strange," she asked, lowering her voice to a whisper, "of all my children it is only Marguerite I have with me? But I have always known she is the saddest of all my children. Georges will never come back to her."

"Perhaps he is dead," Baptiste said.

She shook her head. "No. He is not dead. Don't you believe that I can know such things, Baptiste? He is gone away."

So many people like Georges were going away these days. Many quadroons and octoroons were leaving for the North, for California, for Mexico. It was because with the freeing of the slaves all distinction between them and the free people of color had vanished. All were now counted as the same. New Orleanians counted them so out of bitterness; newly arrived northerners did not understand nor care about such delicate discrimination between castes. To the proud people of color, neither black nor white, and in many cases free for generations, the situation had become intolerable. It would be so for Georges.

"Wherever he went, Georges should have taken Marguerite and their children with him," Marie told Baptiste.

"Men should do many things they do not do," Baptiste said.

Marie nodded in agreement. "She will always consider herself a widow now," she said. "Already she talks of owning a black dress. I will buy her a black dress and a bonnet with a thick veil, and she can call herself the Widow Legendre. It will be a consolation to her."

"Let us have a glass of wine," suggested Baptiste. "It will do you good."

She followed him across the room and stood near him as he poured the wine from the old decanter that had been her mother's given to her by Monsieur Charles. "Monsieur Charles," she murmured unconsciously.

"What?" asked Baptiste.

She smiled. "I was talking to myself. Baptiste, do you believe Marie Philome will come to see me today?"

"I told you she would," said Baptiste. "Let us go sit out on the gallery where it is cooler. Here, I will bring the decanter."

They sat together on a wooden bench on the gallery, and were silent for a few minutes. Marie drained her glass and Baptiste refilled it. "Do you know, I do not mind being old any longer, Baptiste?" she said at last. "Until only the other day I hated being old. Suddenly it does not matter any longer."

"And Marie Philome being young and so like you?" he asked her.

"She was magnificent today," Marie told him. "If only you could have seen her driving those women before her!"

"You are no longer jealous?"

She looked at him. "It may be that I was jealous," she confessed. "If that is true, I am no longer. Baptiste, she was superb!"

Then she was crying, and she did not remember when she had last cried. Baptiste put his arms around her, and she buried her face against his chest. The tears poured from her and her whole body shook with deep and heavy sobs. "You must not!" Baptiste whispered. "You must not!"

As soon as she could stop she looked up at him and tried to smile. "I am a fool," she said hoarsely.

His face was serious. "You are my love!" he told her. "My love!"

"You still love me, Baptiste?" she asked. "Even now?"

"I have always loved you," he said, "and you have loved me, Marie."

"Yes, I have loved you, Baptiste," she said. She was silent again for a moment, and then she said, "Perhaps I have loved you more than anyone. But how can I know now? How can one measure one's loves?"

They were still sitting there when they heard the voices outside. There were people out in the street beyond the gate. The voices grew louder, and there were shouts and laughter, just as there had been outside the prison, only this time the noise was happier, gayer. Then she heard someone cry out, "It is Marie Laveau! Marie Laveau!"

Marie rose and Baptiste with her. The gate opened, the bell above it clinging noisily, and Marie Philome entered the yard. Marie Philome walked quickly, her head high, her immense dark eyes proud and smiling, as were her red lips, her blue skirts swirling about her ankles, the late sun bright on the seven points of her red and yellow *tignon*, and on her gold hoop earrings.

"She is Marie Laveau," Marie whispered to Baptiste, and grasped one of his hands. "She is truly Marie Laveau! Can you not see it? I am young again, Baptiste!"

"There will never be but one real Marie Laveau," Baptiste told her. "There can never be another like you, my dear."